Bought on a short visit to Dublin on Wednesday 5th Sept., 2007. A fine day.

TREASURES OF THE NATIONAL MUSEUM OF IRELAND

IRISH ANTIQUITIES

PATRICK F. WALLACE
AND RAGHNALL Ó FLOINN

EDITORS

GILL & MACMILLAN

IN ASSOCIATION WITH
THE BOYNE VALLEY HONEY COMPANY

Gill & Macmillan Ltd
Hume Avenue
Park West
Dublin 12
with associated companies throughout the world
www.gillmacmillan.ie

© 2002 National Museum of Ireland

0 7171 2829 6

Index compiled by Warren Yeates
Design & print origination by Design Image, Dublin
Colour reproduction by Ultragraphics Ltd, Dublin
Printed by Butler & Tanner Ltd, Frome

1 3 5 4 2

CONTENTS

CONTRIBUTORS

DR PATRICK F. WALLACE has been Director of the National Museum of Ireland since 1988, before which he was the archaeologist in charge of the museum's excavations at Wood Quay, Dublin. He is well known for his work on the Viking Age, especially the archaeology of Dublin, and also for popularising the museum and archaeology on radio and television.

RAGHNALL Ó FLOINN is a curator in the Irish Antiquities Division of the National Museum of Ireland with particular responsibility for the early medieval collections. He has published widely on the subject of medieval Insular metalwork, the archaeology of the early Irish church, and bog bodies.

EAMONN P. KELLY is Keeper of Irish Antiquities at the National Museum of Ireland. He has a particular research interest in the later prehistoric period and has published widely on aspects of Iron Age and Early Medieval Ireland.

MARY CAHILL is a curator in the Irish Antiquities Division of the National Museum of Ireland. She has a special interest in Bronze Age goldwork, the history of collections, and antiquarianism.

VALERIE DOWLING is a senior photographer at the National Museum of Ireland, specialising in fine art photography. She has won several awards for her work which is widely known through the museum's books, calendars and posters.

NOREEN O'CALLAGHAN is a photographer who has worked at the National Museum of Ireland, where her work encompassed studies in all four departments.

AOIFE MC BRIDE has worked in curatorial, educational and research capacities at the National Museum of Ireland and was editorial assistant for this book.

1

THE MUSEUM
ORIGINS, COLLECTIONS
AND BUILDINGS

PATRICK F. WALLACE

The start of a millennium which coincides with a watershed in the development of the National Museum of Ireland makes this an appropriate time for the re-introduction of the treasures of ancient Ireland in a new book. The opening of Collins Barracks, Dublin, as the Museum's headquarters [1:4] and of our branch at Turlough Park House, Castlebar, Co. Mayo [1:5] means that the Museum now has two venues in addition to the Museum of Natural History at Merrion Street (1856) [1:6], and the Museum of Archaeology and History, Kildare Street, Dublin (1890) [1:7]. The year 2002 is also the one-hundred-and-twenty-fifth anniversary of the passing of the first Museum's Act and of the appointment of the first director William Edward Steele in 1877. The recent developments include the passing of the National Cultural Institutions Act in 1997, an increase in staff numbers and the opening of a state-of-the-art conservation laboratory.

To understand the National Museum of Ireland both as an institution and in terms of the traditions from which its collection — particularly that of native antiquities — evolved, is in some ways to understand the complexity of modern Ireland itself. To encounter the archaeological treasures of Ireland is to appreciate national pride in a unique identity rooted over millennia in the achievements of an ancient European culture. Ireland's rich stock of field monuments which encompasses a span of about six thousand years is matched by the quality, range and variety of its archaeological artefacts and treasures.

In European comparative terms, the National Museum of Ireland has a role comparable to its sister institutions in Copenhagen and Edinburgh, having a similar responsibility in the overall national cultural landscape. The National Museum is what may be styled a comprehensive museum and, as the central repository of material culture, is the largest cultural institution in Ireland, significant both in its obligations and in the range and scope of its collections.

The Irish Antiquities division, based at the Museum's Kildare Street, Dublin premises contains the national archaeological collection and includes the treasures of the Irish prehistoric, Celtic, Early Christian and medieval eras. Of these, the prehistoric gold ornaments as well as the early medieval Christian church vessels and reliquaries are fundamental to understanding the character and achievements of ancient Ireland. The collection of prehistoric gold ornaments from the Bronze Age is reputed to be the finest gold collection of native manufacture held in any national museum in Europe outside Athens. Late Bronze Age elements will feature in our review of the metalwork of the succeeding era of the Celtic Iron Age which had a huge cultural (including linguistic) impact on the island. Taking into account Ireland's comparatively late assimilation of this influence, the review of Ireland's Celtic art has also to acknowledge strong influences from Britain.

Christianised from the time of St Patrick in the fifth century, Ireland was not dominated by the Romans nor was it fully urbanised until the tenth century. The country witnessed a flowering of Christianity which blossomed in a monastic milieu from which we have inherited cultural legacies including artworks from a devout and scholarly Golden Age; these include illuminated manuscripts, stone sculpture and metalwork. The present focus is on metalwork because it is almost all held at the Museum; the sculpture is largely *in situ* and the manuscripts are in libraries, principally that of Trinity College, Dublin.

Although the Romans never came to Ireland (officially at least), our survey has to be conscious of their impact and how their world influenced art, technology and belief. It also has to be conscious of the influence of the Vikings who came later and made such profound and lasting contributions in politics, commerce, technology and art in Ireland. As the technological expertise and animal ornament styles of the Scandinavians were absorbed into the repertoire of local craftsmen, the mainland continental European and English influences of their successors, the Anglo-Normans, were similarly assimilated.

While acknowledging these various influences, the distinctiveness and originality of the national treasures define the greatness and, in European terms, the uniqueness of ancient Ireland. It is intriguing to reflect on why these treasures, although so often misunderstood, have continued over the centuries to inspire national pride at home and abroad. This cannot be related to any emphasis in school curricula, which for a variety of reasons, have sacrificed ancient history to modern and current-affairs interests. It is as if a persistent but dimly-understood pride originates from a subconscious folk memory of bad times when tales of ancient achievements gave heart and concepts like the island of saints and scholars emphasised a desire to be regarded as having a distinct identity. One has only to look at the surviving treasures of ancient Ireland to gauge that distinctiveness and its quality. And one has only to be aware of the symbolism of the Young Ireland Movement of the mid-nineteenth century and the products of the later nineteenth-century Celtic Revival to appreciate the longevity of that folk memory. Indeed, even though increased archaeological knowledge also influenced nineteenth-century romantics like Thomas Moore, they nevertheless continued to perpetuate an almost pervasive awareness of a romanticised past.

The origins of collecting ancient artefacts, including the treasures of ancient Ireland, and the establishment of our National Museum are relatively easy to trace from Dublin in the Age of Enlightenment in the early eighteenth century through to the collectors of the nineteenth. The remote origins of the collection, however, go back to late-medieval Ireland, to hereditary keepers who after the collapse of the Gaelic ruling class were charged with the preservation of the relics that now make up a substantial proportion of the medieval treasures of the Museum. Because many of these keepers were descendants of stewards, or *airchinnaigh*, who controlled ancient monastic lands, the tradition of veneration (albeit more because of religious and cultural associations than for any memorial or purely aesthetic reason) in a sense goes back to the original patrons or commissioners and, by implication, to the craftsmen who made the treasures. The Shrine of St Patrick's Bell, for example, was in the possession of its hereditary keepers, the Mulhollands, for at least seven centuries. During the nineteenth century, many reliquaries were bought by collectors and public institutions from such keepers.

In contrast, most of the prehistoric and Celtic period treasures were lost only to be later rediscovered and identified. One Bronze Age gold torc of about 1200 BC was an exception to this pattern. The story goes that on seeing this ornament on display at the home of an old aristocratic family in the north west, a Museum curator enquired in the time-honoured way of servants of the institution as to how, where and by whom the torc was found, only to be told that the family in question had never lost it!

To understand the origins of the Museum itself, how it came about and how it holds the collection of national treasures, we must go back almost three centuries, to the 1730s. The country had then witnessed a century and more of devastation linked to the continental wars of religion and the Stuart cause to which the native aristocracy and its supporters were devoted. Although some survivors of the aristocracy continued to soldier in the armies of France, Spain and Austria, the old Gaelic order which had been conspicuous for its longevity and which effectively had collapsed with the flight of the earls from Ulster in 1607, was now almost completely gone and with it the patronage that had made possible the production and embellishment of Christian treasures for over a thousand years.

The potential of a possible commercial class also declined; many were reduced to the wine trade or piracy. Priests and others were schooled in colleges around Catholic Europe in a tradition that continued up to the foundation of Maynooth College in 1795. The deaths of Gaelic poets like Ó Bruadair (1698), Ó Caoimh (1726), Ó Neachtain (1729), Mac Cuarta (1733) and particularly the poet/musician Turlough O'Carolan (1737) symbolise the turning point that this time was. Some poets and musicians were left, along with other survivors of the old world such as the families who were appointed hereditary keepers of the great relics. The names of these families are known in the cases of at least twenty of the thirty or so reliquaries which survive at the Museum. How such families came to part with the treasures in their care is central to the story of the Museum and its origins in the 1730s.

The old Gaelic order lost its vibrancy to be supplanted by a new, Dublin-centred, mainly Protestant and partly Anglo-Irish world of the Enlightenment which would, in time, rescue the reliquaries from what remained of the milieu in which they had been produced. In this new world such treasures were brought to the attention of antiquarians, collectors, archaeologists, learned societies and eventually in 1890 to a new National Museum where they would be preserved and cherished.

The third decade of the eighteenth century had seen a ripening of colonial nationalism. It also witnessed Jonathan Swift's proposal for the use of Irish manufacture (1720), his *Drapier* letters (1724), and a coming of age of English writing in Dublin with *Gulliver's Travels* (1726) and Berkeley's *Querist*. The first county history (for Co. Down) was published by Walter Harris in 1740. Mercers and Stevens hospitals were opened in Dublin, the first Turnpike Road Acts were instituted, stage-coaches began a service out of Dublin to provincial centres, and the Commissioners for Inland Navigation were put in place. Most symptomatic of the new world and of greatest relevance to our story was the foundation of the Dublin Society for Improving Husbandry and Manufacturing in 1731, the same year in which the Irish Parliament met at College Green for the first time.

The Dublin Society placed agricultural implements, flax-mills and cider-mills on permanent display in a room in the Irish Houses of Parliament in 1733. This museum was later transferred to a building in Shaw's Court, off Grafton Street (1756–67), to 112 Grafton Street (1767–94), and then to the site of what later became the Old Theatre Royal on Hawkins Street (1794–1814). Since 1820 the Dublin Society has been known as the Royal Dublin Society (RDS).

In 1856, with government assistance, the RDS erected the Natural History Museum in Merrion Street. The Society's zoological and geological collections were centrally important to the development of what became the National Museum. The Kildare Street and Natural History premises as well as the art and industrial, geological and zoological collections originate with the Dublin Society, as did much of the original debate about responsibility for the administration of the museum. The Dublin Society is the main parent from which the present institution issued.

The purchase of Leinster House from the Duke of Leinster in 1815 meant that the Society's collection and museum were accommodated in Kildare Street from then. Leinster House remained the headquarters of the Museum until it was appropriated for the Houses of the Oireachtas (parliament) in 1922. The Society used the grounds between Merrion Square and Kildare Street for various exhibitions and agricultural shows until 1886, when that part of its activity was transferred to the present site at Ballsbridge. Leinster House remained the nerve centre of the Museum complex until 1922 up to which date it continued to house the offices and staff of the Museum and Library, its lecture theatre (now the Dáil Chamber) being extensively used.

As befitting an organisation committed to the modernisation of farming, the Dublin Society's museum collection centred mainly on natural history. The first major accession was the purchase of the Leskean mineral collection in Germany in 1792 by Richard Kirwan, acting for the Society. Similar acquisitions of geological and zoological specimens followed in the early nineteenth century. The despatch of the Society's keeper to Donegal in 1826 to collect specimens of 'native entomology and ornithology' represents the first official instance of museum fieldwork in Ireland! Today the Museum's zoologists continue to collect specimens, the Museum's archaeologists mount excavations and investigations and the Museum's art historians and country-life curators attend auctions and record traditional practices and customs around the country.

The RDS museum was open to Society members and the public two days per week up to 1830. That there was a growing desire to accommodate the public is evident from the Treasury's sanction for the Society to open its museum to annual subscribers on the days it was closed to the public. A special Parliamentary Committee reported in 1836 that the public should be entitled to a fuller use of the museum and that the premises should be enlarged to cater for increased public demand in advance of its becoming a national museum. In 1850 there was an outcry when many of the 44,000 visitors, who came to the museum on the two days per week it was open during its annual opening period of nine months, complained of cramped conditions. The Society responded by setting aside £1,000 for the commencement of a new museum building and appointed Dr Alexander Carte to take charge of the natural history collection. Carte fulfilled that task for the next thirty years and played a very significant role in organising the exhibition and the *modus operandi* of that part of the institution.

The origins of the Irish antiquities collection and several of the treasures which are illustrated here lie mainly with another Dublin-based cultural body, the Royal Irish Academy (RIA) which was founded in 1785, and which transferred its collection

to the new museum in 1890. (Incidentally the Museum's ethnographical collection which was mainly drawn from Trinity College also came in at this time.) While the Dublin Society was instrumental in assembling a collection of antiquities, having set up a Committee of Antiquities as early as 1772, and boasting a collection of 'antiquities and works of art' by 1819, it was mainly the Academy which concentrated on the preservation of Irish antiquities. Antiquarians like General Charles Vallancey, and later, archaeologists including George Petrie and Sir William Wilde (father of Oscar) served on its committee, ensuring that the collection grew by donations and purchases. Important papers were published in its *Transactions* and *Proceedings*. The collection was built up around the Cross of Cong, Co. Mayo [6:24], which was presented in 1839, around the same time that two gold torcs from Tara, Co. Meath, were purchased by public subscription [2:28]. The collections of Dean Henry Richard Dawson and Major Charles Sirr were added during the 1840s when the *Domhnach Airgid* was purchased by public subscription. Dean Dawson's collection included a large gold dress-fastener from Castlekelly, Co. Roscommon, a bulla from the Bog of Allen, Co. Kildare, and the gold collars from Ardcrony and Borrisnoe, Co. Tipperary. Major Sirr's collection included other prehistoric gold ornaments. The Ardagh Chalice and hoard were added in 1874. The collection was displayed at the Academy's premises in Dawson Street [1:8–1.11], the items being laid out in the present reading-room, long-room, gold-room (a room set aside for the gold objects and treasures of Early Christian art in the collection) and crypt.

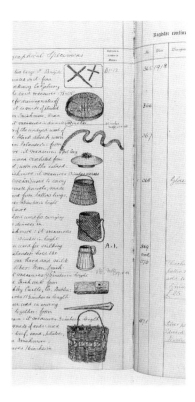

[1:2]
ROYAL IRISH ACADEMY,
REGISTER OF
ANTIQUITIES.

The first corpus of gold ornaments by Sir William Wilde was published in 1862. He probably laid out and arranged the display of the collection while undertaking publication of the catalogue of antiquities (published in 1859 and 1860) for the Dublin visit of the British Association for the Advancement of Science. A more up-to-date gold catalogue was later published by the Keeper of Irish Antiquities, E.C.R. Armstrong in 1920.

Following an agreement between the Government and the Academy, the collection of antiquities was transferred to the new Museum of Science and Art in Kildare Street in 1890 along with the relevant acquisitions registers [1:2, 1:12] and their superintendent, Major MacEniry, an Academy employee who transferred to the civil service. Although within four years of their arrival at the Museum the then director boasted that the objects in the collection 'absorb a large portion of the attention of visitors, for whose benefit and instruction a very detailed system of labelling with printed labels has been commenced', the collection had to wait some years before an altered political climate enabled it to gain pride of place at the Museum.

In earlier years at Kildare Street, the treasures were displayed on the first floor in adjoining galleries fitted with an iron safe and linked by a metal door (which still survives!). Academy specimens were placed on view within a fortnight of their arrival in Kildare Street in special steel cases designed by the Museum registrar, H. Bantry White. Many items of the collection resided in these cases up to the 1980s, though

[1:3] A DEPARTMENT OF AGRICULTURE AND TECHNICAL INSTRUCTION ADVERTISEMENT.

over the century a changed political climate saw them move from the first floor to a more prominent position in the central court [1:31].

The 1890s changed the Museum's regard for the antiquities of ancient Ireland and, in 1905, George Coffey was appointed as the first Keeper of Irish Antiquities. The collection was now a full division of the National Museum (alongside Natural History and Art and Industry), a promotion hastened by the controversy surrounding the Broighter, Co. Derry, hoard, the eventual acquisition of which in 1906 was to change the whole thrust of the institution and to copperfasten its place at the centre of the cultural life of the country.

The Broighter hoard [1:14] is a collection of mainly first-century BC Celtic gold ornaments which was bought by the British Museum, and claimed for Ireland under the normal conditions of treasure trove. The claim was brought to the attention of the Westminster parliament by the Irish leader of the day, John Redmond MP, whose bill to have it transferred to Dublin failed though a Royal Commission was set up in 1898. The Commission recommended that the objects go to Dublin on long-term loan. The British Museum refused and was brought to court by the Crown whose counsel included Sir Edward Carson, later leader of the Ulster Unionists. The court declared the hoard to be treasure trove and Edward VII ordered its return to Dublin in 1903. This was a major victory against what would now be termed cultural imperialism, and in an increasingly nationalist Ireland became hugely symbolic in terms of national cultural pride, and established the Museum in the words of its then director, Colonel G.T. Plunkett, as 'a national museum'. The summer of 1902 saw the arrival of the Addergoole dug-out canoe at the Museum [1:15].

The Museum was the responsibility of the Department of Science and Art, which was also responsible for the South Kensington museums in London, from the enactment of the Dublin Science and Art Museum Act of 1877. In 1900 control passed to the Department of Agriculture and Technical Instruction. After the foundation of the Irish State in 1922, responsibility passed to the Department of Education until it was transferred to the Taoiseach's Department in 1984 and, in 1992 to a new Department of Arts, Heritage, Gaeltacht and the Islands. The dismantling of that Department after the general election of 2002 saw the Museum and the other cultural institutions transfer to the Department of Arts, Sport and Tourism.

The 1877 Act meant that the RDS collection, which had been accumulated over the previous century-and-a-half as well as the premises which housed them, Leinster House, the then new Natural History building and the grounds on which they stood passed to state care and eventually became the National Museum of Ireland and the National Library of Ireland [1:16].

Although set up by the Department of Science and Industry in London, the new museum in Dublin opened its doors at the height of the Celtic Revival in the 1890s [1:17]. In the interests of Irish industrial education and arts facilities, Horace Plunkett and others sought to have the Museum transferred to a Dublin-based department. The Department of Agriculture and Technical Instruction was set up in Dublin in 1900 when responsibility for the Museum was transferred to it. This was in spite of the sincere view of the director, Colonel G.T. Plunkett, that the Museum would do better by not separating from South Kensington. Plunkett, though innovative in so many ways and considered to be among the greatest directors, held fast to the values of a passing era and lost out to the persuasive Horace Plunkett who saw the new department as encouraging 'local freedom, aiming at distinctive national qualities having at its hand, as part of its inspiration, the beautiful and suggestive objects in the museum'.

In 1907 another Plunkett, Count George N., was made director. He was a strong nationalist and Home Ruler who later had to retire when his son, Joseph Mary Plunkett, a signatory of the 1916 proclamation, was executed. The then former director was elected first Sinn Féin MP in the 1918 Roscommon by-election and later first Minister for the Arts in the Dáil of 1919. In Count Plunkett's time (1908) the museum became the 'National Museum' rather than 'the Dublin Museum of Science and Art'. The new title, in Plunkett's words, was more appropriate to an institution in the capital 'as the Museum of Ireland and the treasury of Celtic antiquities' [1:19]. Plunkett began also to rearrange the collections and to give the ancient Irish treasures a more prominent place, claiming 'our work inclines largely towards the collection of things distinctively Irish, both ancient and modern', showing perhaps that museums tend to reflect rather than influence the current time, a trend which is as true now as it ever was, and suggests that we, the present generation of museum men and women, have to rethink some of our emphases, particularly by being more generous in the accommodation of other cultures in providing fuller treatments of all contributions to our common heritage [1:20, 1:21].

The Irish Antiquities Division is close to the soul of the institution and continues to be very much bound up with the development of scientific archaeology and a responsive national collections policy strengthened by necessary legislation, particularly the National Monuments and other acts. Since the first National Monuments Act was passed in 1930, through its revisions of 1954 and 1987, and latterly the National Monuments (Amendment) Act, 1994, the Museum has been responsible for the protection and custody of the portable part of our archaeological heritage. Dr Adolf Mahr, first as Keeper of Irish Antiquities and then as director, was centrally involved with the 1930 Act and with placing the registration of the collection and related archive on the scientific footing recommended by Nils Lithberg's report of 1928. The Harvard Archaeological Expedition came to Ireland with Mahr's encouragement to establish scientific excavation methods for the first time and to explore poorly-understood areas of the past. Large bodies of material and data flooded to the Museum from these works, particularly from crannógs and from prehistoric sites like Creevykeel, Co. Sligo and Knenoge, Co. Meath [1:22]. The Museum later mounted an archaeological campaign to Lough Gara, Co. Sligo in the 1950s, and did most of the extensive work at Wood Quay and the other sites of Viking and medieval Dublin from 1962 to 1981. The Irish Antiquities Division continues to serve as the national repository for archaeological objects. Its staff undertakes fieldwork, and also supervises the intake of artefacts from all the excavations undertaken in the country.

Treasures have continued to be added since the time of Broighter, most notably the Gleninsheen, Co. Clare gold collar in 1932, the Gorteenreagh, Co. Clare, gold collar in 1948 and the Derrynaflan, Co. Tipperary, hoard in 1980. New discoveries are constantly added, most recently the gold hoards from Ballinesker, Co. Wexford, in 1990 and Dooyork, Co. Mayo, in 2001. Important private collections like the Irish gold ornaments in the collection of the Duke of Northumberland which were bought in 1990 and individual treasures like the *Mias Tighearnáin* and the *Miosach* in 1999 and 2001 respectively have also been acquired.

The Kildare Street building, like the National Library built at the same time, was designed by Thomas Newenham Deane and his son Thomas Manly Deane [1:23] and built by the Dublin contractors J. and W. Beckett [1:24]. The main museum building on Kildare Street consists of a large rotunda and gallery which opens onto a great central court and gallery. There are exhibition rooms around the court on the ground floor and off the gallery on the first floor.

The building is constructed of granite from Co. Dublin, faced with sandstone from Mount Charles, Co. Donegal, which is also featured in the window and door details. Polished granite from Bessbrook, Co. Armagh, is used externally on the columns of the dome. Groups of statues executed in Portland stone originally adorned the Museum parapets but weathered so badly that they have long since been removed.

The sandstone in the exterior is being renewed by a mortar that includes sandstone of the same colour and texture in the aggregate. Inside, the gallery of the rotunda is supported on pillars of mainly Irish marble except for a few Italian examples. Irish marbles originally displayed at the Great Dublin Exhibition of 1853 are incorporated in the central court. Some of the internal door architraves were executed in majolica by Burmantofts of Leeds — whites, yellows and blues dominating smaller portions of greens and browns. Some of the more intricate carving of classical scenes on the doors were executed by the Italian, Carlo Cambi of Siena [1:25]; others were carved by John Milligan of Dublin, the firm also responsible for the museum's oak floors.

The mosaic floors on the ground floor with their scenes of classical mythology and allegory were laid by Oppenheimers of Manchester [1:26]. The wrought-iron supports for the glass roof were constructed by McLoughlins of Dublin; Edmundsons of Capel Street were responsible for the original gaslight fittings and the electric fittings which were soon to replace them. The heating system was devised by Musgraves of Belfast and installed by Hodges of Dublin.

A century ago the Museum presented a very different appearance to the visitor than it does today. Field guns captured by Lord Gough from the Sikhs were displayed in the rotunda, but were later removed [1:27]. The rotunda displayed copies of classical statuary and ceremonial carriages [1:28]. The centre court contained a group of classical models presented by the artist, John Henry Foley, and plaster casts of high crosses [1:18]. The statue of Lieutenant Hamilton defending the British Embassy at Kabul in 1879 by Charles Bell Birch dominated a scene which also included the red coats of the Irish yeomanry [1:29]. The faded colours of the Clare militia, as well as embroidered robes from the Imperial Palace at Peking, were suspended from the gallery. The magnificent collection of Irish antiquities recently presented by the Royal Irish Academy was displayed in rooms off the gallery on the first floor of the centre court. The Museum, Library and Leinster House shared the same grassed courtyard, dominated by a huge bronze statue of Queen Victoria. Leinster House was then part of the Science and Art complex and contained the offices of the Museum and Library staffs. Leinster House and the Museum with its frequent lectures and *conversazione* evenings occupied a significant position in the social life of turn-of-the-century Dublin, a position which the present Museum is trying to regain a century later. The visits of crowned heads and other dignitaries copperfasten the Museum's place in the public mind [1:30], while participation in major international exhibitions and smaller touring exhibitions of our own collections help fly the cultural flag abroad.

While now justifiably regarded as treasures of ancient Ireland, the two hundred or so items discussed and illustrated here were not made for museums. They were, without exception, produced by the finest craftsmen of their day and were preserved and venerated because of the beliefs associated with their shape and symbolism and the wealth that was lovingly lavished upon their production. Some were even placed in burials. The Late Bronze Age gold hoards are themselves even thought to have been substitutes for burials!

Spanning a period of some five thousand years and made to the highest standards, there is about nearly all of the objects selected for discussion here a monumentality and sanctity which makes a national museum of antiquities the most fitting repository. They are, after all, the best expressions of their ancient times.

While the treasures remind us of our transience, their current location in the Museum highlights the human desire to preserve what is best from the past. In their own time the medieval treasures would have been kept in castles or great churches and while now, in the prevailing view of this time, they rightly find themselves in the galleries of the National Museum [1:31, 1.32], this may not be for ever — we can only guess at how such treasures will fare in the distant future. We must hope that by preserving and studying them as best we can while they are in our care we will ensure that future generations will continue to see in them the uniqueness and artistry of the craftsmen of ancient Ireland.

∞

The selection of artefacts and their accompanying texts have been left to the discretion of the individual contributors. It is hoped the chapters and the respective personal selections will provide an overall impression of the richness and variety of the national collection. These essays along with the introductory chapter on the history of the Museum and its collections should make it clear why the collection of Irish antiquities is so important to Ireland and so central to the *raison d'être* of the Museum. It is not intended here to provide an overall history or archaeology of Ireland, but rather to offer a text-aided pictorial impression of the principal archaeological artefacts in the collection.

Illustrations

[1:1] Royal Irish Academy Museum, Dawson Street, Dublin.
Exhibition case with bog body from Gallagh, Co. Galway. The bog body, found in 1821, was exhibited in the 'crypt' or basement of the Academy's museum and was known as the 'Irish Mummy'.

[1:2] Royal Irish Academy, Register of Antiquities.
When Major Robert J. MacEniry moved with the antiquities collection to the Museum from the Academy in 1890 he brought with him the related catalogues and registers. These included his own manuscript *Catalogue* of the Petrie collection (1874), W.F. Wakeman's *Catalogue* of the same collection (1867). The Academy also provided a *Donations Book* (1785–1856) as well as its *Register of Antiquities* (1846–53) and the wonderful RIA *Register of Antiquities* commenced in 1859. The latter along with the boxes of *Antiquities Dockets* form the basis of the registration system which still obtains. A page from the *Register of Antiquities* (1886–1928) illustrated here shows a collection of Irish ethnographical specimens collected in 1918 by Henry Crawford and presented by him to the Royal Irish Academy. Also to be seen is a coloured drawing of a glass bead found in June 1918 by C. Kean, museum attendant, in the water at the Pigeon House Fort, Dublin.

[1:3] A Department of Agriculture and Technical Instruction advertisement.
This is a Department of Agriculture and Technical Instruction advertisement for ancient bones. The department had responsibility for the museum from 1900 until the foundation of the Irish State in 1922.

[1:4] Museum of Decorative Arts and History, Collins Barracks, Dublin.
Dublin's former Royal Barracks was handed over to the Irish Free State by the British in 1922. The nineteen-acre site has an esplanade fronting onto the River Liffey and, reputedly, was the oldest continuously-occupied military barracks in Europe until refurbished for the National Museum of Ireland in 1997. It was designed by Thomas Burgh and enlarged in the mid-eighteenth century. The founder of Irish republicanism, Wolfe Tone, was put to death here in 1798. Three floors of exhibition galleries are open on two of the wings of the best surviving square — Clarke Square. The eighteenth-century riding school is also used for exhibitions and a conservation laboratory has been opened at the western end of the site. The main galleries will be located in a new headquarters building on the site of one of the original squares which was demolished for health reasons over a century ago. *Inset:* A view of Clarke Square through the north archway.
Dunlevy 2002.

[1:5] MUSEUM OF COUNTRY LIFE, TURLOUGH PARK, CASTLEBAR, CO. MAYO.

The Venetian Gothic building of the Fitzgerald family was built in 1865 and its gardens have been refurbished for the Museum's folklife collection for which the Office of Public Works designed a new museum building nearby as well as storage and conservation areas. Now known as the Museum of Country Life, this is the only branch of the National Museum outside Dublin and is located at Turlough on the Dublin road near Castlebar. The original house was designed by Thomas Newenham Deane, the architect who was also to design the Museum's Kildare Street building; it serves as the main office as well as the education/reception area and is used to show visitors how families like its original owners lived. This contrasts with the main exhibition in the new building which deals with traditional crafts, beliefs and everyday life in rural Ireland in the century or so since the Great Famine.

≈

[1:6] MUSEUM OF NATURAL HISTORY, MERRION STREET, DUBLIN.

The foundation stone was laid in March 1856 by the Lord Lieutenant and a lecture was delivered by Dr Livingstone on his 'African discoveries'. 'The day was remarkably fine, and 'the gathering was numerous and brilliant'. This building was designed by Frederick V. Clarendon. It is the oldest purpose-built museum building in Ireland and even on the opening day was regarded as 'the National Museum of Ireland'. Actually, *objects d'art* were exhibited in the building when it first opened in 1857 because the National Gallery was not yet ready. It contains many types of specimens and comprises two main exhibition galleries — the lowermost dealing with the mammals and birds of Ireland and the upper (*inset*) (overseen by whale skeletons), which is mainly devoted to animals of more exotic origin. The natural history stores are in Beggar's Bush barracks and the earth science collections will go on show at Collins Barracks. The main picture shows the present entrance which was made in the 1920s; the building was originally entered from the side.

O'Riordan 1986.

≈

[1:7] MUSEUM OF ARCHAEOLOGY AND HISTORY, KILDARE STREET, DUBLIN.

Designed by Sir Thomas Newenham Deane and his son Thomas Manly Deane, the building was opened to the public in 1890. The lower picture shows the 200-foot-long Kildare Street elevation, which has been restored by the Office of Public Works. The present main entrance to the rotunda is through a double iron gate. The original main entrance would have been through the main gates to Leinster House, the yard of which opened to both the National Museum and Library. The intention is to have the definitive entrance to the Museum through the present 'back' door in the fine Kildare Place elevation.

Mac Lochlainn, O'Riordan and Wallace 1977; Crooke 2000.

≈

[1:8] ROYAL IRISH ACADEMY MUSEUM, DAWSON STREET, DUBLIN: EARLY MEDIEVAL ANTIQUITIES.
View of the way the Cross of Cong, the copy of St Manchan's Shrine and the Shrine of St Patrick's Tooth were exhibited in the long room of the Royal Irish Academy, Dawson Street. The Academy's *Case Inventory* was commenced in 1882 and gives lists of objects on display in the long room, the gallery of the reading room and the crypts. Distinctions are drawn between objects in 'presses' and 'table cases' and whether they were in 'trays', 'desks' or 'drawers' in the long room. There were 'presses' as well as 'recesses' and 'drawers' in the reading room with objects (especially silver coins) on 'shelves', or in 'cabinets' or 'rail cases', the latter pair having 'drawers'. In the less formal crypts distinctions were drawn between 'cases', 'iron stands', 'the floor' and 'the transverse wall', with many objects on shelves. The dug-out canoes and other wooden objects, some of which feature in William Wilde's *Catalogue*, were placed on these iron stands.
O'Raifeartaigh 1985; Crooke 2000.

[1:9] ROYAL IRISH ACADEMY MUSEUM, DAWSON STREET, DUBLIN: THE GOLD ROOM.
Many of the gold objects were located in what is called the 'old strong room' (i.e. the long room). There was a *Register of objects in the strong room of the Museum* as well as an *Inventory of the Collection* which listed 'the gold acquired up to 1881'. In the *Register*, distinctions are made between 'wall cases', 'desk cases' and a 'window case', each of which was fitted with 'drawers'.
O'Raifeartaigh 1985; Crooke 2000.

[1:10] ROYAL IRISH ACADEMY MUSEUM, DAWSON STREET, DUBLIN: PREHISTORIC ANTIQUITIES.
View of the south and east sides and centre of the long room in the old Academy museum. Note the cauldron from Castlederg, Co. Tyrone on the floor, the stone axes and bronze antiquities in the wall cases and the shield.

[1:11] ROYAL IRISH ACADEMY MUSEUM, DAWSON STREET, DUBLIN: EARLY MEDIEVAL ANTIQUITIES.
The Ardagh Chalice as displayed at the Academy and, in the foreground, a collection of Early Christian handbells. This is a view of the north-west side and centre area of the long room. Sir William Wilde compiled a manuscript *Catalogue of Ecclesiastical Antiquities* between 1856 and 1866. W.F. Wakeman compiled a *Catalogue* of specimens in the collection of the Royal Irish Academy which in 1894 was advanced to galley stage with a preface by Valentine Ball (Director), who described this exercise as 'preparing labels'. Material for two volumes appears to have been prepared, the first being typeset at the Museum's own printshop. Although never definitively published, these Catalogues are still a fundamental part of the Museum's basic register.
O'Raifeartaigh 1985; Crooke 2000.

[1:12] WATERCOLOUR SHOWING GROUP OF EARLY MEDIEVAL ANTIQUITIES.

This watercolour includes the Navan harness mounts [see also 5:11], crozier crooks, the Aghaboe figure [5:34], the Clonmacnoise Crozier [6:31] and the Armagh Bell. Unsigned and undated but probably one of a series of watercolours commissioned by the Academy from the artist James Plunket around 1845-6.

[1:13] VISIT OF PRINCESS BEATRICE TO THE NATIONAL MUSEUM.
BELOW RIGHT: EARLY VIEW OF ROYAL IRISH ACADEMY COLLECTION
IN THEIR NEW CASES IN KILDARE STREET.

This drawing by J.H. Bacon was made from a sketch by Enoch Ward in 1900 when Princess Beatrice came to the Museum during Queen Victoria's visit to Dublin. It shows George Coffey showing the Ardagh Chalice in the presence of Colonel G.T. Plunkett (Director) and H. Bantry White as well as Lord Cecil (*extreme left*) and Minnie Cochrane.

The letter below shows that the Queen herself did not visit the Museum. Below (*right*) is a view of one of the galleries showing the Late Bronze Age horns, the Loughnashade trumpet, the harps and Early Iron Age horse-bits and leading pieces in their new cases in Kildare Street with, in the distance, a selection of Early Christian handbells.

[1:14] BROIGHTER HOARD, CO. DERRY.
Early Iron Age, first century BC

Modern photograph of the famous Early Iron Age hoard which threw considerable light on Ireland, its technology, beliefs and international contacts around the first century BC. Legal and related events following its discovery were to have major repercussions for the Museum and its widespread acceptance as the National Museum of Ireland. The part played by the State's Counsel, Sir Edward Carson, the later leader of Ulster Unionism, in the return of the hoard to Ireland was not inconsiderable.
Warner 1982, 29–30; Raftery 1983.

[1:15] ARRIVAL OF THE ADDERGOOLE DUG-OUT CANOE, LURGAN, CO. GALWAY,
AT THE MUSEUM IN THE SUMMER OF 1902.

The discovery of the canoe at Lurgan, Addergoole, Co. Galway, was recorded by Dr T.B. Costello of Tuam, Co. Galway, the previous year. The view is from inside the grounds of Leinster House, looking across Kildare Street towards Molesworth Street. The canoe was brought by rail to Dublin and from the station to Kildare Street on specially linked carts pulled by horses. It was raised on brackets on the wall of the centre court; timber-framed showcases were later fitted underneath. Most recently, these showed medieval wooden statues before the canoe was lowered to its present position in 1994. The canoe has been radio-carbon dated to about 2200 BC, making it one of the oldest specimens known. It was carved from a huge oak tree and was paddled probably by as many as half a dozen kneeling warriors possibly on a parade occasion.
Costello 1902, 57–9.

[1:16] Old gate to Leinster House.

The gate was taken down in 1889 as part of the building programme for the new Museum and Library complex. Note the theatre and music-hall posters and the builder's sheds in the yard to the right of the gateway. The new gates and railing may be seen in the previous photograph [1:15]. Note the RDS emblem (statue of Minerva) on top of the archway.
Griffin and Pegum 2000, 7–9.

❧

[1:17] Centre court, Kildare Street on opening night, 1890.

This is how the centre court was dressed for the opening ceremony at 4 p.m. on 29 August 1890. The upper photograph shows the attendants, a policeman, a tradesman and an overseer. The museum was opened by the Lord Lieutenant, the Earl of Zetland. The architect, Thomas Newenham Deane, was knighted and the director, Valentine Ball, was awarded a lesser honour on the occasion of the opening.

❧

[1:18] Kildare Street, centre court with high crosses.

Photograph showing casts of high crosses made in the 1890s. Note also the casts of Italian Renaissance panels on the far end wall which were only taken down in the last few years.

❧

[1:19] Count Plunkett with the Museums Association, 1912.

Count George N. Plunkett with members of the Museums Association on the steps of the rotunda during their visit to the Museum in 1912. In his address to them, the Lord Mayor felt they 'would give a fillip to the great Gaelic revival going on in Ireland'. The Museum had previously hosted the Association's visit in 1894 when its director, Valentine Ball, was President. Ball was director from 1883 (when he succeeded Dr William Edward Steele who was director from 1878) until 1895 when he was succeeded by Colonel G.T. Plunkett, late of the Indian Army.

❧

**[1:20] Decorative ironwork on roof: spandrels and railings,
first floor gallery, Kildare Street.**

This view across the gallery of the centre court shows the ironwork of the great late-Victorian hall with its glass roof before it was finally darkened for conservation reasons. Note the large iron spandrels, the ornate capitals of the cast-iron columns and the classical motifs on the rails.

❧

**[1:21] Viking ship at Kildare Place 1998 (*top*). Mary McAleese,
President of Ireland and HRH Prince Joachim of Denmark at the opening of
the *Viking Ships* exhibition (*bottom*).**

Replica of the Viking-age coastal-trading boat known as the *Roar Ege*. This was brought to Dublin on a Danish Royal Navy ship for display outside the Museum at Kildare Place in 1998 to highlight the *Viking Ships* Exhibition opened by Mary McAleese, President of Ireland in the presence of HRH Prince Joachim of Denmark.

❧

[1:22] Dr Adolf Mahr (*extreme left*) at the
Early Bronze Age cemetery of Keenoge, Co. Meath, in 1929.

In 1928 Mahr came to the Museum from the Natural History and Prehistoric Museum in Vienna. He was an expert on the early Iron Age who quickly established himself in the English-speaking archaeological world, becoming President of the Prehistoric Society, to whom he gave a long address in 1937 presenting an assessment of Irish prehistory as it then stood. He also published an album of *Christian Art in Ancient Ireland* to coincide with the Eucharistic Congress in Dublin in 1932. He was instrumental in the acquisition by the Museum of the Bender Collection of Oriental tapestries and silks and influenced a whole generation of younger Irish archaeologists, particularly after he became director in 1933, up to which time he had been Keeper of Irish Antiquities. More than anyone, he is the founding figure of modern Irish archaeology as much as George Petrie, Sir William Wilde and George Coffey are the founders of the subject in general. Sadly, he was caught up in German politics of the thirties and left Dublin in 1939, never to return to his desk in Kildare Street.

❧

[1:23] Kildare Street: architect's plans of the Museum of Science and Art.

Thomas Newenham Deane (1828–99) was born in Cork where his father was also an architect. Educated at Trinity College, Dublin, he was made a partner in his father's practice along with Benjamin Woodward in 1851. They were influenced by John Ruskin and had a role in the Gothic Revival in England. Their best designs are the museum at Trinity College, Dublin (1854–7) and the museum at Oxford (1854–60). Turlough Park House, Castlebar, belongs to this phase of their work. They also designed the Kildare Street Club, Dublin. Deane later formed a practice with his son, Thomas Manly, with whom he designed the Museum and Library buildings and at the opening of which he was knighted.

Two competitions had to be held to find a design. Entries were selected under mottos, 'Crom-a-Boo' [*sic*] the motto of the Fitzgeralds being that of the winners, T.N. Deane's design. Deane's design has been called 'an accomplished exercise in Victorian Palladianism', the rotunda apparently being inspired by Schinkel's Altes Museum in Berlin which was built sixty years earlier.

O'Dwyer 1987, 23–24; O'Dwyer 1997.

❧

[1:24] Kildare Street: building in progress.

The foundation stone for the new Museum was laid by the Prince of Wales on the afternoon of 10 April 1885. Guided by the director, Valentine Ball, this seems to have been a more prestigious occasion than the actual opening over five years later. The building work was carried out by J. and W. Beckett of South King Street, Dublin, whose work is shown at two different stages here: the first (*above*) with the masons' huts and the back of the old entrance and the second (*below*) with the building nearly finished.

O'Dwyer 1987, 23–24.

❧

[1:25] KILDARE STREET: CARVED WOODEN DOOR PANELS.

There are approximately 33 doors in the Museum in Kildare Street carved by Carlo Cambi of Siena. The carved panels feature a wealth of motifs referring to art, mythology, science and industry and of the thousand or so carved panels few are the same in either shape or design. Many of the panels are marked with Cambi's stamp and the architects' names.

McCarthy 2002, 71–9.

[1:26] KILDARE STREET: SIGNS OF THE ZODIAC ON THE ROTUNDA FLOOR.

The mosaic floors in the rotunda feature signs of the zodiac. They were installed by Ludwig Oppenheimer of Manchester who was responsible for all the mosaic floors with their classical motifs on the ground floor in Kildare Street.

[1:27] KILDARE STREET: SIKH GUNS IN THE ROTUNDA.

These field guns were captured from the Sikhs by the British Army in 1846 and presented to Sir Hugh Gough (later Lord Gough), commander in chief of the British Army in India. They were subsequently loaned to the Museum where they were displayed in the Rotunda, Kildare Street, later they were moved to the colonnade outside and more recently two were sent to Army Headquarters at McKee Barracks, Dublin. Many of the classical figures are modelled from the collection of John Henry Foley (1818–74), regarded during his lifetime as the leading sculptor in Ireland.

[1:28] KILDARE STREET: CARRIAGES IN THE ROTUNDA, INCLUDING THE LORD CHANCELLOR'S COACH.

The coach on the right was manufactured by Philip Godsall of London and imported to Ireland in 1790. It was used by Lord Clare, the Lord Chancellor of Ireland and was exhibited in the Rotunda from 1899–1929. In 1982 it was restored at the Museum.

Strickland 1921, 61–67; McEvansoneya 2000, 80–87.

[1:29] KILDARE STREET: CENTRE COURT.

The striking feature of Lieutenant Walter Richard Pollock Hamilton by Charles Bell Birch shows its subject defending the British Embassy in Kabul in 1879.

[1:30] KILDARE STREET: VISITS BY FOREIGN DIGNITARIES.

Queen Beatrix of the Netherlands and Prince Klaus visited in 1990 (*top*). King Carl XVI Gustaf of Sweden and Queen Silvia visited in 1992 (*lower left*). The then Crown Prince Akihito and Crown Princess Michiko of Japan came to the Museum in 1985 (*lower right*).

[1:31] VIEW OF CENTRE COURT, KILDARE STREET, WITH THE DERRYNAFLAN HOARD.

This first showing of the recently-found Derrynaflan hoard (displayed in the centre of the photograph) attracted great crowds to the Museum in 1980. The Ardagh Chalice was placed in the smaller case beside it for comparative purposes. Note the Derrynaflan bucket (acquired two years earlier) in the right foreground, the Kavanagh Charter Horn to the left behind the replica of St Manchan's Shrine, and the gold ornaments in the six showcases behind. The use of perspex-topped cases was then an early attempt to break from the older timber-framed glass case.

❧

[1:32] MEDIEVAL IRELAND, 1150–1550 EXHIBITION, KILDARE STREET.

Opened in 2001, the *Medieval Ireland 1150–1550* exhibition builds on experiences of using interpretative planners, architects and conservators with educators and curators in an integrated way. This approach was first tried in the *The Way We Wore* exhibition at Collins Barracks and later developed at the Museum of Country Life in Castlebar. The exhibition displays the collections in three segments — warfare, everyday life (rural and urban) and the Museum's great holdings of medieval ecclesiastical treasures. The view here shows that part of the exhibition devoted to warfare.

❧

[1:4]
**MUSEUM OF DECORATIVE ARTS AND HISTORY,
COLLINS BARRACKS, DUBLIN.**

[1:5]

MUSEUM OF COUNTRY LIFE, TURLOUGH PARK, CASTLEBAR, CO. MAYO.

[1:6]
MUSEUM OF NATURAL HISTORY,
MERRION STREET, DUBLIN.

[1:8]
ROYAL IRISH ACADEMY MUSEUM, DAWSON STREET, DUBLIN: EARLY MEDIEVAL ANTIQUITIES.

[1:9]
ROYAL IRISH ACADEMY MUSEUM, DAWSON STREET, DUBLIN: THE GOLD ROOM.

ROYAL IRISH ACADEMY MUSEUM, DAWSON STREET, DUBLIN: EARLY MEDIEVAL ANTIQUITIES.

[1:11]

ROYAL IRISH ACADEMY MUSEUM, DAWSON STREET, DUBLIN: PREHISTORIC ANTIQUITIES.

[1:10]

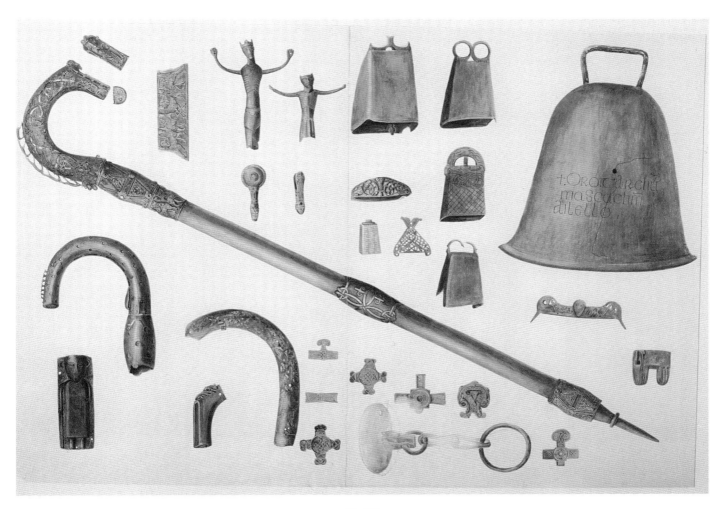

[1:12]

WATERCOLOUR SHOWING GROUP OF EARLY MEDIEVAL ANTIQUITIES.

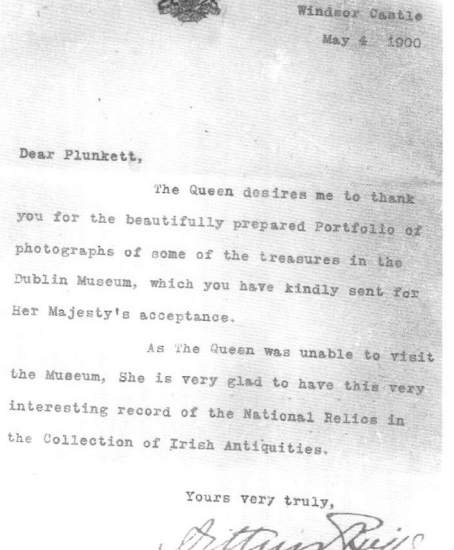

Windsor Castle
May 4 1900

Dear Plunkett,

The Queen desires me to thank
you for the beautifully prepared Portfolio of
photographs of some of the treasures in the
Dublin Museum, which you have kindly sent for
Her Majesty's acceptance.

As The Queen was unable to visit
the Museum, She is very glad to have this very
interesting record of the National Relics in
the Collection of Irish Antiquities.

Yours very truly,

[1:13]

VISIT OF PRINCESS BEATRICE TO THE NATIONAL MUSEUM.

BELOW RIGHT: EARLY VIEW OF ROYAL IRISH ACADEMY COLLECTION IN THEIR NEW CASES IN KILDARE STREET.

[1:14]

BROIGHTER HOARD, CO. DERRY.

Early Iron Age, first century BC.

[1:15]
ARRIVAL OF THE ADDERGOOLE DUG-OUT CANOE, LURGAN, CO. GALWAY, AT THE MUSEUM IN THE SUMMER OF 1902.

[1:16]

Old gate to Leinster House.

[1:17]
CENTRE COURT, KILDARE STREET ON OPENING NIGHT, 1890.

[1:18]

Kildare Street, centre court with high crosses.

[1:19]

Count Plunkett with The Museums Association, 1912.

[1:20]

DECORATIVE IRONWORK ON ROOF: SPANDRELS AND RAILINGS, FIRST FLOOR GALLERY, KILDARE STREET.

[1:21]
VIKING SHIP AT KILDARE PLACE 1998 (*TOP*).
(Photograph above courtesy of Independent Newspapers)
MARY MCALEESE, PRESIDENT OF IRELAND AND HRH PRINCE JOACHIM OF DENMARK AT THE OPENING OF
THE *VIKING SHIPS* EXHIBITION (*BOTTOM*).

[1:22]

DR ADOLF MAHR (*EXTREME LEFT*) AT THE EARLY BRONZE AGE CEMETERY OF KEENOGE, CO. MEATH, 1929.

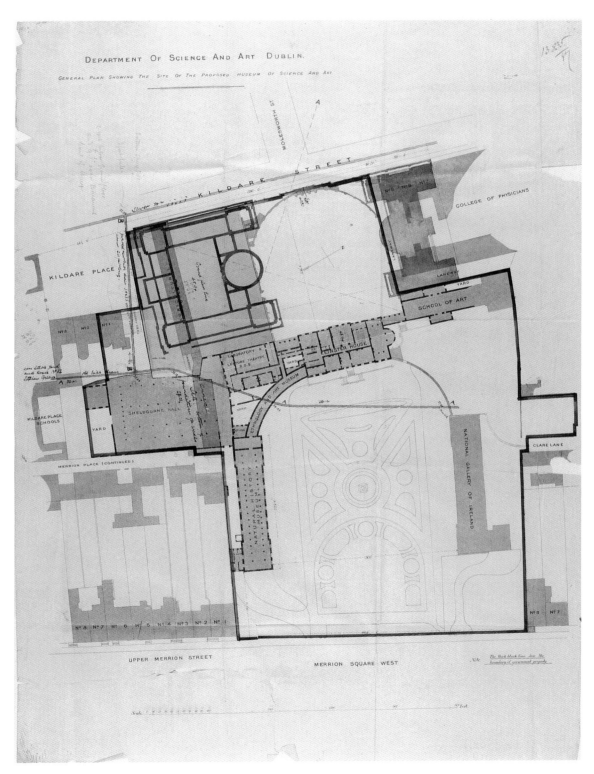

[1:23]

KILDARE STREET: ARCHITECTS' PLANS OF THE MUSEUM OF SCIENCE AND ART.

[1:24]

KILDARE STREET: BUILDING IN PROGRESS.

[1:25]

KILDARE STREET: CARVED WOODEN DOOR PANELS.

[1:26]

KILDARE STREET: SIGNS OF THE ZODIAC ON THE ROTUNDA FLOOR.

[1:27]

KILDARE STREET: SIKH GUNS IN THE ROTUNDA.

[1:28]

KILDARE STREET: CARRIAGES IN THE ROTUNDA; INCLUDING THE LORD CHANCELLOR'S COACH.

[1:29]

KILDARE STREET: CENTRE COURT.

[1:30]

KILDARE STREET: VISITS BY FOREIGN DIGNITARIES.

(Photograph lower right courtesy of Independent Newspapers)

[1:31]
VIEW OF CENTRE COURT, KILDARE STREET, WITH DERRYNAFLAN HOARD, 1980.

[1:32]
MEDIEVAL IRELAND, 1150–1550 EXHIBITION, KILDARE STREET.

2

PREHISTORIC ANTIQUITIES

FROM THE STONE AGE TO THE END OF THE MIDDLE BRONZE AGE

EAMONN P. KELLY

In October 1968, the late Professor G.F. Mitchell visited the site of a quarry at Mell, on the outskirts of Drogheda, Co. Louth to study a deposit of gravel that had been carried there by an ice sheet sometime before 70,000 BC. Professor Mitchell collected a number of flints from the gravel, which he took with him for further study in the laboratory. Later, on closer examination, Professor Mitchell realised that the largest piece of flint was of greater interest than he had first assumed. The Mell flake [2:3] was made by human hands and although it was not actually fashioned in Ireland but transported here in gravel carried by an ice sheet, it is the earliest artefact to have been found in Ireland.

On present evidence, it was not until around 7000 BC, during the Mesolithic period, that the earliest human settlers came to live in Ireland. These were hunters whose tools and equipment were fashioned from stone, wood, bone, animal hides and other natural raw materials, much of which have not survived. Excavation has produced tiny blades and points called microliths, which were used by the earliest colonists in composite harpoon-like implements together with scrapers and stone axes fashioned by grinding a sharp edge on a suitably shaped pebble. By around 4500 BC composite tools appear to have been replaced by larger flake implements called Bann Flakes, named after the river Bann along whose valley they were first found in Ireland. One such Bann Flake was found on a farm at Cloonarragh, Co. Roscommon and in another field close by was discovered a beautifully polished stone spearhead of the

[2:1]
STONE SPEARHEAD,
CLOONARRAGH,
CO. ROSCOMMON.
Late Mesolithic
4300-3900 BC.

same period [2:1]. Made usually from slate or mudstone, only around a dozen objects of the type have been found in Ireland, although the form appears to have been distributed widely. Measuring 37.8 cm in length, the Cloonarragh spearhead is made from black baked hornfels, of great hardness, carefully polished and ground to produce an object of elegant form and symmetry. The quality of its finish and the care and attention lavished on its manufacture suggest that the Cloonarragh spearhead may have had significance beyond mere functionality.

By around 3700 BC farming replaced the hunting and gathering economy of Mesolithic Ireland and the large numbers of polished stone axes that survive from the Neolithic period bear witness to the extensive woodland clearance that began at this time. The stone axe was an indispensable general tool, supplemented occasionally for more specialist work by polished stone chisels and adzes. A wide variety of axes were produced, most of which were polished overall. Fine-grained rock was sometimes quarried and the axes were first shaped roughly by chipping, flaking or pecking before being ground and polished on a grinding stone using a mixture of sand and water. Axe factories at Rathlin Island and Tievebulliagh Mountain, Co. Antrim, utilised a rock called porcellanite and the products of these factories were traded over long distances. Two porcellanite artefacts originating in Co. Antrim were among a large number of stone axes found on the river Shannon at Killaloe, Co. Clare, perhaps lost by persons using the crossing place on the river [2:4]. One of these is an axe of a common shape and form having a narrow rounded butt and curved cutting edge, but another is narrow and elongated suggesting that it may have functioned as a chisel rather than an axe.

The economic importance of the stone axe is reflected in the probable use of some larger examples to signify the power, wealth and prestige of their owners. Occasionally, exotic stone axes made from rare and attractive material were acquired such as the jadeite axes found at Raymoghy, Co. Donegal, Nenagh, Co. Tipperary and Paslickstown, Co. Westmeath [2:5]. The raw material for these axes originated probably in the Piedmont area of Alpine Italy and comparable finds have been made in greater numbers in Britain. The material from which the Paslickstown axe is made appears to be particularly close to that of an axe found at Daviot, Invernesshire, Scotland.

Further confirmation of the status of stone axes comes from their deposition in Neolithic burials. Diminutive axes have also been found in burial contexts while some perforated examples are likely to have functioned as amulets or may have been used in a ritual context. Among objects found in the Passage Tomb known as Cairn R2, Loughcrew, Co. Meath was a tiny porcellanite axe measuring a mere 2.2 cm in length. The context of its discovery and its diminutive size indicate that the object was for ritual use. Two collections of antiquities, one from the vicinity of Garvagh, Co. Derry and the other from the vicinity of Ballymena, Co. Antrim each contain a small axe the scale of which suggests that they were not made with a utilitarian function in mind. The Ballymena example was almost certainly an amulet as it is perforated to facilitate a suspension cord [2:6].

At various times during the Neolithic period, different burial rites were followed. Megalithic tombs, large burial monuments built of stone, were popular mainly in the northern half of the country where the commonest types of burial monuments are called Court Tombs, Portal Tombs, and Passage Tombs. In the southern half of the country single burials placed in cists beneath round cairns occur.

Besides stone axes, Neolithic tombs contain a range of other ritual objects that accompanied the dead. Among the outstanding products of the knapper's art are beautifully made points for javelins that appear to be associated mainly with the builders of Court Tombs. Around one hundred and fifty examples are known and the find sites are concentrated in the north east of the island where good quality flint is to be obtained. Kellysgrove, Co. Galway lies at the southern end of the distribution where, at a depth of thirteen feet in a bog, a javelin head was discovered by a man cutting peat [2:7]. It is not made of flint but of partially desilicified chert that presented a greater challenge to its maker. Of elongated lozenge shape, the flat surfaces were polished to an even smoothness before a combination of careful flaking and chipping sharpened the edges.

An outstanding artistic achievement is the flint macehead from a Passage Tomb at Knowth, Co. Meath, which bears elaborate raised decoration [2:8]. A difficult and laborious process whereby the hard background was reduced so as to leave the decoration standing in relief was employed to produce it and the technical virtuosity and finesse involved demonstrate that one is dealing with the work of a master craftsman. No other decorated Neolithic macehead has been found in Ireland and, although a number have been found in Britain, none possesses the outstanding quality of the Knowth find. However, the possibility that the Knowth example is an import cannot be discounted. In Ireland, other maceheads occur which are of a type associated with the users of Passage Tombs. Although undecorated they are masterly works of art fashioned beautifully from specially selected stone. Elegant examples such as those from near Bushmills, Co. Antrim and Lough Fea, Doohatty, Co. Monaghan are of a type similar to finds from the north of Britain, in particular Orkney where Passage Tombs are also found [2:9]. Small amulets that appear to be modelled on maceheads are part of the ritual equipment found in Irish Passage Tombs [2:10]. Phallus-shaped amulets also occur along with beads made from a variety of carefully chosen stone.

Phallus-shaped objects found near the entrances to the Passage Tombs at Newgrange and Knowth, Co. Meath may have been associated with ceremonial rites concerned in part with fertility, emphasising the continuity of society [2:11]. Unlike the Newgrange object, which is plain, the Knowth find is highly decorated. Comparable decorated objects of bone or antler are known from Knowth and Fourknocks I, Co. Meath and plain examples with domed heads that may also have possessed a similar symbolic significance occur widely in Passage Tombs.

Neolithic household goods included undecorated, often shouldered, pottery bowls used for storage and cooking while finely decorated vessels were made to accompany burials. Small Necked Vessels with elaborate designs are associated with single burials placed in cists beneath round cairns. One such burial at Baunogenasraid, Co. Carlow that contained the unburnt remains of an adult male of large stature was accompanied by a vessel of supreme excellence [2:12]. The rim is decorated with bands of elongated impressed triangles while the entire surface of the bowl is adorned with a series of concentric-arc motifs. The general impression given by the ornamental style employed on vessels of this type is that of the imitation of basketry.

Prehistoric basketry and other artefacts made from organic material survive only in exceptional circumstances and are rendered all the more precious both by their rarity and for the tantalising insight they provide into the rich material culture of ancient communities. In 1967, a bog at Aghintemple, Co. Longford yielded a Neolithic woven bag that contained a small stone axe. Only fragments of the bag survived and its overall size and form could not be determined. However, during the same year, a better-preserved woven bag was found over eleven feet deep in a bog at Twyford, Co. Westmeath [2:13]. With two handles, it is circular, made by a simple coiling technique using naturally available vegetal material.

Due to a lack of survival we can tell nothing about the form of dress of Neolithic people but the assortment of beads and amulets found in tombs suggests that attention was lavished on attire and personal adornment. This is borne out further by finds made on two male skeletons buried in a cist beneath a round cairn at Knockmaree, Phoenix Park, Dublin [2:14]. Both wore necklaces made of periwinkle shells, one of 195 and the other of 274 shells. Strung in two opposing asymmetrical rows, with the domed surfaces to the outside to create a pleasing aesthetic effect, the shells of both necklaces are graduated in size towards the midpoint where the larger shells are placed.

As well as a new technology, the earliest metal-smiths brought with them a new burial practice in the form of a new type of megalithic monument known as a Wedge Tomb. They also brought in a new distinctive, decorated pottery called Beaker Pottery, made usually in the form of tall vessels, although bowls, sometimes on legs, are also known.

When the knowledge of metalworking was introduced to Ireland around 2500 BC, the possibility of producing a whole new range of tools and weapons was presented.

The earliest metal objects such as flat axes were made from pure copper, which could be cast easily and hardened by hammering.

Gold could simply be hammered into sheets of the required shape and size and the raw material was probably acquired from alluvial deposits. Some copper may have been collected on the surface but quite soon mines were dug for the extraction of ore. One such copper mine at Ross Island, Killarney, Co. Kerry was in use by at least 2400 BC. Having first been shattered by setting a fire against the rock-face and then throwing water on the heated surface, the ores were prised from the surrounding rock using hammers and wedges. Once carried to the surface in baskets the ore was crushed before being smelted to produce ingots which were later turned into tools.

The earliest groups of gold objects in Ireland began to be produced probably between 2200 and 1800 BC. Although ear-rings, bracelets, a gold pin and decorated gold bands and plaques are known [2:15], overwhelmingly the earliest forms produced were discs, sometimes found in matching pairs, and neck ornaments known as lunulae, which predominate.

About twenty gold discs measuring between 1.1 cm and 11.4 cm in diameter are known, almost all of which are decorated, the motifs consisting of concentric lines, concentric rows of dots, crosses, triangles and zigzags. The ornament on one group of discs is dominated by a ladder-patterned cruciform motif. This group contains a pair of discs found at Rappa Castle, near Ballina, Co. Mayo with which comparisons can be drawn with Beaker-phase material found in Britain [2:16]. The Rappa Castle discs may therefore be among the earliest Beaker-phase gold objects to have been produced in Ireland. The presence of a pair of perforations near the centres of the discs, together with the thinness of the metal, suggests that they were attached to a backing, possibly a garment worn on special occasions. The finest Irish examples are a pair of gold discs from Tedavnet, Co. Monaghan [2:17].

Other very early Irish gold artefacts include a pair of unlocalised basket-shaped objects that may have served as hair ornaments, but which are more likely to be ear-rings. They can be compared with similar finds from Beaker burials in Britain for which a continental background seems likely.

The lunula might be regarded as the most characteristic gold object of the Irish Early Bronze Age. Using thinly beaten sheets, gold was fashioned into crescent shapes with expanded horn terminals set at right angles to the plane of the crescent. Incised or punched decoration, confined normally to the horns and the internal and external edges, consists usually of fields of simple geometric patterns. These patterns can be compared with decoration found on pottery such as Beaker pottery and Bowl Food Vessels as well as that found on certain flat copper-alloy axes and kite-shaped spearheads. More than one hundred lunulae are known from Western Europe of which more than eighty have been found in Ireland. Lunulae have been classified into three groups designated as Classical, Unaccomplished and Provincial. The most proficiently-executed examples, which also display the greatest symmetry in the layout of their ornament, are of the Classical type, an exceptionally fine example of which is said to have been found at Rossmore Park, Drumbanagher, Co. Monaghan [2:18]. Other impressive examples are those from Trillick, Co. Tyrone [2:19] and near Killarney, Co. Kerry [2:20]. A lunula from Ballinagroun, Co. Kerry [2:21] is unusual in that close examination confirms that accomplished decoration was erased and replaced some time later by a scheme which is less expert in its execution. The reason for this remains inexplicable.

Unaccomplished lunulae use less metal and display a lesser degree of skill in their manufacture although the type appears to be related closely to the Classical type. These two types were manufactured in Ireland and examples found abroad are likely to be Irish exports. By contrast, only one example of the third group, designated as the Provincial type, has been found in Ireland and examples of the type may be of foreign manufacture, based on Irish prototypes. Provincial lunulae tend to be thicker and more rigid and display greater variation in the decorative motifs employed.

Gold was not the only material used to produce high status objects of personal adornment. Among the earliest Bronze Age finds are buttons made from fossil wood of jet or lignite which can be polished to a lustrous black finish. The buttons have distinctive V-shaped perforations at the back for attachment to a garment that was worn presumably on special occasions. Jet and lignite was also used to produce crescent-shaped, multi-strand necklaces with spacer beads such as an incomplete example found at Comber, Co. Down. Similar necklaces, the form of which closely mirrors the lunula, as well as examples made of amber, have been found in Britain and further afield.

The earliest copper objects were cast in single-piece stone moulds and then later, two-piece stone moulds were developed. A further development was mixing or alloying copper with tin to produce a harder metal — bronze. In time tools and weapons of increasing complexity came to be made and much attention was concentrated on developing effective designs to secure the objects, mainly axes, to their handles. Initially, this was done by means of flanges — raised edges — which ensured a more secure grip. The very earliest axes are plain, but from early in the Bronze Age decoration came to be applied to many of them, usually in the form of punched or hammered geometric patterns. The continuing importance from Neolithic times of the axe is illustrated by the discovery of a decorated example, found in a bog at Brockagh, Co. Kildare, retained in a leather sheath [2:22]. A leather thong was also discovered. The axe is flat with a widely-splayed blade decorated on the two main surfaces with areas of herring-bone design formed of punched vertical rows. Low hammered-up flanges and a slight stop-ridge across the axe were designed to assist secure hafting. However, the fact that the axe was found in a leather sheath suggests that it was hafted only on certain occasions. Together with stone battle-axes and axe-like copper alloy objects known as halberds, decorated axes may have been used on ceremonial occasions to designate rank and status. This may represent the continuation of a tradition that extends back to the production of ceremonial stone axes and maceheads during the Neolithic period.

Halberds look similar to daggers of the period; unlike the daggers, however, they were hafted at right angles to the shaft in the manner of an axe. Around 350 examples are known from Ireland where they are widely distributed [2:23]. They also occur in Britain and across Europe from Scandinavia to the Mediterranean. Other products of the metal-smiths included sickles, awls, spearheads and razors.

The construction of Wedge Tombs gradually ceased around 2200 BC and was replaced by separate burials of one or more persons. Thereafter burial was either in simple pits or in stone-lined graves known as cists that sometimes formed cemeteries. In keeping with earlier burial practices the remains were cremated but, in a new development, unburnt bodies were also interred, usually in a crouched position. The positioning of the body recalls the foetal position adopted by a child in the womb and this may relate to a concept of rebirth in the afterlife. Highly decorated pots, sometimes with lids, known as Food Vessels, accompanied the dead and very occasionally other personal possessions [2:24]. Gradually, cremation became popular once more and the burnt bones were placed in large decorated pots called urns that were inverted in the graves [2:25]. A range of different types of urns known as Vase Urns, Encrusted Urns, Collared Urns and Cordoned Urns were used and, in some cases, Food Vessels and miniature vessels called Pygmy Cups or Incense Cups [2:26] were placed with them, accompanied occasionally by ceremonial stone battle-axes,

DETAIL OF [2:19]
GOLD LUNULA, TRILLICK, CO. TYRONE.
Early Bronze Age, c. 2000 BC.

DETAIL OF [2:20]
GOLD LUNULA, NEAR KILLARNEY, CO. KERRY.
Early Bronze Age,
c. 2000 BC.

daggers, pins and beads. Faience is a type of blue glass that originated in Egypt and occasionally beads made from the material have been found in Irish Bronze Age burials. Quoit-shaped, segmented and star-shaped forms are known.

Apart from burial sites, a range of Early Bronze Age ritual monuments were built including Stone Circles, Stone Alignments and single Standing Stones. A new type of rock art occurs and despite some similarities between the motifs used in Passage Tomb art, striking differences occur. Consisting of geometric designs characterised by cup-shaped depressions enclosed by one or more concentric circles the art is found carved on rock outcrops and boulders. In some areas the coincidence between the distribution of Rock Art and local copper sources has been noted. At Drumirril located on the Co. Monaghan border with Co. Louth there is an important complex where more than seventy separate decorated stones have been found which appear to have survived land clearance due to their location within a former deer park. A decorated boulder, the surface of which is covered extensively with carved and pocked decoration, was acquired by the National Museum of Ireland in 1994 having been discovered during land clearance at Kilwarden, Co. Kildare [2:27].

The centuries between 1500 and 900 BC saw a period of development and innovation, and from about 1200 BC climatic deterioration together with other factors may have been responsible for widespread change. It may also have been a time of insecurity as small settlements of the period that have been found, containing circular houses, are often sited on small islands, promontories or lake-edges, enclosed by banks, walls or palisades. The dead were cremated and sometimes placed in undecorated urns, often buried at the centre of small ring ditches. In some places burials are also found without urns, in graves called boulder burials — structures made of boulders in the manner of small megalithic tombs. Ritual Stone Circles and Alignments were also constructed, many of which appear to have been laid out so as to allow for the observation of phases of the sun and moon.

A carved wooden figure made of yew wood, found in a bog at Ralaghan, Co. Cavan, provides further insight into the religious practices of the time. The figure was almost certainly an idol of a type that was used over a wide area of Europe where similar figures have been found dating from Middle Bronze Age to Early Iron Age times.

A second important phase of Bronze Age gold working occurs at this time and the output of the Middle Bronze Age goldsmiths was impressive. As in the earlier phase ornaments were produced from sheet gold, but the use of gold bars, either plain or with hammered flanges, constituted an important addition to the repertoire of the goldsmiths. New techniques were deployed to produce multifaceted ornaments by twisting thin strips of gold sheet and gold bars into an array of neck ornaments, ear-rings, bracelets, armlets and rings used as hair ornaments known as tress rings. Two spectacular twisted torcs were found on the Hill of Tara where the occurrence of numerous earthen barrows or burial monuments suggests that the hill was of ritual and political importance during the Bronze Age [2:28].

An unusual technique whereby gold wire of D-shaped cross-section was wound around a cylindrical leather core was employed to fashion a neck ornament found in a hoard at Derrinboy, Co. Offaly [2:29]. Gold objects such as torcs and ear-rings which were fashioned by twisting are otherwise plain, while sheet ornaments, such as armlets, are decorated generally with ribbed decoration formed by careful hammering and punching by means of the repoussé technique. More finely ribbed sheet objects such as bracelets and tress rings appear to have been decorated by chasing, a technique of working gold ornament from the front. In bronze working, the use of two-piece moulds of stone, and later of clay, allowed for significant improvements in the range and form of metal objects that could be made. A wide variety of bronze weapons and tools were manufactured, some of which were extremely large.

Spearheads of various forms were in use, as were axes of a type known as palstaves, and a range of smaller tools that have occasionally been found in hoards. One such hoard of note, which would seem to have been the stock in trade of a metal-smith, was found at Bishopsland, Co. Kildare, and it illustrates the range of bronze objects available during this period. Included are a variety of axes, chisels, a sickle, double-edged saw, anvil, vice, finger rings, bracelet, tweezers, flesh hook, a possible toilet article resembling an ear pick and up to forty fragments of wire and miscellaneous bronze fragments.

An important weapon of the period is the rapier which developed from the shorter daggers of an earlier period. Although weak hafting may have marred its effectiveness, the rapier was a formidable thrusting and stabbing weapon. The great skills of the bronze smiths are outstandingly illustrated in the rapier found near Lissan, Co. Derry, cast in a two-piece stone mould and finished by hammering; a wooden handle was then secured in place by two rivets [2:2]. It is the longest rapier known from Bronze Age Europe and, due to its extreme length and delicacy, great technical mastery was required in its production. In particular, the utmost control was required during the casting process to prevent differential cooling of the mould, which would have cracked the blade. Similar technical skills were required for the production of large basal-looped spearheads, some of which are of such a length that they must have been produced for ceremonial rather than utilitarian purposes. Measuring 68.2 cm. in overall length, a basal-looped spearhead found near Maghera, Co. Derry, is the longest to have survived from Ireland [2:2]. It is socketed, with an elongated triangular blade, and loops are placed at the angles formed by the socket and the flat base of the blade. Most finds of this type for which details of discovery are known are from wet or watery places such as bogs, rivers and lakes, suggesting the likelihood of deliberate ritual deposition.

[2:2]
RAPIER AND SPEARHEAD,
TULLYNURE, NEAR LISSAN
AND NEAR MAGHERA,
CO. DERRY.
Middle to Later Bronze Age,
1400–1000 BC.

ILLUSTRATIONS

[2:1] STONE SPEARHEAD, CLOONARRAGH, CO. ROSCOMMON.
Late Mesolithic, 4300–3900 BC.

Found on the surface of a ploughed field the spearhead is long and slender, flat on each face with bevelled edges. Its point is sharp and the butt is narrow and slightly rounded. The rock was identified as baked hornfels of porcellanite texture, of great hardness which is unlikely to have been obtained in Co. Roscommon. Its elegant beauty elevates it to the category of an artwork and it must have been a prized possession, perhaps denoting the rank of an important dignitary within a late Mesolithic hunting-band.
1968:208. L. 37.8 cm.
Lucas 1971, 191; Woodman et al 1999, 81–3.

[2:2] RAPIER, NEAR LISSAN, CO. DERRY, AND SPEARHEAD, TULLYVURE, NEAR MAGHERA, CO. DERRY.
Middle to Later Bronze Age, 1400–1000 BC.

The rapier was found in a bog in the townland of Tullyvure, near Lissan, Co. Derry. The rapier may date between 1400–1000 BC and for long has been regarded as the finest object of its class from Western Europe. It is of a class known as Group III rapiers of which almost three-quarters of the group have been found in Britain, the remaining examples being Irish. The Lissan rapier has a trapezoidal butt in which one rivet survives. The long elegant blade has a lozenge-shaped cross-section with bevelled edges.
1912:15. L. 79.7cm.
Anon 1846, 255; Wilde 1861, 442–3; Burgess & Gerloff 1981, no. 387, 54.

The spearhead with loops at the base of the blade found near Maghera, Co. Derry, is the second largest of its class to have been found in Ireland and it dates to between 1300–1000 BC. The object is by no means cast as proficiently as the rapier. Casting flaws near the base mean that part of the bevelled edge is absent and there is a hole in the socket while a section below the point is a cast-on repair. W18. L. 68.2 cm.
Wilde 1861, 497.

[2:3] FLINT FLAKE, MELL, CO. LOUTH.
Palaeolithic, 400,000–300,000 BC.

The Mell flake is a heavy trapezoidal flint flake with a width greater than its breadth. When striking produces a flint flake, a distinctive convex area known as a bulb of percussion is produced immediately below the point of impact. This feature is present on the Mell flake demonstrating that it was fashioned by human hands. It is not a tool but a piece of knapper's waste that is most closely comparable with the lithic products of the Clactonian and Acheulian cultures of southern Britain. These stone-working industries are associated with the activities of early hominids and the Mell flake could date as early as 400,000 BC. It was probably fashioned on land that now forms the basin of the Irish Sea where an advancing ice sheet picked it up. When the ice retreated melt-water deposited it near the Irish coast in gravel. 1972:65. L. 8.5 cm; W. 6.0 cm.
Mitchell & Sieveking 1972, 174–7.

[2:4] PORCELLANITE AXE AND CHISEL, KILLALOE, CO. CLARE.
Neolithic, 3800–2500 BC.

These beautifully polished objects from the river Shannon were among hundreds of artefacts acquired by the National Museum of Ireland during the 1930s through the energetic efforts of Mr A.B. Killeen, an engineer with the Electricity Supply Board. Made in an axe factory in Co. Antrim, in the north east of the island, the artefacts travelled a long distance before finding a watery end on the bed of the Shannon at an important crossing-place. They were found in the course of dredging work associated with the construction of a hydroelectric power station. The axe has a pointed elliptical cross-section, a narrow rounded butt and a curved cutting edge. 1934:103. L. 16.4 cm.

The curved cutting edge is at the wider end of the chisel, which has an oval cross-section tapering to a narrow circular butt. 1934:104. L. 20.7 cm.
Unpublished.

[2:5] JADEITE AXE, PASLICKSTOWN, CO. WESTMEATH.
Neolithic, 3600–2500 BC.

One of a small number of exotic imports probably from the Alpine region of northern Italy. It is unlikely to have reached Ireland in a single-stage journey and there may have been a long interval between the time of its manufacture and its arrival in the Irish midlands. The surface has a highly-polished marble finish and is of a mottled green colour. The axe is flat and thin with a pointed butt broken in antiquity. The Paslickstown axe is clearly a prestige object whose beauty and rarity would have set its owner apart in status and wealth. 1901:42. L. 19.4 cm; max. W. 9.0 cm; max. T. 1.6 cm.
Smith 1963, 69; Cooney & Mandal 1998, 105.

[2:6] THREE AXE AMULETS: LOUGHCREW, CO. MEATH; LISNASCREGHOG, GARVAGH, CO. DERRY AND BALLYMENA, CO. ANTRIM.
Neolithic, 3800–2500 BC.

The precise circumstances of discovery of the axes found at Lisnascreghog and near Ballymena are unknown. The Lisnascreghog axe has a sharp cutting edge and may have functioned as a fine tool although it is more likely to have served a ritual function. The Ballymena axe has a blunt edge and a hole by means of which it was worn as an amulet. The tiny Loughcrew axe has a fine cutting edge but its diminutive scale must surely mean that it served a ritual purpose and the context of its having been found in a Passage Tomb further underlines the point. The Loughcrew axe dates to between 3300 and 2800 BC, while the broader date range may be applied to the remaining axes. 1942:971; 1933:253; 1937:3380. L. 2.2 cm; 6.93 cm; 2.53 cm.
Unpublished.

[2:7] CHERT JAVELIN HEAD, KELLYSGROVE, CO. GALWAY.

Neolithic, 3800–2700 BC.

Found in a bog at Kellysgrove, Co. Galway. As is the case with Neolithic arrowheads, javelin heads of the period may be leaf-shaped or lozenge-shaped. The Kellysgrove example is lozenge-shaped, the butt end being shorter than the end containing the tip, which is damaged. The finely serrated edges provide a contrast with the main surfaces, which are finely polished. It seems likely that the point would have been employed on a relatively light shaft as a projectile rather than as a spear (which could serve equally as a thrusting weapon). Javelin heads range in length up to a maximum of around 25 cm. 1958:149. L. 13.6 cm; T. 0.6 cm.

Lucas 1960, 20–21; Collins 1982, 111–33.

[2:8] DECORATED MACEHEAD, KNOWTH, CO. MEATH.

Neolithic, 3300–2800 BC.

Found in the eastern chamber of the main Passage Tomb at Knowth, Co. Meath, this is an object that shows a refinement of design, sophistication and technical ability of an exceptionally high order. It is made from pale grey flint with some brown-coloured patches. Of compact hammer-shape, with a roughly trapezoidal plan, there is a cylindrical perforation for the handle located towards the narrow end. All six surfaces bear decoration in low relief carved with incredible finesse. The sides bear spiral designs that continue on to the upper and lower surfaces respectively to curve around the shaft hole. On the upper surface there is a c-shaped scroll that may represent the eyes of a human face with the shaft hole representing a gaping mouth. The ends each bear a series of interlocking elongated lozenges. No macehead with comparable decoration has been found elsewhere in Ireland although comparisons can be drawn with finds from northern and western Britain in particular. E70:31361. L. 7.9 cm; max. W. 5.4 cm; D. of perforation 1.7 cm.

Eogan & Richardson 1982, 123–38; Simpson 1988, 27–52.

[2:9] TWO STONE MACEHEADS, BUSHMILLS, CO. ANTRIM
AND LOUGH FEA, DOOHATTY, CO. MONAGHAN.

Neolithic, 3300–2800 BC.

Stone-working reached a very high standard, as shown by the perforated maceheads made of carefully selected stone from near Bushmills, Co. Antrim and Lough Fea, Doohatty, Co. Monaghan. Both are of the so-called Orkney pestle type. A cylindrical perforation is set nearer the narrower end of each and both have dome-shaped ends and concave sides. The Bushmills macehead is made from a mottled grey-green stone of considerable hardness and the larger domed end is damaged, possibly by hammering. Knowles, Coll. 568. L. 8.42 cm; max. W. 5.34; D. of perforation 1.79 cm.

Lucas 1968, 100–101; Simpson 1988, 36.

The Lough Fea macehead was found at the bottom of a bog, probably in Doohatty townland. It is a finely-polished specimen made from a very hard, whitish, gneissose rock that is not found locally. 1965:119. L. 10 cm; max. W. 6.3 cm; D. of perforation 2 cm.

Simpson 1988, 37.

[2:10] STONE BEADS AND PENDANTS, CARROWKEEL, CO. SLIGO.
Neolithic, 3300–2800 BC.

Finds from Passage Tombs show that attractive coloured stone was traded over long distances to be made into beads and pendants that may have possessed symbolic significance. Semi-precious stone such as jasper and serpentine as well as limestone and steatite was used to fashion the beads and pendants discovered in the Passage Tomb cemetery at Carrowkeel, Co. Sligo, and similar objects made from carnelian have been found elsewhere. Some of the Carrowkeel pendants are modelled on maceheads while others notched at one end represent phalli. The pattern of deposition of beads and pendants at Carrowkeel suggests that only a small number would be strung for each wearer. Examination of beads and pendants from the Passage Tomb known as the Mound of the Hostages at Tara suggests that beads and pendants were strung alternately. The largest Carrowkeel pendant illustrated is 3 cm in length. E624:21–55; 1953:7.
Macalister et al 1912, 339; Gogan 1930, 90–91; Herity 1974, 126–32.

⚘

[2:11] PHALLUS-SHAPED STONE, KNOWTH, CO. MEATH.
Neolithic, 3300–2800 BC.

During the excavation of a Passage Tomb cemetery in 1970 a phallus-shaped stone was found in a small depression outside the western tomb of the main mound at Knowth. Unlike a similar find from Newgrange, Co. Meath the Knowth object is decorated. Most of the body has a series of arched grooves, which terminate at a channel which runs down from the top to the bottom. Like comparable decorated objects of bone or antler from Knowth and Fourknocks I, Co. Meath and more widespread plain objects with domed heads, the Knowth phallus-shaped stone would have a ritual function associated with fertility. The phallus-shaped pendants [2:9], some of which have similar grooved decoration, are also clearly related. The emphasis on fertility was probably in order to stress social and family continuity in the face of the death of individuals. E70:31362. L. 25.5 cm.
Eogan 1974, 47; Shee-Twohig 1981, 125–6; O'Connor 1983, 74; Eogan 1984, 26, 29–30; Eogan 1986, 143–4, 179–80.

⚘

[2:12] POTTERY VESSEL, BAUNOGENASRAID, CO. CARLOW.
Neolithic, 3500–3400 BC.

A decorated pottery vessel, a toggle of fossil wood and the worked long bone of an animal accompanied a male burial in a cist at the centre of a cairn excavated at Baunogenasraid, Co. Carlow. The handmade ware is fairly fine although the protrusion of mica grits on the inner surface gives it a speckled appearance. The outer surface has been smoothed carefully and fired to a reddish-buff colour. The rim projects horizontally inwards and is decorated with bands of impressed decoration. The entire body of the pot bears a field of incised concentric decoration perhaps applied using a curved edge of some kind. Around fifty similar vessels are known and the Baunogenasraid vessel displays a highly individual decorative treatment unparalleled on Irish Neolithic pottery. E111:9. D. 13.6 cm; H. 6.8 cm.
Raftery 1974, 298–302; Herity 1982, 295.

⚘

[2:13] Circular handled bag, Twyford, Co. Westmeath.

Neolithic, 3800–2500 BC.

Found in a peat bog at Twyford, Co. Westmeath, the bag was made by coiling spirally long slivers of wood which are bound together by lighter grass-like material. The two sides were woven together along a seam. Long straws plaited together form the two handles. The handles have a total length each of 20 cm and are 9 cm wide where they join the body of the bag. The Twyford bag is remarkably similar to a bag in the museum's collections acquired at the beginning of the last century in Australia. The Aboriginal bag (1902: 189) is decorated with a dyed whirligig design but it is not possible to tell if the Twyford bag was originally coloured or patterned in any way. The Australian bag underlines the persistence of simple but effective technology over a broad geographical and chronological range. 1967:115. Original D. *c.* 40 cm.
Raftery 1970, 167–8.

[2:14] Two shell necklaces, Knockmaree, Co. Dublin.

Neolithic, 3600–3400 BC.

The exquisite workmanship of Neolithic artists working in a variety of media including stone and pottery shows that they were a stylish and sophisticated people. The two shell necklaces found with two male skeletons at Knockmaree in the Phoenix Park, Dublin, show the inventiveness used to produce simple but attractive items of personal adornment using easily available natural materials. Each shell was ground against a stone to create a second opening in the shell-wall. The shells are those of the flat-topped or blunt winkle (*Littorina littoralis*), an inedible species that is found commonly around the coasts, their shells being washed up in thousands after storms. When fresh, the shells may be yellow, red, brown, green, purple and almost black but the Knockmaree shells have now faded to a dull brownish hue. It is clear from the way the shells are graded that they were selected carefully and it is likely that shells of different colours were chosen to produce a varied and pleasing effect.

The Knockmaree grave also contained a barbell-shaped bone object, a flint knife and an animal bone. Although no pottery was present the burial is closely related to that from Baunogenasraid, Co. Carlow [2:12]. X145. L. of longest necklace 1.56 cm.
Wilde 1857, 180–83, 191–2.

[2:15] Five gold bands, Belville, Co. Cavan.

Early Bronze Age, 2300–2100 BC.

The records of the Royal Irish Academy note that these objects were found in the bed of a tributary of the river Erne in the townland of Belville, Co. Cavan in 1852. Although unparalleled in the Irish record they can be regarded as amongst the earliest gold objects known from Ireland. They are of sheet gold decorated with simple patterns of raised lines and dots. Their purpose is unknown but the perforated examples may form two pairs to be attached to a backing material. The longer object may have been an ornament for the head or forehead. W71, W72, W75, W76, W78–81. L. of longest band 29.6 cm; Wt. 11.21 g.
Armstrong 1920, 91; Eogan 1994, 19.

[2:16] PAIR OF GOLD DISCS, RAPPA CASTLE, CO. MAYO.

Early Bronze Age, 2200–2000 BC.

This pair of gold discs was acquired by the Royal Irish Academy in 1856 but nothing about the find circumstances has been recorded. They are two of twenty-one gold discs known from the Early Bronze Age, many of which occur as matching pairs. Although their precise function is not known, the perforations suggest that they were to be attached to a backing material. The decoration of most is based on a centrally placed cross-shaped motif with concentric patterns of zig-zags, lines and rows of dots filling each disc to its edge. Finds of similar objects from graves in England indicate a relationship with Beaker pottery and a very early date for the production of this type of gold ornament. W267, W271. D. 7.6 cm and 8.1 cm; Wt. 6.93 g and 9.09 g.
Armstrong 1920, 84; Eogan 1994, 19.

❧

[2:17] PAIR OF GOLD DISCS, TEDAVNET, CO. MONAGHAN.

Early Bronze Age, 2200–2000 BC.

Discovered in the roots of an old tree, this pair of discs is the largest and most sophisticated of the Early Bronze Age discs known from Ireland. A complex arrangement of raised lines, rows of dots and zig-zags has produced a central cross surrounded by concentric patterns similar to other discs but much more elaborate in composition and, technically, far superior. The combination of the techniques of repoussé, punching and polishing, together with the slight doming of the surfaces, highlights and gives a depth and texture to the discs not seen on other pieces. 1872:34, 35. D. 11.3 and 11.5 cm; Wt. 22.5 and 22.8 g.
Armstrong 1920, 84; Cahill 1983, no. 6.

❧

[2:18] GOLD LUNULA, ROSSMORE PARK, CO. MONAGHAN.

Early Bronze Age, c. 2000 BC.

This exceptionally fine lunula is said to have been found at Rossmore Park, Drumbanagher, Co. Monaghan, but no details of its discovery have been recorded. Its perfect shape and brilliant execution capture the essence of the craft of goldsmithing as practised in Ireland in the Early Bronze Age. The beating of the gold into the crescentic shape, which is thickened slightly at the edges, is a remarkable skill in itself. The decorative scheme relies on a simple pattern of hatched triangles and groups of lines, but the balance and symmetry achieved testify to the expertise of the master craftsman who undertook its production. SA 1928:715. W. 21.5 cm; Wt. 58.12 g.
Unpublished.

❧

[2:19] GOLD LUNULA, TRILLICK, CO. TYRONE.
Early Bronze Age, c. 2000 BC.

Found under a rock, in 1884, this is another very fine example of the exceptional expertise achieved by Ireland's early goldsmiths. The shape of the lunula is close to the ideal crescentic form. The detailed layout and precise incision of the designs has been accomplished with considerable skill and finesse. The motifs used are a brilliant composition of hatched triangles, lozenges, criss-cross lines and zig-zags. The subtle combination of form and decoration has resulted in a prestige object which would have imbued the wearer with special power and symbolic bearing and instilled in the observers an awareness of the status and influence of the wearer. 1884:495. W. 21.0 cm; Wt. 47.89 g.
Armstrong 1920, 55–6.

[2:20] GOLD LUNULA, NEAR KILLARNEY, CO. KERRY.
Early Bronze Age, c. 2000 BC.

This fine lunula was found in the late eighteenth century but the circumstances have not been recorded. A lunula is a crescentic collar made of sheet gold and is the most common object of gold in the Irish Early Bronze Age. In setting out the decorative scheme the goldsmith aimed to achieve a symmetrical pattern which compares closely in detail from one side to the other. This has been very skilfully realised using a set of geometrical motifs in which the blank spaces are also an integral part of the design. W2. W. 22.6 cm; Wt. 99.5 g.
Armstrong 1920, 50; Taylor 1970, 38–81

[2:21] GOLD LUNULA, BALLINAGROUN, CO. KERRY.
Early Bronze Age, c. 2000 BC.

Unusually, this lunula shows evidence of having been decorated on two occasions. Close examination confirms that the first layout was erased and replaced by a scheme which is less expert in its execution. The crescentic shape has been skilfully beaten from a small bar or ingot. The lunula also shows evidence of having been folded at its widest point and then folded over several times. This feature and the evidence of redecoration suggest that the lunula may have been in use over a long period. 1998:74. W. 23.4 cm; Wt. 78.34 g.
Cahill forthcoming; Taylor 1970, 51.

[2:22] Decorated copper axe in leather sheath and leather thong, Brockagh, Co. Kildare.

Early Bronze Age, 1900–1700 BC.

The axe is a typical example of a type called 'Derryniggan' of which more than 300 are known, two-thirds of them decorated. Axes of this type generally have low cast flanges, stop ridges, thin rounded butts and widely-splayed blades. The Brockagh axe was found at a depth of twelve feet in a bog which also preserved its leather sheath and thong. The sheath is made from rawhide with the hair side placed on the inside and stitched up the front with a narrow leather thong. With the sheath was found a leather strap-like thong 47.5 cm in length. 1994:59–61. The axe is 14.7 cm in length and the sheath is a little longer at 18.5 cm.
Harbison 1969, no. 1671, pl. 68, 26; Rynne 1961–3, 459–61.

[2.23] Bronze Halberd, Greaghnafarna, Co. Leitrim and Bronze Dagger, Athlone, Co. Westmeath.

Early Bronze Age.

The halberd, which was found six feet deep in a bog at Greaghnafarna, Co. Leitrim, probably dates to between 2000 and 1700 BC. The halberd has a slightly curved blade and there is a strengthening midrib running the length of it. Originally the halberd was hafted at right angles to a wooden handle and held secure by means of three large rivets, two of which survive in the original rivet holes. The third rivet is damaged and torn. 1964:44. L. 40.2 cm.
Lucas 1967, 6-7.

The dagger, despite its superficial resemblance, may be earlier, dating from 2500–2000 BC. It was found during dredging of the bed of the River Shannon at Athlone. The dagger is flat with slightly bevelled edges. The dagger would have been hafted to a hilt of wood, horn or bone. The original four rivets are still present and there is a notch that probably assisted hafting. W252. L. 15.5 cm.
Wilde 1861, 486.

[2:24] Group of food vessels (*left to right*): Danesfort, Co. Kilkenny; Stonepark, Co. Mayo; Greenhills, Co. Dublin and Lisnamulligan, Co. Donegal.

Early Bronze Age, 2000–1800 BC.

Food Vessels are funerary pots and the belief that they contained food to accompany the dead led to their being so-named. Two basic types were produced, having either a bowl or a vase profile, and both types are decorated with fields of incised geometric ornament, usually arranged in horizontal zones. Bowls have a northerly and easterly distribution and, while this is true also of vases, the vases show a greater penetration into the west and south of the island. The Stonepark vessel may have been placed in an isolated burial, but the other three pots were found in cemeteries. No details were recorded in respect of the Greenhills find. The remaining three were placed in cists, although the burial rite at Danesfort was cremation while the Stonepark and Lisnamulligan pots accompanied crouched inhumations. All but the Lisnamulligan pot is of vase type but there are clear differences between them.

The Danesfort vessel is biconical in profile and bears finely-incised decoration on the exterior surface and rim. The design is dominated by a series of semi-elliptical patterns made up of closely-spaced lines that are set against a background field of inverted V motifs arranged in horizontal rows. There is a conical lid with a strap handle and the lid is decorated overall with radiating zones of impressed decoration. 1886:90–90a. H. of vessel 13.5 cm, H. of lid 6.2 cm.
Ó Ríordáin & Waddell 1993, no. 537.

The decorated vase from Stonepark, Co. Mayo bears unusual decoration over most of its exterior consisting of a series of oval impressions. Incised ornament occurs on the rim. 1933:341. H. 14.0 cm.
Ó Ríordáin & Waddell 1993, no. 558.

The fine tall vase from Greenhills is decorated externally and internally on the upper neck with rows of impressed triangles and cord impressions. 1945:373. H. 16.8 cm.
Ó Ríordáin & Waddell 1993, no. 421.

As is generally the case, none of the vase bases is decorated. However, the Lisnamulligan vessel is one of many bowl types that bears decoration on its circular flat base. Designs may consist of cruciform patterns, concentric rows of zig-zags or related star-shaped patterns, designs that are reminiscent of those found on Early Bronze Age gold discs. The Lisnamulligan design is an eleven-pointed star surrounded by concentric cord-impressed rings. The bowl has a rounded profile and on its sides there are alternating bands of cord-impressed lines and low false relief produced by using impressed triangles. 1989:45. H. 9.3 cm.
Ó Floinn 1989, 17.

❧

[2:25] THREE CINERARY URNS (*LEFT TO RIGHT*): GORTEREGHY, CO. ANTRIM, BALLYCASTLE, CO. ANTRIM AND BALLYCONNELL, CO. WICKLOW.
Early to Middle Bronze Age, 1900–1300 BC.

Cremation is the burial rite associated with the urn tradition and British influences may be detected in the adoption of the new fashion. The Ballyconnell and Gortereghy urns were inverted over cremated remains in pits while the Ballycastle urn was placed in a cist. The urns are of different types and are not all of the same date; those from Ballycastle and Ballyconnell date to between 1900–1700 BC, while that from Gortereghy dates to 1700–1300 BC.

At a mere 23.5 cm tall the Ballycastle vessel is the smallest of the three. It is a decorated Collared Urn, a type whose distribution has a marked concentration in the north-east corner of Ireland. The collar design is one of large triangles filled alternately with a series of horizontal and diagonal lines while the neck has a series of individual criss-cross motifs. The body is incised with a criss-cross pattern that is applied haphazardly. 1898:78. H. 23.5 cm.
Kavanagh 1976, no. 1.

The Ballycastle urn is broadly contemporary with an Encrusted Urn from Ballyconnell, Co. Wicklow. Encrusted Urns have more lavish decoration than other types and they are more widely distributed, being absent only from the far west of the island. The Ballyconnell pot has five horizontal zones formed of applied decoration. Each zone is sub-divided by chevrons and diagonal lines, while on the collar there are applied bosses. Within each zone there are incised herring-bone and crosshatched designs. 1956:1. H. 33.0 cm.
Kavanagh 1973, no. 84.

By far the largest urn is that from Gortereghy, Co. Antrim which is 47.2 cm tall. Known as a Cordoned Urn it is of a type that seems to have developed from Collared Urns, with which it shares a similar though less restricted distribution. Three channels divide the pot into horizontal bands of which one band bears a cord-impressed series of blank chevrons highlighted by a background of diagonal lines. 1905:258. H. 47.2 cm.
Kavanagh 1976, no. 4.

❧

[2:26] MINIATURE VASES OR PYGMY CUPS, GREENHILLS, CO. DUBLIN AND DUNLECKNY, CO. CARLOW.

Early Bronze Age, 2000–1800 BC.

Miniature vessels of various types are found in Early Bronze Age graves, in all but one instance accompanying a cremation. In some instances a miniature vessel has been the only pot found to accompany a burial but more often the type occurs alongside pottery of other types. The type has been found with urns of all forms (although the single association with a Collared Urn is doubtful), and with vase Food Vessels. It does not appear to be associated with bowl Food Vessels however. Two of the finest examples are the vessels from Greenhills, Co. Dublin and Dunleckny, Co. Carlow.

The Greenhills vessel was found in a grave under an Encrusted Urn, beside of which there was a vase Food Vessel. The grave was in a cemetery located on an esker ridge in Co. Dublin. The miniature vessel has a flared neck above a sloping shoulder and a recessed base. Before the pot was decorated the potter decided to alter the original design by filling five circular holes in the neck. The neck is now decorated on the flared interior down to the level of the shoulder with rows of false relief chevrons inter-spaced with vertical milling. There is a groove on the rim and another on the shoulder. The exterior of the neck bears a field of incised criss-cross decoration while the rest of the vessel is decorated elaborately overall with false relief, incised lines and cord impressions. SA 1898:18. H. 7.6 cm.
Kavanagh 1977–8, no. 25; Ó Ríordáin & Waddell 1993, no. 423.

The Dunleckny vessel was found in a cist uncovered during railway construction near Bagenalstown, Co. Carlow in 1847. The miniature pot was said to have contained the cremated bones of a child and it was discovered within an urn that contained the remains of an adult. The cup-shaped vessel, which has a small handle, is decorated with very fine incised ornament executed with precision and sophistication. The slightly rounded out-turned rim carries finely-incised parallel lines bounded by rows of chevrons. The main design scheme radiates vertically up the body of the vessel from the base in broadening zones bearing two alternating patterns, one a tiny honeycomb motif, the other a series of horizontal rows of milling. W14. H. 5.5 cm.
Kavanagh 1977–8, no. 7; Ó Ríordáin & Waddell 1993, no. 458.

[2:27] DECORATED BOULDER, KILWARDEN, CO. KILDARE.

Early Bronze Age, 2500–1700 BC.

Whereas Neolithic rock carvings occur in the context of funerary monuments, Early Bronze Age rock art is found on outcrops and isolated boulders. One such boulder is that from Kilwarden, Co. Kildare, which is decorated extensively with geometric designs.

A basic pattern is repeated many times over across the surface using different scales and combinations of elements. It consists of a series of concentric circles alternating with concentric rings of cup-marks. At the centre of each pattern lies a single cup-mark from which a channel runs radially from the centre to the outermost edge. 1994:58. L. 145 cm.
Unpublished.

[2:28] TWO GOLD TORCS, TARA, CO. MEATH.

Middle Bronze Age, 1200–1000 BC.

Found at the Rath of the Synods, Tara, Co. Meath, in 1810, these magnificent torcs which, between them, contain over a kilogram of gold, are the finest of their class from Ireland. They are of exceptionally large size and are further elaborated by the addition of extensions to the terminals, a feature which is not recorded elsewhere. Torcs of this type are made from bars of square or rectangular section, the angles of which have been hammered up to produce flanges. The even twisting of such a long bar requires considerable expertise and understanding of the working properties of the metal. W192, W173. D. 43.0 and 37.3 cm; Wt. 852.0 and 385.1 g.

Armstrong 1920 159; Eogan 1967, 132–3, 139, 164; Cahill 1983, no. 9.

[2:29] HOARD OF GOLD ORNAMENTS, DERRINBOY, CO. OFFALY.

Middle Bronze Age, 1400–1200 BC.

This hoard of unusual objects was found during turf-cutting at Derrinboy, Co. Offaly. The necklet which is made from gold wire wrapped over a leather thong is a unique piece. The wire was produced by hammering and has been estimated to be 15m in length. The armlets are made from heavy sheet gold, decorated with elaborate patterns of parallel rows of raised ribs. The smaller rings are also of heavy sheet and decorated with closely spaced, finely incised lines. The armlets closely resemble similar objects known from Denmark and suggest links between Ireland and the Baltic area which the trade in amber also supports. 1959:693–698. Dims. of necklet 35.4 cm x 26.4 cm.

Raftery 1961, 55–8; Eogan 1983, 42–3.

[2:3]

FLINT FLAKE, MELL, CO. LOUTH.

Palaeolithic, 400,000–300,000 BC.

[2:4]

PORCELLANITE AXE AND CHISEL, KILLALOE, CO. CLARE.

Neolithic, 3800–2500 BC.

[2:5]

JADEITE AXE, PASLICKSTOWN, CO. WESTMEATH.

Neolithic, 3600–2500 BC.

[2:6]

THREE AXE AMULETS: LOUGHCREW, CO. MEATH; LISNASCREGHOG, GARVAGH, CO. DERRY AND BALLYMENA, CO. ANTRIM.

Neolithic, 3800–2500 BC.

[2:7]

CHERT JAVELIN HEAD, KELLYSGROVE, CO. GALWAY.

Neolithic, 3800–2700 BC.

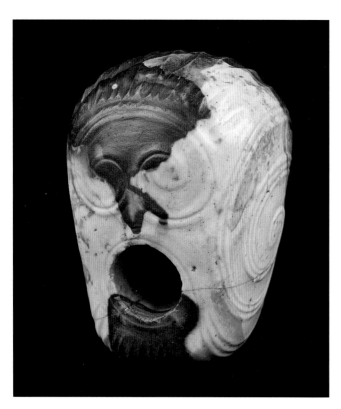

[2:8]
DECORATED MACEHEAD, KNOWTH, CO. MEATH.
Neolithic, 3300–2800 BC.

[2:9]
TWO STONE MACEHEADS, BUSHMILLS, CO. ANTRIM AND LOUGH FEA, DOOHATTY, CO. MONAGHAN.
Neolithic, 3300–2800 BC.

[2:10] *facing page*
STONE BEADS AND PENDANTS, CARROWKEEL, CO. SLIGO.
Neolithic, 3300–2800 BC.

[2:11]

PHALLUS-SHAPED STONE, KNOWTH, CO. MEATH.

Neolithic, 3300–2800 BC.

[2:12]

POTTERY VESSEL, BAUNOGENASRAID, CO. CARLOW.

Neolithic, 3500–3400 BC.

[2:13] *top*
CIRCULAR HANDLED BAG, TWYFORD, CO. WESTMEATH.
Neolithic, 3800–2500 BC.

[2:13] *left*
CIRCULAR HANDLED BAG, AUSTRALIA.
Nineteenth century AD.

[2:14] *facing page*
TWO SHELL NECKLACES, KNOCKMAREE, CO. DUBLIN.
Neolithic, 3600–3400 BC.

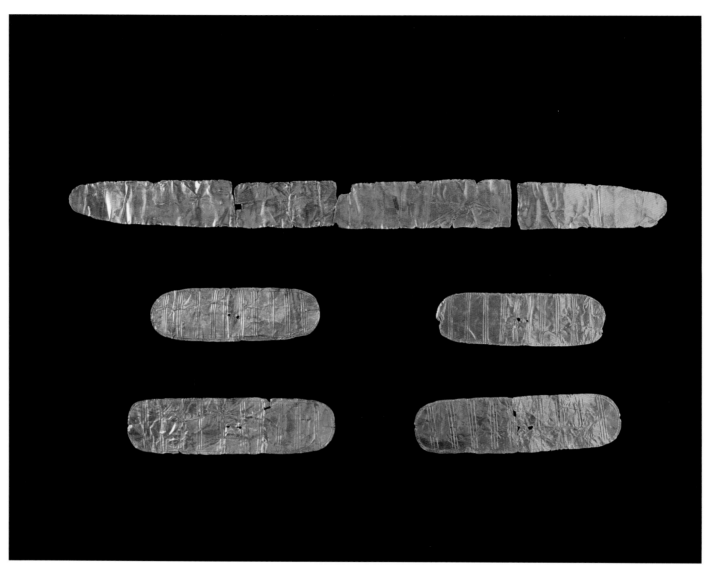

[2:15]

FIVE GOLD BANDS, BELVILLE, CO. CAVAN.

Early Bronze Age, 2300–2100 BC.

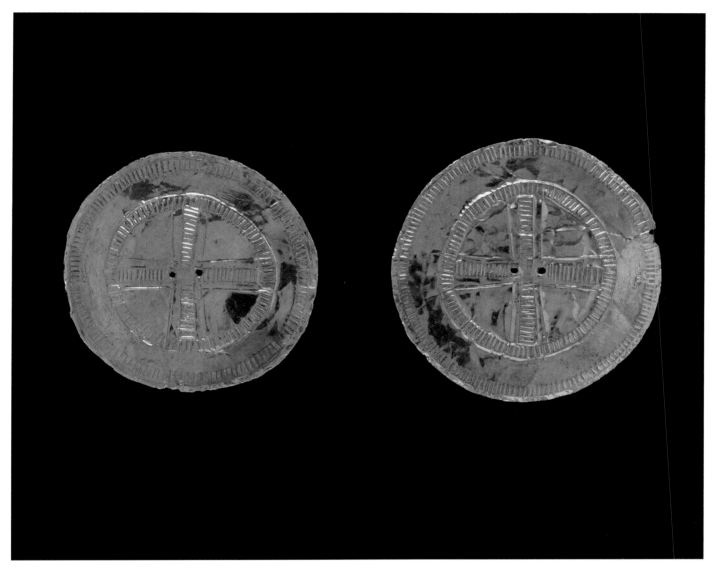

[2:16]

PAIR OF GOLD DISCS, RAPPA CASTLE, CO. MAYO.

Early Bronze Age, 2200–2000 BC.

[2:17]

PAIR OF GOLD DISCS, TEDAVNET, CO. MONAGHAN.

Early Bronze Age, 2200–2000 BC.

[2:18]
GOLD LUNULA, ROSSMORE PARK, CO. MONAGHAN.
Early Bronze Age, c. 2000 BC.

[2:19]
GOLD LUNULA, TRILLICK, CO. TYRONE.
Early Bronze Age, c. 2000 BC.

[2:20]
GOLD LUNULA, NEAR KILLARNEY, CO. KERRY.
Early Bronze Age, c. 2000 BC.

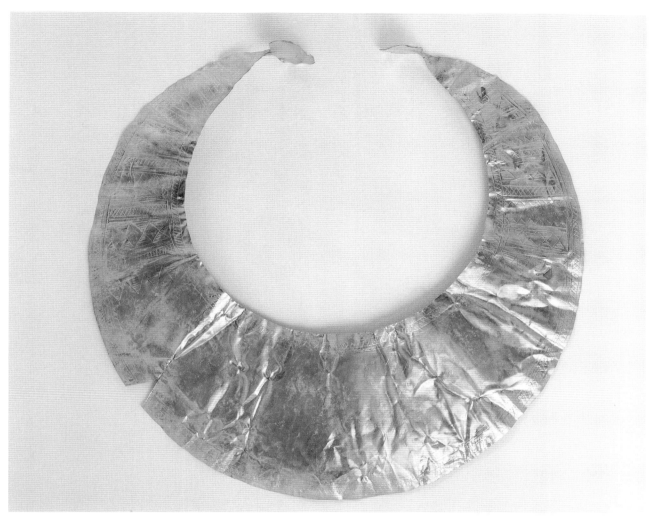

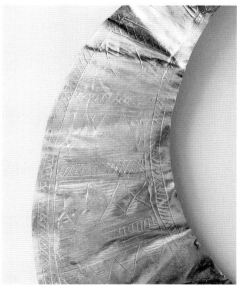

[2:21]
GOLD LUNULA, BALLINAGROUN, CO. KERRY.
Early Bronze Age, c. 2000 BC.

[2:22]
DECORATED COPPER AXE IN LEATHER SHEATH AND LEATHER THONG, BROCKAGH, CO. KILDARE.
Early Bronze Age, 1900–1700 BC.

[2:23]
BRONZE HALBERD, GREAGHNAFARNA, CO. LEITRIM AND BRONZE DAGGER, ATHLONE, CO. WESTMEATH.
Early Bronze Age.

[2:24]
GROUP OF FOOD VESSELS (*LEFT TO RIGHT*): DANESFORT, CO. KILKENNY; STONEPARK, CO. MAYO;
GREENHILLS, CO. DUBLIN AND LISNAMULLIGAN, CO. DONEGAL.
Early Bronze Age, 2000–1800 BC.

[2:25]
THREE CINERARY URNS (*LEFT TO RIGHT*): **GORTEREGHY, CO. ANTRIM,
BALLYCASTLE, CO. ANTRIM AND BALLYCONNELL, CO. WICKLOW.**
Early to Middle Bronze Age, 1900–1300 BC.

[2:26]
MINIATURE VASES OR PYGMY CUPS, GREENHILLS, CO. DUBLIN AND DUNLECKNY, CO. CARLOW.
Early Bronze Age, 2000–1800 BC.

[2:27]

DECORATED BOULDER, KILWARDEN, CO. KILDARE.

Early Bronze Age, 2500–1700 BC.

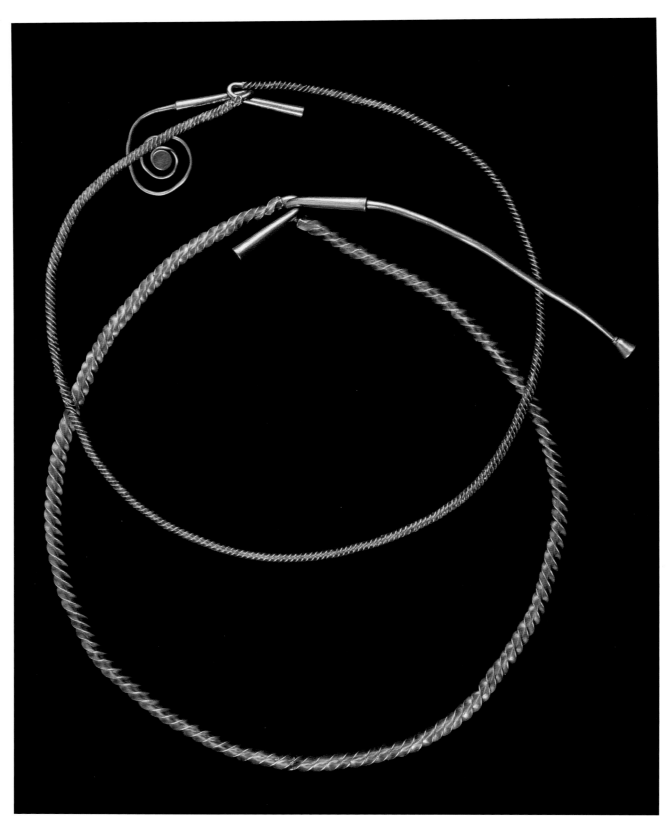

[2:28]

TWO GOLD TORCS, TARA, CO. MEATH.

Middle Bronze Age, 1200–1000 BC.

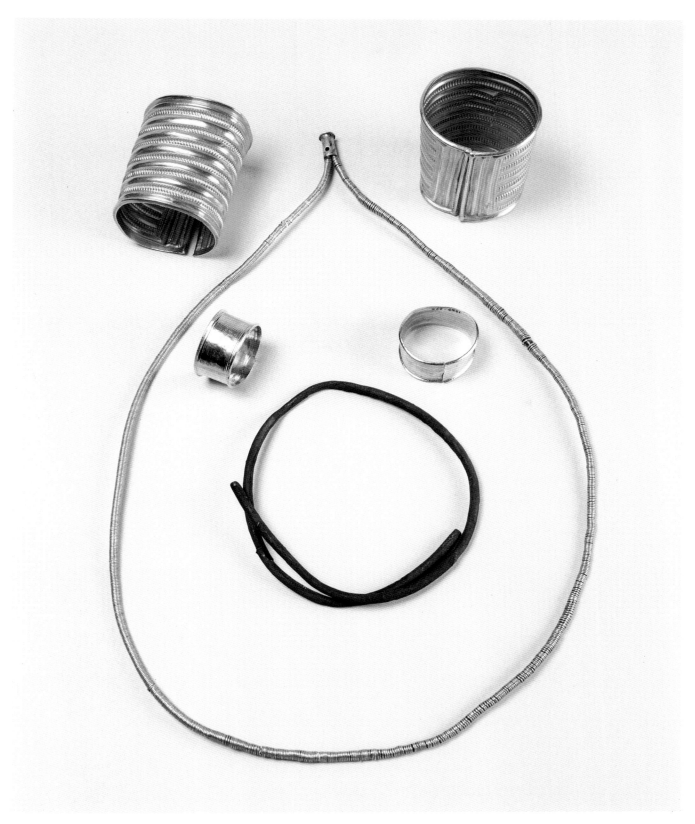

[2:29]
HOARD OF GOLD ORNAMENTS, DERRINBOY, CO. OFFALY.
Middle Bronze Age, 1400–1200 BC.

3

BEFORE THE CELTS

TREASURES IN GOLD AND BRONZE

MARY CAHILL

The nature of material culture is such that archaeologists tend to compartmentalise, to subdivide on grounds of date, similarity, dissimilarity, typology, provenance and many other factors. This can lead to an artificial impression that prehistory can be divided into neat chunks during which certain things happened or particular developments took place, but with little reference to what preceded or followed. Because of the way evidence survives especially as it relates to material culture — patchy and incomplete — it is not always possible to follow closely the technical and morphological changes which gave rise to what are perceived as significant changes and new types of object. Survival and recovery seriously influence our understanding, particularly in a country where the rate of survival and recovery of metal artefacts is high but, unfortunately, is very poor for many types of organic materials. This is very much the case in looking at the period known as the Bronze Age. For convenience and ease of understanding the Bronze Age is subdivided into three main phases — Early, Middle and Late Bronze Age — but no discussion of any particular phase can pick up at a specific date and close at another.

When dealing with the latest phase of the Bronze Age in Ireland — the Dowris phase (900–600 BC) — it is impossible not to be impressed by the range and quality of the material that has survived, especially in bronze and gold. The largest hoard of Bronze Age bronze objects found in Ireland was discovered in the 1820s at Dowris, near Birr, Co. Offaly. Containing at least 218 bronze tools and weapons, the importance of the find is reflected in the fact that the find-place lends its name to the final phase of the Irish Late Bronze Age.

Placing such objects in a cultural setting can be very difficult because they have been deposited away from the centres of production and settlement and are not used as grave goods. This causes problems in determining function and in interpretation. In a museum setting it is easy to observe and be struck by the inherent beauty, the fine craftsmanship and the intricate detail but, at the same time, to lose sight of the landscape and the people and to become detached from the realities of life as it was at a remote period of prehistory. In this book, very few of the objects which illustrate this phase of the Bronze Age have been found during the course of archaeological excavation. Many were found during the nineteenth century and have no record of their finding other than the name of the place. Still, in spite of these limitations it is possible to outline the course of developments in technology and changes in burial and settlement patterns and to note outside influences.

We have already seen that the introduction of metallurgy brought about great changes in society and introduced a whole new assemblage of tools, weapons and personal ornaments. While finished objects are present in the archaeological record in large numbers, our knowledge of the procurement of resources for the later phases of the Bronze Age is slight. Although much effort has been expended in trying to identify the sources of the immense quantities of gold used during the Dowris period, we still cannot say with certainty where the ores were sourced and we know nothing of how the processes of ore production, manufacture and distribution were organised. As far as the craft of goldsmithing is concerned, we can only infer from the objects, some of which are unfinished, from some scrap pieces and from what we know of the working of gold in later periods. Two pieces of scrap gold found in an excavation at Lough Gur Co. Limerick, come from a site dated 1400–1300 BC, but there is insufficient evidence to propose a workshop at this site. The discovery of small pieces of scrap, including fragments of sheet and wire, in the fill of a number of pits at Haughey's Fort, Co. Armagh, dated by radio-carbon to the period c.1260–910 BC, is highly suggestive of goldworking activity on the site. Goldsmiths usually employ all sorts of devices to catch and trap the tiniest amounts of waste for recycling, so the survival of these fragments is fortunate.

Although it is difficult to propose absolute continuity in goldworking between all phases of the Bronze Age as the nature of the material suggests episodes of activity, it is unlikely that the craft ever died out completely. What seem like gaps in production may be more a matter of archaeological visibility than anything else, as the sudden re-introduction of a highly specialised craft seems unlikely. The recently-determined radio-carbon date for the gold wire-covered leather necklet from Derrinboy, Co. Offaly [2:29], brings it back in date to c. 1400 BC and closer to the period when lunula production ended. A date for the box which accompanied the Killymoon dress-fastener also brings the date for this type back a century or so to c. 900 BC suggesting that another perceived gap in the record may not exist in reality. Nevertheless, dramatic changes in form took place and great technical innovation and new styles of decoration were introduced during this period, many of which show the independent creativity of the Irish smiths, while others clearly point to considerable influence from Europe. Whether this influence was by direct contact or through some form of secondary communication is not known, but the links are undeniable. The same general principles apply to work in bronze although continuity of production is not an issue.

One of the most striking aspects of goldworking in this period is the skill with which the smiths could use the metal. At one extreme, minute quantities of gold were used to produce the fine foils that cover bullae, split-ring ornaments and discs [3:14, 3:18, 3:21]; while at the other extreme immense quantities were lavished on a single object such as the dress-fasteners from near Clones and Castlekelly which together weigh over 1500 grams (50ozs Troy) [3:6 and 3:7]. It is assumed that most of the objects produced in gold were intended to be worn as personal ornaments — to adorn the person for adornment's sake — or as statements of status and rank in society. Their use may have been restricted to certain persons on occasions of particular significance. They were only very rarely used to accompany the dead, but were disposed of in bogs and on dry land, sometimes under rocks. The types of objects produced in gold such as collars, bracelets, dress-fasteners, ear ornaments and others are rarely and, in many cases, never seen in bronze. It seems as if bronze was not considered an appropriate material for certain objects. In other words there are no 'cheap' versions in bronze or other metals, further emphasising the special role which gold has played throughout prehistory and later.

The most imposing of the sheet gold ornaments are the large gold collars which antiquarians called 'gorgets' [3:19–3:25]. Of the nine which survive, seven are in the national collection although not all of them survive intact. They are remarkable pieces of gold craft combining sheet-working skills, repoussé and chasing, raising and stamping, twisting and stitching. Each one is different, some finer than others, but all display the individuality of the maker who while retaining the basic form and utilising a restricted range of motifs, could nevertheless vary the design to such a degree that each collar is quite distinctive. It is highly likely that the motifs both individually and in composition with one another held some symbolism, but the meanings are lost to us. The presence of a small punched hole on either side of the upper inner edge of the collar and a gold link which survives in the collar from Borrisnoe, Co. Tipperary, show that they were intended to be worn on the chest, the position being determined by the length of a cord or chain which held the collar in place across the back of the neck. We can only assume that the wearing of such imposing ornaments was not a daily occurrence but that they were

DETAIL OF [3:19]
GOLD COLLAR,
ARDCRONY,
CO. TIPPERARY.
*Late Bronze Age,
800–700 BC.*

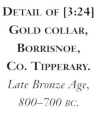

DETAIL OF [3:24]
GOLD COLLAR,
BORRISNOE,
CO. TIPPERARY.
*Late Bronze Age,
800–700 BC.*

used as important symbols of rank and authority. Their restricted distribution, confined (with one exception) to the area around the lower Shannon basin, suggests a society which controlled access to the resource or was rich enough in other goods that it could trade for the raw materials. The quality of the craftsmanship is such that workshops of highly skilled and experienced goldsmiths must have been capable of being supported by the local community.

The majority of collars show evidence of having been folded in two prior to disposal. The line of folding is slightly off-centre. Can this be interpreted as a ritual decommissioning of the object? What events triggered the act of deposition? Was it an act in which the whole community had a role or was it a secret ceremony undertaken by a priestly élite? These are questions which archaeology may never be able to answer but even in our own time many important events — inaugurations, coronations, consecrations, interments — are orchestrated and regulated by a series of rituals, so it is certain that Late Bronze Age society in Ireland was governed by its own calendar of ceremonial events.

The purpose to which certain objects were put has not always been easy to explain. Antiquarians in the eighteenth and nineteenth centuries proposed functions for certain objects according to how they viewed prehistoric society, often by reference to their own education which would have been biased in favour of the study of classical literature and mythology. Thus what today is regarded as a large dress-fastener [3:6, 3:7] was described as a *patera* — a vessel from which the gods might drink or pour a libation. Dress-fasteners such as these and the example from Killymoon, Co. Tyrone [3:8], are thought to be derived from a Scandinavian type which functioned with a pin, the Irish type perhaps using double buttonholes into which the terminals are inserted. The largest examples recorded weigh over 1,300 grams and are unlikely to have been worn although they may have been used as symbols of authority as well as representations of real wealth. The objects which were sometimes described as cosmetic boxes are now recognised as extravagant ear ornaments called ear-spools [3:9, 3:10]. Other split-ring ornaments [3:11, 3:13, 3:14] can also be identified as ornaments for the ears.

One of the most exciting archaeological discoveries of the nineteenth century was the finding, during the course of railway construction, of a huge hoard of gold objects at Mooghaun North, Co. Clare [3:17]. Its discovery on an old lake shore within a short distance of the great hill-fort at Mooghaun which has been dated by excavation to the Late Bronze Age suggests an important relationship between the two locations. Although the original number of objects cannot be established as most of them were sold off and melted down, the hoard contained large

GOLD COLLAR FROM A HOARD [3:17] FOUND AT MOOGHAUN NORTH, CO. CLARE.
Late Bronze Age, 800–700 BC.

[3:1]
BRONZE SWORD,
BALLYHARNEY,
CO. WESTMEATH.
*Late Bronze Age,
900–700 BC.*

numbers of bracelets, gold collars and neck rings, together numbering over two hundred pieces. In bullion terms alone this hoard represents an enormous resource which it seems the local community was prepared to offer or sacrifice by its ritual abandonment in what must have been regarded as a sacred place.

While work in gold continued to develop throughout the Late Bronze Age, there was also a parallel, and in numerical terms, a much more massive bronze-working industry which flourished during the same period. The tools and weapons that appeared in the Early Bronze Age were further developed and improved, simpler forms were overtaken by the continuous advances in product design and functionality which went hand in hand with improved metal working skills and more complex casting techniques. Over time axeheads, spearheads and daggers developed into fully socketed forms, which could be more securely hafted. Specialist and all-purpose tools such as chisels, gouges, punches, tweezers, sickles and knives were manufactured in large numbers. The addition of lead to bronze and the use of clay moulds enabled large, sophisticated objects to be produced using complex casting techniques.

Lakeside settlements and the use of artificial islands or crannógs and small natural islands were a feature of Late Bronze Age society, while the construction of large defended hill-top enclosures suggests that it was a period of violent uncertainty. The production of vast numbers of weapons, especially swords, reinforces that view. Unlike the rapiers of an earlier age, which are for thrusting and stabbing, swords are slashing weapons and this may suggest a change from fighting on foot to warfare between warriors mounted on horseback. A fine example is the exceptionally long specimen from the river Inny at Ballyharney, Co. Westmeath [3:1], the condition of which, especially the sharpness of the hilt flanges, suggests that it was unfinished and had never been used. Spearheads developed into slender weapons with elongated blades and decorated sockets, many of which were also destined to be deposited in rivers and lakes. Some, perhaps, were made deliberately for that purpose rather than for any utilitarian requirement. In addition to swords and spears, socketed axes were produced in large numbers and, although they may have functioned primarily as tools, their use as weapons cannot be discounted.

The bronze smiths' skills were also equally well developed in sheet bronze as evidenced by the enormous cauldrons of riveted sheet which have been discovered. Two types were made which could have been suspended over a fire or heated by adding hot stones. Wooden cauldrons carved from poplar or alder are known, the contents of which may have been heated in a similar way. Meals prepared in cauldrons, such as the one from Castlederg, Co. Tyrone [3:26], may have been consumed on ritual or ceremonial occasions and so the cauldrons need not be regarded simply as domestic utensils. Their eventual abandonment in bogs is part of the same ritual forsaking of rare and valuable objects which is the lasting impression of the Dowris period. Elaborate flesh-hooks, which may have been used for the removal of hot meat, may also be regarded as ritual regalia. The first shields were introduced with fine examples in sheet bronze such as the one from Lough Gur, Co. Limerick [3:27], demonstrating the superior skills of the Late Bronze Age craftsmen.

Among the most impressive objects of cast bronze are the large horns, which are the oldest known musical instruments from Ireland. Two types are known — one is played from the side of the horn (like a flute), while the other is blown through a mouthpiece at the narrower end. Horns cast in one piece and others made from two or more parts have been found. Until recently the horns were thought to be limited in terms of the range of notes and tone that they could produce. However, experimental work using exact replicas has shown that they are sophisticated musical instruments. To play them requires considerable skill. A hoard of four horns from Drumbest, Co. Antrim [3:2], was found in a bog, once again drawing attention to the use of watery locations for the final deposition of valuable metalwork. The fine end-blown example illustrated can be contrasted with the side-blown horn from Derrynane, Co. Kerry [3:2]. Together with pear-shaped objects known as crotals found in the Dowris Hoard [3:3], horns may have been used in the rites of a fertility cult associated with the bull, echoes of which may survive in the early medieval tale *Táin Bó Cuailnge* (The Cattle Raid of Cooley) which features magical bulls. The cult may have had its origins in the Mediterranean during the Bronze Age, where the background of much of the Irish gold and bronze work of the period seems to lie ultimately.

The vast collection of over two hundred axeheads, spearheads, crotals, horns and cauldrons in the Dowris hoard represents a considerable amount of wealth, not just in the amount of metal it contained but also in terms of the effort required to produce the raw materials and the finished objects. Yet at some point, it must be presumed, in the judgment of the local leaders, it became necessary to jettison this remarkable collection of material either as a single-episode deposition or as a series of smaller deposits. This depositional event at Dowris can be replicated on a lesser scale in the discovery of smaller hoards of valuable metalwork during the Dowris phase from all over the country. Some hoards may have been deposited ritually as offerings to appease the gods, while others may simply represent private possessions hidden in times of danger. Hoards containing scrap metal may have been founders' hoards, collected for re-processing, while those which appear to contain trade goods may represent merchants' hoards.

[3:2]
TWO BRONZE HORNS, DRUMBEST, CO. ANTRIM AND DERRYNANE, CO. KERRY.
Late Bronze Age, 800–600 BC.

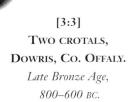

[3:3]
TWO CROTALS, DOWRIS, CO. OFFALY.
Late Bronze Age, 800–600 BC.

[3:4]
ORNAMENT OF
HORSEHAIR, CROMAGHS,
ARMOY, CO. ANTRIM.
Late Bronze Age,
900–500 BC.

The very large number of hoards and single objects found in rivers and bogs suggests a ritual interest in wet environments, perhaps related to the deterioration in the climate. It is likely, however, that a number of complex economic and social reasons were responsible for the practice of hoarding.

It is the chance discovery of so many of these hoards that, until recently, gave this period its essential character but one that seemed very remote from the settlements and dwelling-places of the people. In recent years, due to the development of new infrastructure, extensive excavations have been taking place all over the country. These have led to the identification of both settlement and burial sites, resulting in a more complete view of society during this period. Sites of domestic habitation have produced coarse pottery similar to that found on Middle Bronze Age settlements, often coated in soot. These everyday cooking vessels were used occasionally as containers for the cremated bones of the dead and were buried in low mounds surrounded by a shallow circular ditch. The use of radiocarbon dating has further refined the differentiation and separation of site types, enabling the identification of burial sites of different forms as well as habitation sites and sites which may have been used for large assemblies.

The climatic conditions that prevailed throughout the Bronze Age encouraged the growth of bogs and throughout the Bronze Age surfaced trackways, usually of wood, were constructed across bogs. Continuous growth of peat preserved the track-ways together with associated items such as two wooden wheels found in a bog at Doogarrymore, Co. Roscommon, which once formed part of a cart used in the fourth century BC. Much of the evidence for leather working and wood working has survived in bogs and this shows that skills in working these materials were also highly developed, as the leather shields and wooden shield-formers indicate.

Amber is used for necklaces of graduated beads and has been found in hoards containing both gold ornaments and bronze tools or weapons. Its attractive, lustrous appearance and its exotic origin must have made it a very desirable commodity but one which had to be traded for a material of similar value. In finding its way to Ireland from the Baltic region, the amber route may also have been instrumental in introducing other influences such as the use of sunflower pins and dress-fasteners and elements of the motif repertoire used in decorating both gold and bronze. Exceptional preservation of amber has been possible because of the deposition in bogs or waterlogged places as demonstrated by the necklace from Tooradoo, Co. Limerick [3:14].

Other exceptionally rare survivals are the organic remains found with a hoard of bronze tools, a sunflower pin and a razor at Cromaghs, Co. Antrim. As well as pieces of a large woollen textile with evidence of stitching, it also contained tassels of delicately woven fine horse hair — a unique find which may have been part of a belt [3:4]. Imposing objects of personal adornment, while not as common in bronze as in gold, have also been found. One of the most unusual, found in a bog near Roscommon town [3:5], is composed of bronze rings forming chains linked to one another, gathered into circular medallions attached to cast, open-work shoulder plates. This outstanding object is similar to others known from central Europe and, together with other objects such as the buckets from the Dowris hoard, demonstrates that ideas and influences as well as objects were transported and traded over long distances.

These influences were ultimately responsible for significant changes in terms of material culture during the later centuries of the first millennium. The gradual change from a mainly bronze-working economy to one based on the use of iron as the preferred metal took some time but the changes were irreversible and affected all aspects of society. Eventually, as the following chapter will discuss, iron was used primarily for the production of tools and weapons while bronze was restricted mostly to objects of a more decorative nature. Gold working was almost completely abandoned and was never again used in Ireland to the same extent or with the same sense of, seemingly, uncontrolled bounty.

[3:5]
BRONZE CHAIN COLLAR, NEAR ROSCOMMON CASTLE, CO. ROSCOMMON.
Late Bronze Age, 1000–700 BC.

ILLUSTRATIONS

[3:1] BRONZE SWORD, BALLYHARNEY, CO. WESTMEATH.

Late Bronze Age, 900–700 BC.

This long, well-made sword of cast bronze was found during dredging operations on a shoal at the left bank of the river Inny, Ballyharney, Co. Westmeath. On each face a fine groove runs parallel to each edge of the leaf-shaped blade. The hafting plate has rounded shoulders, originally with three rivets on each shoulder. The rivets, one of which is missing, are slender and cylindrical. The tang is flanged and has a long median slot. The terminal is roughly straight. All the edges of the hafting plate are sharp, suggesting that the sword was unused when placed in the river. Slightly more than twenty swords of this type have been found in Ireland and it is a native version of a widely distributed continental form. 1965:57. L. 76 cm. *Lucas 1968, 111–13.*

[3:2] TWO BRONZE HORNS, DRUMBEST, CO. ANTRIM AND DERRYNANE, CO. KERRY.

Late Bronze Age, 800–600 BC.

These two fine horns provide excellent contrasts in a number of respects. The Drumbest end-blown horn is from a hoard of four instruments of which two are side-blown and two end-blown. Using clay moulds, it was cast in two pieces, the blown end being cast-on to the bell end. Two zones of four grooved lines occur at the bell end and a ring is fitted to a loop located towards the blown end. It has a somewhat S-shaped profile. 1893:17. Full L. 89.5 cm.

MacAdam 1860, 100; Coles 1963, 330, 340–43, 353; Kelly 1983, no. 25a; Eogan 1983, no. 39, 54–5.

The Derrynane horn appears to have been a single find. It has a C-shaped profile and the side-blown mouthpiece is located on the concave surface, one third of the way along from the closed end, which has a ridged, domed terminal. There are six cones and four holes at the bell end. Between the mouthpiece and the closed end there is a ring in a loop and another occurs on the closed end terminal itself. The object has been repaired at the mouthpiece. W12. Full L. 88.0 cm.

Wilde 1861,629; Coles 1963, 337, 351.

[3:3] TWO CROTALS, DOWRIS, CO. OFFALY.

Late Bronze Age, 800–600 BC.

Found in boggy ground at Dowris, Co. Offaly. The two cast bronze objects, known as crotals, are part of a huge hoard of more than two hundred objects including axeheads, spearheads, horns and cauldrons. In all, forty-eight crotals were discovered and, apart from two other Irish examples, all the objects of this type have been found in the Dowris hoard. A large and a small specimen are illustrated and most of the Dowris crotals are of the larger type. They each contain a pebble or piece of baked clay that results in a musical sound when the crotal is shaken. They may have been rattles used in rituals of a fertility cult related to the bull. SA 57.ia. and 1882: 40. L. 13.5 cm and 7.22 cm; D. of ring 3.9 cm and 3.0 cm.

Eogan 1983, no. 119, 136–41.

[3:4] ORNAMENT OF HORSEHAIR, CROMAGHS, ARMOY, CO. ANTRIM.

Late Bronze Age, 900–500 BC.

In May 1904, deep in a bog at Cromaghs, Armoy, Co. Antrim, a turf-cutter found a group of bronze objects wrapped in a woollen cloth. The metal objects consisted of a sunflower pin, axe, gouge, and a razor still retained in its leather case. The woollen textile has survived only partially and seems to have consisted of two pieces of cloth sewn together. An extraordinary part of the hoard consisted of two tasselled fringes that would have finished the ends of a woven textile, probably a belt. In the better-preserved example, nine bunches of horse hair are bound around by more horsehair. After a short distance each of these subdivides into five smaller bunches, each of which ends in a horsehair ball. The Cromaghs find confirms the artistry of the Late Bronze Age craftsmen working in a range of materials and indicates that the garments worn on ceremonial occasions may have been of a more than appropriate standard with which to show off gold, bronze and amber jewellery. 1906:13. L. of largest fragment 30.2 cm.

Coffey 1906, 119–24; Eogan 1983, no. 38, 52–4.

[3:5] BRONZE CHAIN COLLAR, NEAR ROSCOMMON CASTLE, CO. ROSCOMMON.

Late Bronze Age, 1000–700 BC.

Found in a bog near Roscommon Castle, Co. Roscommon. There are three main elements consisting of bands of rings, two shoulder plaques and two rings or medallions that would have been suspended front and back. The medallions have a cruciform design and hollowed conical bosses in the centre. The cast openwork plaques are rectangular and curved to sit on the shoulders. Conical bosses occur spaced evenly on the upper surface of the plaques. Five bands of chain join the shoulder plaques to the medallions to the front and back, and seven rows of chain are suspended for a short distance below the medallions. The chains are formed of cast triple rings joined by loops made of bent metal strips. The object is ceremonial rather than utilitarian and it has its ultimate background in central Europe where chain link ornaments of various kinds have been found. Late Bronze Age finds from Ireland indicate that chain link ornaments of various kinds may have been in use here also. No other examples of shoulder plaques have been found but similar types of medallion, triple and double rings, and perforated rings with buffer projections are all clearly related to the Roscommon find. W1. L. of collar 39.4 cm.

Wilde 1861, 576–7; McEvoy, 1997; Eogan 2001, 231–40.

[3:6] GOLD DRESS-FASTENER, NEAR CLONES, CO. MONAGHAN.

Late Bronze Age, 900–700 BC.

Found near Clones, Co. Monaghan and acquired by Trinity College, Dublin, in 1820, this magnificent object of exceptional size and weight consists of a solid, cast 'bow' or 'handle' attached to two sub-conical terminals. The terminals are decorated with rows of concentric, raised lines. Incised against the innermost rib on the underside is a row of hatched triangles. The upper surface is decorated by a pattern of punched dots placed centrally in a series of incised, concentric circles. The bow is plain except for an area near the junction with the terminals which is decorated with rows of parallel and oblique lines bordered by a double zig-zag. The surfaces have been highly polished giving this object a very rich, lustrous appearance. IA/L/1963:1. L. 21.27 cm; Wt. 1032.64 g.

Cahill 1998, 55–9.

[3:7] GOLD DRESS-FASTENER, CASTLEKELLY, CO. GALWAY.

Late Bronze Age, 900–700 BC.

Found in gravel under a bog at a depth of *c.*20 feet at Castlekelly, Co. Galway, in 1819, this is another fine specimen of an exceptionally large and heavy dress-fastener. It consists of a hollow 'bow' or 'handle' attached to two terminals. The surfaces of the terminals are covered with the impressions of the planishing hammer which give a mottled appearance to the gold. Decoration is confined to the outer edges of the terminals and to a small area above the bow/terminal joint. Although an impressive piece, it may be that this specimen is unfinished. This would accord with the apparent lack of finish on the terminals. W122. L. 28.1 cm; Wt. 524.35 g.
Cahill 1998, 45–8.

[3:8] GOLD DRESS-FASTENER AND WOODEN BOX, KILLYMOON, CO. TYRONE.

Late Bronze Age, 900–700 BC.

The alder box which provided protection for the gold dress-fastener is a very rare survival. They were found together in a bog in 1816 at Killymoon, Co. Tyrone. Both box and lid were carved from single pieces of alder without any great skill, but clearly with the intention of providing a secure niche for its precious contents. The dress-fastener is undecorated but very well made and finished. Over sixty dress-fasteners survive from Ireland. The method of use is not properly understood but they may have functioned using loops or double buttonholes. They vary considerably in size, some weighing over 1 kg. 1967:234, 239a–b. Box L. 21.4 cm; Dress-fastener L. 9.6 cm; Wt. 102.9 g.
Armstrong 1920, 33; Cahill 1983, no. 15.

[3:9] PAIR OF GOLD EAR-SPOOLS, NEAR MULLINGAR, CO. WESTMEATH.

Late Bronze Age, 800–700 BC.

This pair of ear-spools is said to be from near Mullingar, Co. Westmeath. Objects of this type have been described as boxes although when intact it was impossible for them to function as such. It has now been recognised that they are ear-spools, worn in the distended lobe of the ear and held in place by the pressure of the stretched lobe. They are made from fine sheet gold and consist of a cylindrical side piece and two closing discs. These are decorated with patterns composed mainly of concentric circles and raised bosses closely related to the motifs familiar from gold collars and bronze ornaments. 1884:8–9. D. 5.8 and 5.6 cm; Wt. 18.7 and 15.95 g.
Armstrong 1920, 89; Cahill 1983, no. 17; Cahill 2000, 8–15.

[3:10] HOARD OF GOLD ORNAMENTS, BALLINESKER, CO. WEXFORD.

Late Bronze Age, 900–700 BC.

Although this hoard was originally disturbed during site clearance at Ballinesker, Co. Wexford, it was not discovered until the topsoil was redistributed. It consists of two dress-fasteners, a bracelet, three ear-spools and part of a fourth. The dress-fasteners and bracelet are substantial pieces of solid gold. They are very well made, but undecorated and lightly polished. Of the ear-spools, two are a matching pair of cylindrical form while the others are a complete bobbin-shaped spool and a fragment of another. The decoration of the ear-spools is closely comparable to the gold collars. 1990:62–68. W. of largest dress-fastener 14.70 cm; Wt. 280.0 g; D. of ear-spool 7.25 cm; Wt. 33.6 g; Wt. of hoard 666.0 g.
Cahill 1994, 21–3; Cahill 2001, 8–15.

[3:11] HOARD OF EAR-ORNAMENTS, ARBOE AND KILLYCOLPY, CO. TYRONE.

Late Bronze Age, 800–700 BC.

This group of four split-ring ornaments with discs was found with other objects in the area of Arboe and Killycolpy, Co. Tyrone, in the early nineteenth century. Each one consists of a cast ring, the ends of which have been worked into discs. The ring is decorated with deep, tightly-spaced grooves bordered by panels of incised cross-hatching. Many uses, from musical instruments to dress-fasteners, have been proposed for these objects which are known only from Ireland. Recently, it has been suggested that they may have been worn as ear ornaments, fitting into the loop of the perforated and distended ear lobe. 1967:235–238. W. of largest 4.32 cm; Wt. 43.95 g.
Raftery, 1970, 169–74; Eogan 1972, 196.

[3:12] TWO GOLD FOIL-COVERED LEAD SPLIT-RING ORNAMENTS IN A CERAMIC CONTAINER, ANNAGHBEG (OR MONASTEREADAN), CO. SLIGO.

Late Bronze Age, 800–700 BC.

The hoard was found on the shore of Lough Gara at Annaghbeg (or Monastereadan), Co. Sligo. The discovery of a specially made ceramic vessel to contain these split-ring ornaments is most unusual. The rings are composed of a lead core over which a thin gold foil cover has been attached. The inner edges of the lead rings are carefully incised so that the foil can be pressed into the grooves as it folds inwards towards the centre. This produces a pattern of rayed lines on the foil while keeping it in place. The rings narrow towards the opening and are decorated with a simple, incised diamond pattern on each side. These rings form a matching pair and may have been worn in the ears. 1989:8–10. D. of rings 2.4 cm; Wt. 23.84 and 23.92 g.
Unpublished.

[3:13] TWO GOLD FOIL-COVERED LEAD SPLIT-RING ORNAMENTS, NO LOCALITY, IRELAND.

Late Bronze Age, 800–700 BC.

It has been recorded that these split-ring ornaments were found in a cinerary urn, but the place and circumstances are not known. The lead core of each ring has been covered by a fine gold foil which has been expertly decorated with minute, complex patterns of criss-cross lines, hatched triangles interspersed with groups of lines and rows of dots. The foils have been folded over the inner edges of the rings and concealed in the hollow. Although not a matching pair, they were made by a highly accomplished craftsman. While there are no associated finds which would indicate the function of these rings, if worn in the ear through a distended lobe, the decoration could be shown to its best advantage. W258–259. D. 2.6 and 4.2 cm; Wt. 21.58 and 72.19 g.

Armstrong 1920, 93.

[3:14] HOARD OF ORNAMENTS, TOORADOO, CO. LIMERICK.

Late Bronze Age, 800–700 BC.

This hoard of ornaments was found in a bog called Cnoc na bPoll in the townland of Tooradoo, Co. Limerick. It contains four bronze rings, four gold foil-covered lead split-ring ornaments, a lignite bead, and an amber necklace. While the function of the bronze rings is not fully understood, they could have functioned as personal ornaments. The foil-covered split rings, which bear some simple decoration, could have been worn in the ears or tied in the hair. The necklace of 105 graduated amber beads must have been a truly prized possession, as the amber — a rare and costly material — would have been imported from the Baltic. SA 1927:2a–l. W. of largest bronze ring 3.35 cm.

Gogan 1932, 58–71; Eogan 1983, 104–105.

[3:15] HOARD OF GOLD ORNAMENTS, KILMOYLY NORTH, CO. KERRY.

Late Bronze Age, 900–700 BC.

When found in a bog at Kilmoyly North, Co. Kerry, in 1940, these objects — three bracelets and a dress-fastener — were in an oak box which, unfortunately, has not survived. Two of the bracelets are solid with expanded terminals, while the third is made from a thick, c-shaped band. Gold bracelets of various forms are very common in the Irish Late Bronze Age — over two hundred have been recorded. The dress-fastener is solid with deeply hollowed terminals. None of the objects is decorated. It is not unusual to find small hoards of gold ornaments deposited in bogs during this period. 1940:2a–d. W. of largest bracelet 9.30 cm; Wt. of hoard 57.85 g.

Raftery 1940, 56–7.

[3:16] HOARD OF GOLD ORNAMENTS, LATTOON, CO. CAVAN.

Late Bronze Age, 900–700 BC.

This group of gold ornaments was found deep in a bog at Lattoon, Co. Cavan, in 1919. The objects are two dress-fasteners, two bracelets and a disc of fine gold foil. The bracelets are solid and have slightly expanded terminals while the dress-fasteners are also solid and have deeply dished, expanded terminals. The disc is made from an exceptionally thin foil and is elaborately decorated with a complex pattern of concentric circles, hatched triangles and herring-bone patterns. When complete the foil would have been slightly domed and would have covered a disc of copper or bronze making a very impressive display. 1920:24–8. D. of disc 12.05 cm; Wt. 5.96 g.

Armstrong 1920, 47–8; Eogan 1981, 148; Eogan 1983, 64–5.

[3:17] HOARD OF GOLD ORNAMENTS, MOOGHAUN NORTH, CO. CLARE.

Late Bronze Age, 800–700 BC.

In 1854 an enormous hoard of gold ornaments was found at Mooghaun North, Co. Clare, during the building of a railway. Most of the hoard was dispersed by the workmen through jewellers who provided ready cash for the bullion value. As a result the original number of objects cannot be accurately assessed but numbered several hundred. Only thirty-four originals (fourteen in the British Museum) have survived, but many of the lost objects were replicated before being melted down. The hoard contained mostly small bracelets together with collars, neck-rings and ingots. The burial of such a vast amount of gold must have represented a considerable loss to the community which produced it. The proximity of the find-place to Mooghaun Lough suggests that this massive hoard was deposited ritually in an act of propitiation. NMI Reg. nos. W22–27, W91–92, W117–118, W175–176, SA1904:2, 1936:3696–3697, 1960:675; BM Reg. nos. WG32, 1857.6–27.1–13. W. of largest collar 18.00 cm; Wt. 223.16 g. (This image includes all the British Museum originals.)

Armstrong 1920, 14–20; Eogan 1983, 69–72.

[3:18] GROUP OF GOLD FOIL-COVERED BULLAE (*FROM LEFT*): BOG OF ALLEN, CO. KILDARE; ARBOE/KILLYCOLPY, CO. TYRONE; RIVER BANN, CO. ANTRIM; KINNEGOE, CO. ARMAGH; NO LOCALITY, IRELAND.

Late Bronze Age, 800–700 BC.

These heart-shaped objects consist of a core of base metal or clay, covered in finely decorated gold foil. Called bullae after the amulets well known from classical Europe, they were intended to be worn as pendants as each one can be strung through the cylindrical opening at the top. They are decorated with various combinations of concentric circles, geometric motifs and gold wire filigree. Whether or not they were intended to protect the wearer may never be known, but as they are of extremely rare occurrence we can assume that they were prized possessions which confirmed the status and wealth of the wearer. W265, IA/305/53, 1906:160, 1906:447, W264. L. of largest 6.4 cm; Wt. of largest 146.9 g.

Armstrong 1920, 92–3; Eogan 1998, 17–26.

[3:19] GOLD COLLAR, ARDCRONY, CO. TIPPERARY.

Late Bronze Age, 800–700 BC.

Found in 1842 in a bog in the parish of Ardcrony, Co. Tipperary, this is one of nine large gold collars (or fragments of collars) to have survived. Although now incomplete, it is also one of the most skilfully crafted. Its structure and decoration follow the usual form — a one-piece collar to which large terminals have been attached by gold wire stitching. The collar shows evidence of having been folded in two, perhaps as part of the deposition ritual. The decoration, especially the rope pattern on the collar, is extremely fine and delicate in its execution, demonstrating a level of skill rarely surpassed in the Irish record. W16. W. 26.0 cm; Wt. 132.52 g.

Armstrong 1920, 57; Cahill 1995, 63–65.

[3:20] GOLD COLLAR, NO LOCALITY, IRELAND.

Late Bronze Age, 800–700 BC.

No details of the discovery or find place have been recorded for this collar which was formerly part of the collection of Henry R. Dawson, Dean of St Patrick's, Dublin. It survives in two fragments. This conforms with several other collars which show evidence of having been folded in antiquity. Between the raised ribs are four rows of thick, single rope patterning. The surviving frontal disc is decorated with round bosses set in concentric circles, while the lower disc has a simple pattern of rays. The twisted gold wire stitches which attached the terminals to the collar are visible. W20. W. 25.7 cm; Wt. 231.4 g.

Armstrong 1920, 58.

[3:21] GOLD COLLAR, GLENINSHEEN, CO. CLARE.

Late Bronze Age, 800–700 BC.

Found in a rock cleft in 1932 at Gleninsheen, Co. Clare, this collar is an exceptional example of the highly developed goldsmithing skills displayed by Irish craftsmen in the Late Bronze Age. While conforming closely to the pattern of ornamentation prescribed for such collars, the smith, by varying the detail of the motifs, has achieved a *tour de force*. In particular, the frontal terminal discs are of superb craftsmanship. The layout and execution of the designs incorporating concentric circles, rope patterns and conical and round bosses, have been expertly achieved. It also appears to have been folded in two before deposition in a rock fissure on the Burren. 1934:85. W. 31.4 cm; Wt. 276 g.

Gleeson 1934, 138–9; Cahill 1983, no. 21.

[3:22] GOLD COLLAR, CO. CLARE.
Late Bronze Age, 800–700 BC.

Said to have been found in Co. Clare, this exceptionally heavy collar was acquired by the Royal Irish Academy with the collection of Major Henry Sirr in 1841. It is a very unusual example for a number of reasons. It is made of very heavy sheet gold. It has only three raised ribs, each of which is decorated with three rows of round bosses instead of being left plain. There are no rope patterns between the ribs, the narrow space between them being decorated with only a single row of short punched strokes. The final product is a heavy, inflexible collar which, it has been suggested, may relate to a studded leather prototype. W21. W. 27.0 cm; Wt. 514.1 g.
Armstrong 1920, 58; Raftery 1967, 70.

[3:23] GOLD COLLAR, TORYHILL, CO. LIMERICK.
Late Bronze Age, 800–700 BC.

This collar was found at Toryhill, Co. Limerick. Unfortunately, nothing is known of the find circumstances other than that the object was in two pieces when found. It has lost its terminals but whether in antiquity or at the time of discovery is not known. In spite of these losses it is clear that, when complete, this collar would have been a very splendid piece. The breadth of the collar is wider than is usual and the workmanship is of a very high standard, although the rope patterns are relatively simple. It has eleven raised ribs which is considerably more than any other collar, making the multi-stranded effect much more impressive. W18. W. 24.7 cm; Wt. 38.23 g.
Armstrong 1920, 58.

[3:24] GOLD COLLAR, BORRISNOE, CO. TIPPERARY.
Late Bronze Age, 800–700 BC.

Found in 1836 under a bog at Borrisnoe, Co. Tipperary, this collar was collected by Dean Dawson and acquired by the Royal Irish Academy with his collection. Although complete it has suffered damage in antiquity including ritual folding prior to deposition. The collar is decorated with a pattern of rope motifs while the discs favour a concentric layout featuring bosses set in circles. The collar retains a unique feature, i.e. a small loop of gold wire, which enabled the collar to be held securely in place by linking one side to the other across the back of the neck using other gold links or a cord of organic material. W17. W. 25.0 cm; Wt. 137.96 g.
Armstrong 1920, 58; Cahill 1995, 66, 88.

[3:25] Hoard containing a gold collar, two gold lock-rings, two bracelets and an ear-ornament, Gorteenreagh, Co. Clare.

Late Bronze Age, 800–700 BC.

This hoard was found by a man clearing stones from a field in 1948 at Gorteenreagh, Co. Clare. It may represent the personal jewellery of an individual. The collar was in a disassembled condition but all the component parts are present. The collar has three raised ribs and a single row of short strokes between the ribs. The terminals are decorated with patterns of bosses set in concentric circles. The lock-rings, thought to have been worn in the hair, are made from fine gold wire and are the two largest and finest found in Ireland. The bracelets are small with slightly expanded terminals. The sixth object, which previously was thought to be a small dress-fastener, is now thought to be an ear ornament. 1948:320–330. W. of collar 25.0 cm; Wt. 358.43 g; D. of lock-rings 9.9 cm; Wt. 95 g.

Raftery 1967, 63–5; Eogan 1968, 93–148.

[3:26] Bronze cauldron, Castlederg, Co. Tyrone.

Late Bronze Age, 700–600 BC.

Found in a bog at Castlederg, Co. Tyrone, this superb example of the sheet-metalworker's craft is formed of offset bands of metal held in place by horizontal rows of conical rivets. The base is rounded, the profile is incurving at the shoulder and ends in an everted rim that is decorated with four rows of small holes. There are two large suspension rings in loops on the rim. More than thirty cauldrons have been found in Ireland of which more than half are of the type represented by the Castlederg cauldron, a type based ultimately on Greek and Oriental prototypes. The conical headed rivet form appears to be derived from central Europe. 1933:119. D. 56.0 cm.

Hawkes and Smith 1957, 182; Kelly 1983, no. 24.

[3.27] Bronze shield, near Lough Gur, Co. Limerick.

Late Bronze Age, c.700 BC.

Found in a bog between Ballinamoona and Herbertstown, near Lough Gur, Co. Limerick. Beaten from a flat sheet of bronze, the corrugated surface was then beaten from behind. There is a central raised boss surrounded by seven concentric ridges, inter-spaced by six rings of hemispherical bosses. The rim is strengthened by turning in the edge. There is a handle on the back behind the boss, held in place by two domed rivets that fit unobtrusively into the inner ring of bosses. Similar rivets hold two sling loops in position. Affording as it does less protection against sword slashes than would the leather shields of the period, the object may have functioned mainly as a parade shield. A proposal that the object was wrapped in textile when deposited would not appear to be correct. 1872:15. D. 71.3 cm.

Coles 1962, 167, 183; Kelly 1983, no. 23a.

[3:6]

GOLD DRESS-FASTENER, NEAR CLONES, CO. MONAGHAN.

Late Bronze Age, 900–700 BC.

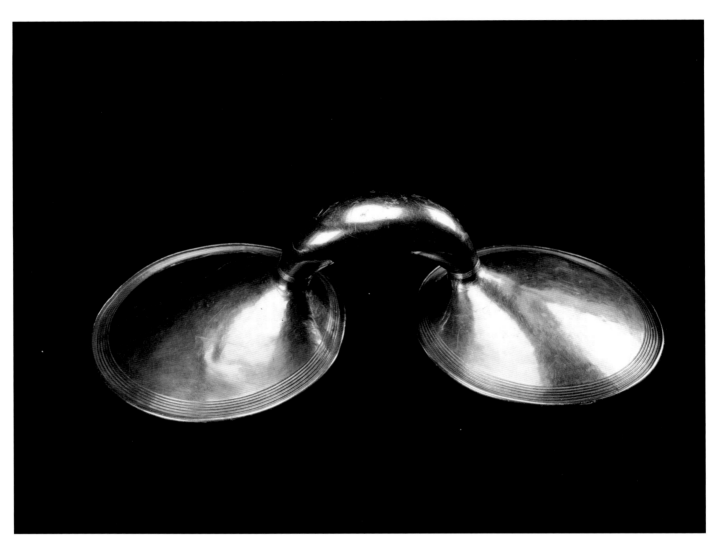

[3:7]
Gold dress-fastener, Castlekelly, Co. Galway.
Late Bronze Age, 900–700 BC.

[3:8]
Gold dress-fastener and wooden box, Killymoon, Co. Tyrone.
Late Bronze Age, 900–700 BC.

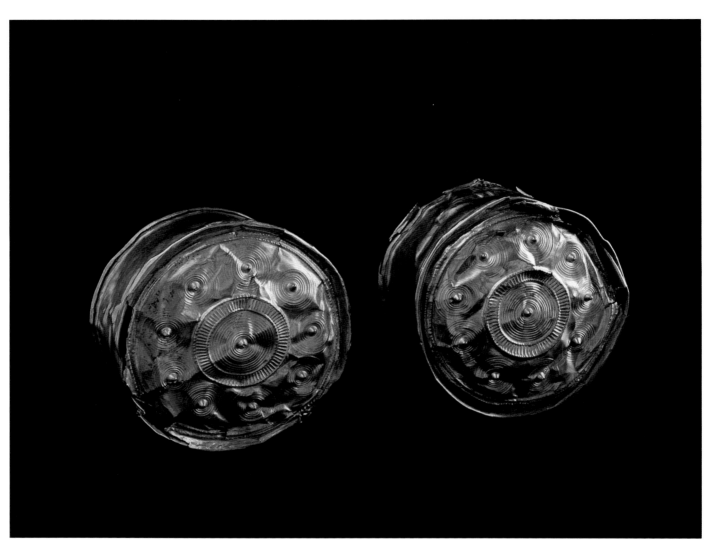

[3:9]

PAIR OF GOLD EAR-SPOOLS, NEAR MULLINGAR, CO. WESTMEATH.

Late Bronze Age, 800–700 BC

[3:10]
HOARD OF GOLD ORNAMENTS, BALLINESKER, CO. WEXFORD.
Late Bronze Age, 900–700 BC.

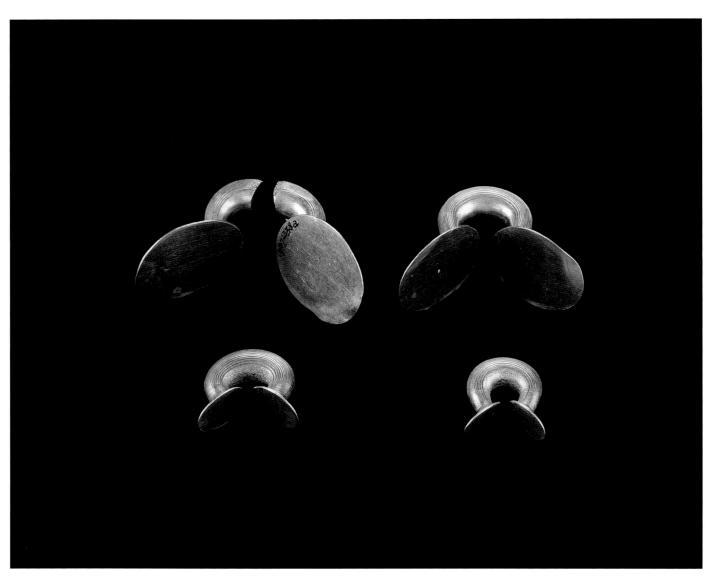

[3:11]
HOARD OF EAR-ORNAMENTS, ARBOE AND KILLYCOLPY, CO. TYRONE.
Late Bronze Age, 800–700 BC.

[3:12]

**TWO GOLD FOIL-COVERED LEAD SPLIT-RING ORNAMENTS IN A CERAMIC CONTAINER,
ANNAGHBEG (OR MONASTEREADAN), CO. SLIGO.**

Late Bronze Age, 800–700 BC.

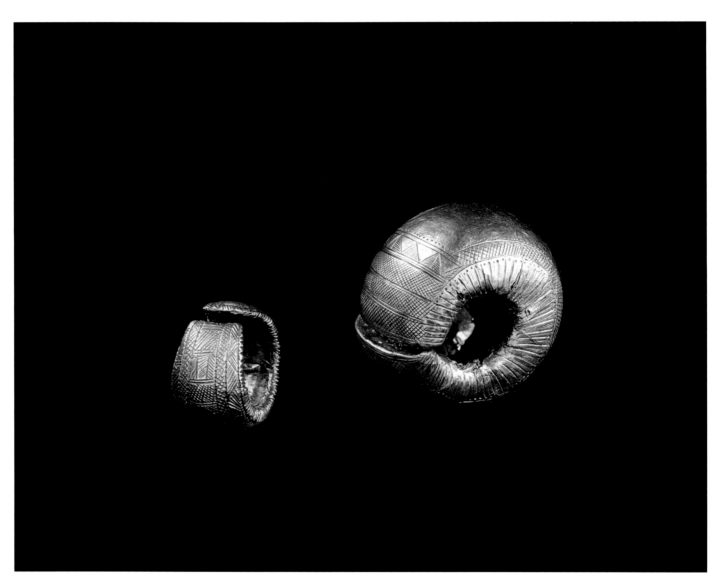

[3:13]
TWO GOLD FOIL-COVERED LEAD SPLIT-RING ORNAMENTS, NO LOCALITY, IRELAND.
Late Bronze Age, 800–700 BC.

[3:14] *facing page*
HOARD OF ORNAMENTS, TOORADOO, CO. LIMERICK.
Late Bronze Age, 800–700 BC.

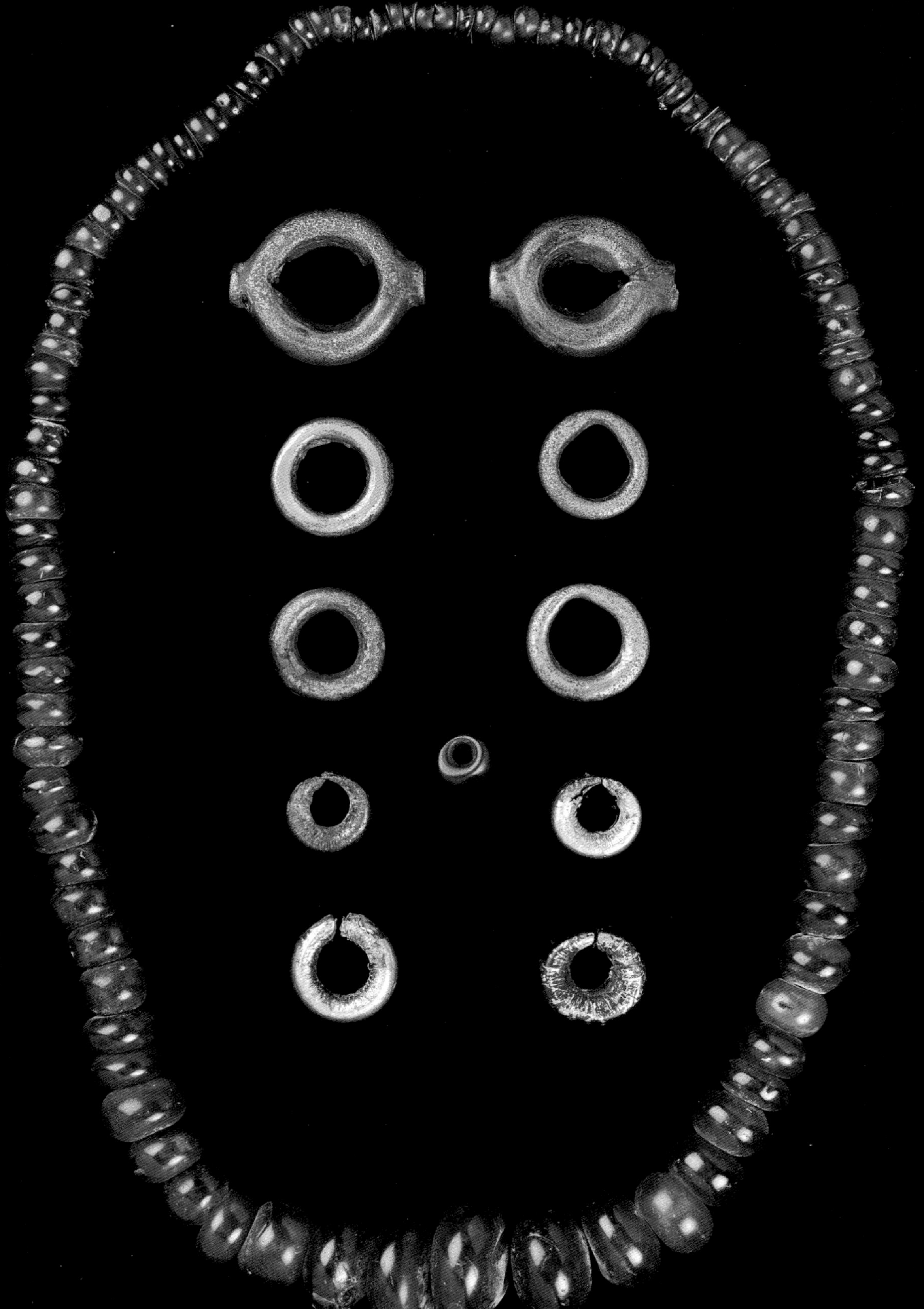

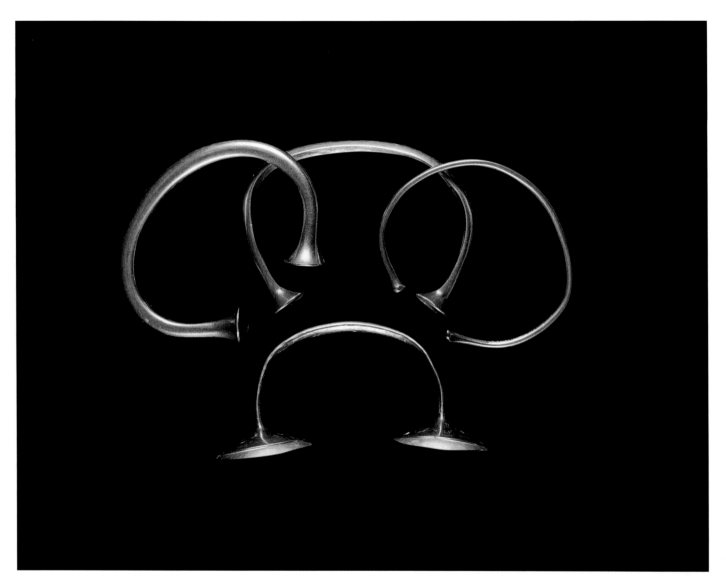

[3:15]

HOARD OF GOLD ORNAMENTS, KILMOYLY NORTH, CO. KERRY.

Late Bronze Age, 900–700 BC.

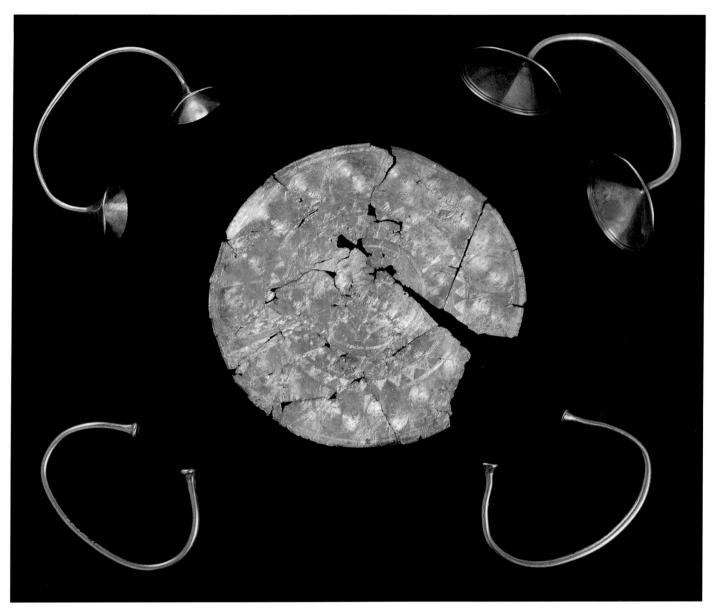

[3:16]

HOARD OF GOLD ORNAMENTS, LATTOON, CO. CAVAN.

Late Bronze Age, 900–700 BC.

[3:17]
HOARD OF GOLD ORNAMENTS, MOOGHAUN NORTH, CO. CLARE.
Late Bronze Age, 800–700 BC.

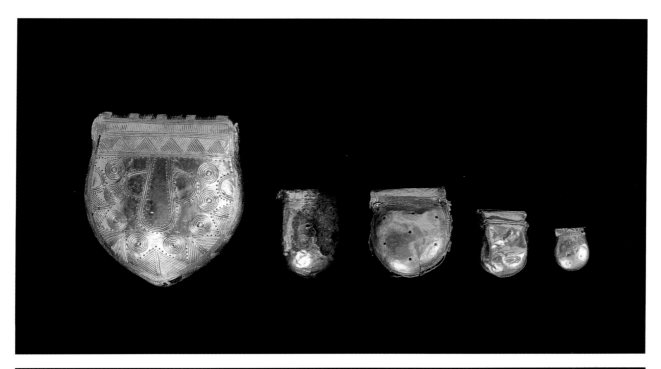

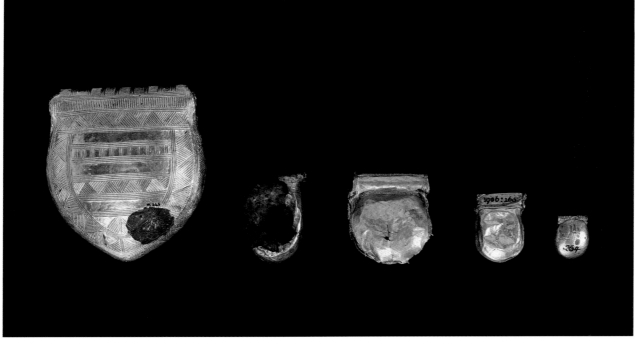

[3:18]

GROUP OF GOLD FOIL-COVERED BULLAE (*FROM LEFT*): BOG OF ALLEN, CO. KILDARE; ARBOE/KILLYCOLPY, CO. TYRONE;
RIVER BANN, CO. ANTRIM; KINNEGOE, CO. ARMAGH; NO LOCALITY, IRELAND.

Late Bronze Age, 800–700 BC.

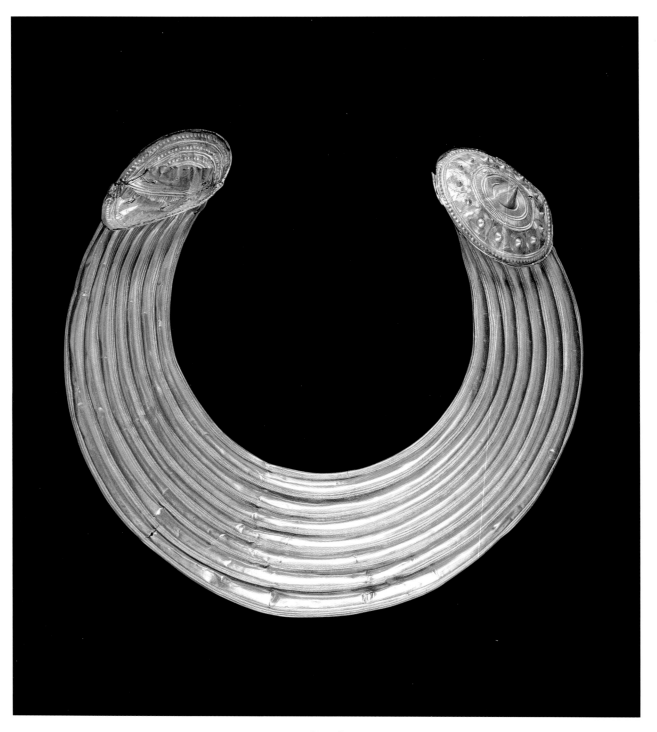

[3:19]

GOLD COLLAR, ARDCRONY, CO. TIPPERARY.

Late Bronze Age, 800–700 BC.

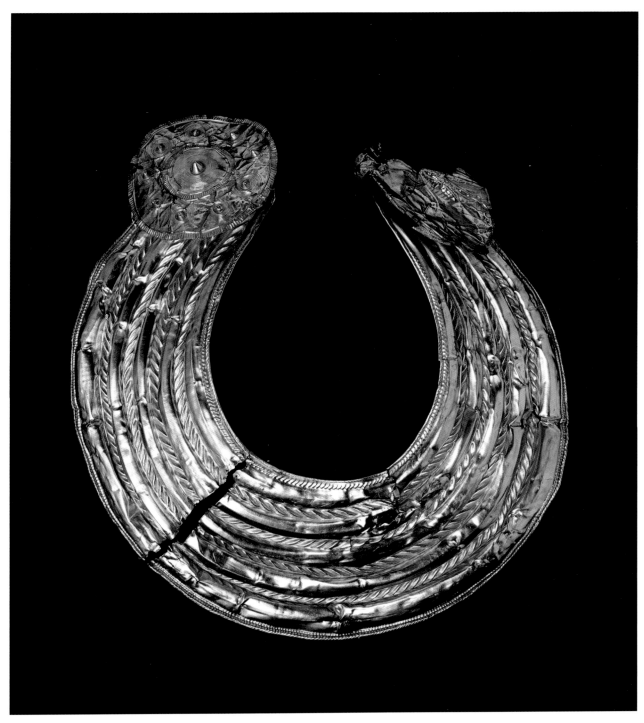

[3:20]

GOLD COLLAR, NO LOCALITY, IRELAND.

Late Bronze Age, 800–700 BC.

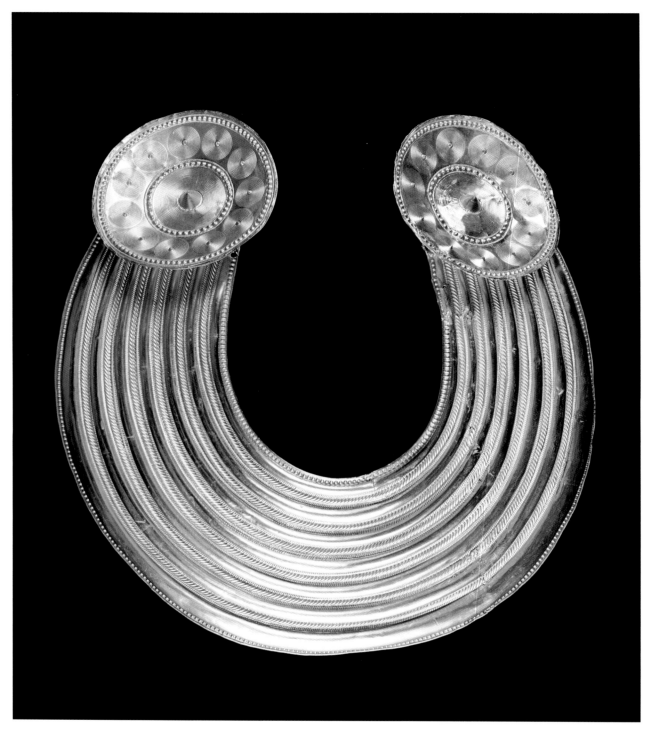

[3:21]

GOLD COLLAR, GLENINSHEEN, CO. CLARE.

Late Bronze Age, 800–700 BC.

[3:22]

GOLD COLLAR, CO. CLARE.

Late Bronze Age, 800–700 BC.

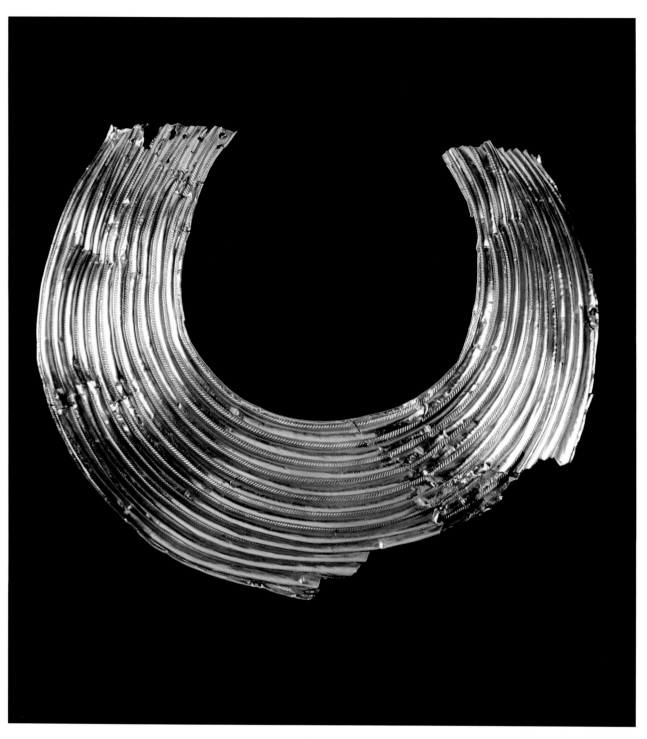

[3:23]
GOLD COLLAR, TORYHILL, CO. LIMERICK.
Late Bronze Age, 800–700 BC.

[3:24] *facing page*
GOLD COLLAR, BORRISNOE, CO. TIPPERARY.
Late Bronze Age, 800–700 BC.

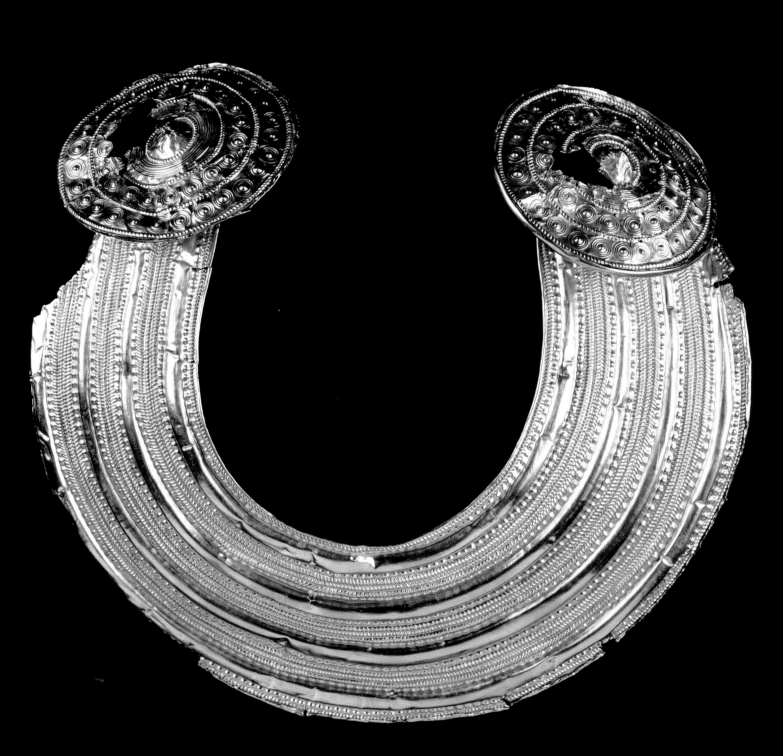

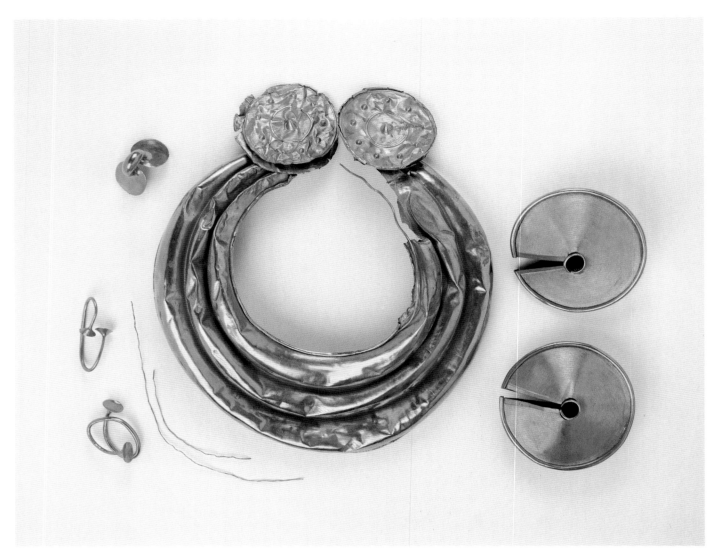

[3:25]
**HOARD CONTAINING A GOLD COLLAR, TWO GOLD LOCK-RINGS,
TWO BRACELETS AND AN EAR-ORNAMENT, GORTEENREAGH, CO. CLARE.**
Late Bronze Age, 800–700 BC.

[3:26]
BRONZE CAULDRON, CASTLEDERG, CO. TYRONE.
Late Bronze Age, 700–600 BC.

[3.27]
BRONZE SHIELD, NEAR LOUGH GUR, CO. LIMERICK.
Late Bronze Age, c.700 BC.

4

THE IRON AGE

EAMONN P. KELLY

The Iron Age in Ireland is not just a period that saw the introduction of a new metalworking technology; it is also a period during which objects were made and decorated using an art style that, in Britain and on the continent, is associated with Celtic peoples. At the end of the Iron Age when Ireland entered into the historical era its population spoke a Celtic language and its institutions and traditions reflect practices that were recorded among Celtic societies elsewhere. Celtic art was clearly introduced to Ireland but the existing evidence does not support the notion that this coincided with the introduction of a Celtic language by invading population groups. It may well be that the use of the Irish language predates the appearance of Celtic art in Ireland by some considerable length of time; but the question remains a vexing one that is not possible to answer using archaeological methodology.

During the Dowris Phase of the Irish Late Bronze Age the appearance of certain metal artefacts shows that before the end of the seventh century BC cultural influences reached Ireland from the continental iron-using Hallstatt culture, probably by way of southern Britain. This is evidenced by the appearance of objects having a continental Hallstatt background, such as a new type of Irish bronze sword and fittings known as chapes that were used to strengthen the closed ends of sword scabbards. Other Hallstatt types include two unlocalised cast bronze bracelets of the 'nut-moulded' type and three others of the same type found in Co. Antrim. A penannular bracelet that has knobbed terminals, from a hoard discovered in Kilmurry, Co. Kerry, may also be included, as may certain ritual objects known as flesh-hooks, the best example of which was found at Dunaverney, Co. Antrim.

By around about 500 BC the Dowris culture was in major decline in Ireland and one cause of this may have been the presence of intrusive peoples who are detected but faintly in the archaeological record. It was probably around this time that the technology for the mining, smelting and production of iron artefacts was first introduced. On the continent at this time, Hallstatt society had been replaced by the La Tène culture, which is characterised by richly ornamented artefacts in metal, stone and other media. This ornament is rendered in the mature Celtic art style that originated in eastern France and the Rhineland during the fifth century BC. It is a highly stylised curvilinear art based mainly on classical vegetable and foliage motifs such as leafy palmette forms, vines, tendrils and lotus flowers together with spirals, S-scrolls, lyre and trumpet shapes. La Tène art was given its greatest expression on the personal ornaments and weapons of a warrior aristocracy and its occurrence in Ireland is generally regarded as confirming the essentially Celtic nature of the island's culture during the final prehistoric and Early Medieval periods. Many of these finds may be regarded as casual losses but others appear to have been deposited deliberately in ritual contexts such as burials and votive deposits in watery locations and at shrines.

Few settlement sites of the Iron Age have been excavated in Ireland and little is known about the way of life of the ordinary people. That there may have been considerable continuity of settlement patterns from the Late Bronze Age is suggested by the use of crannógs or dwellings on artificial islands in lakes, and lakeside habitation. A number of ritual sites which were also seats of political power are known, the most important being Tara, Co. Meath; Cruachain, Co. Roscommon; Emain Macha, Co. Armagh and Dún Ailinne, Co. Kildare. These were sites that had been of importance at an earlier time, evidenced at Tara by the presence of extensive funerary monuments of Neolithic and Bronze Age date. The major Iron Age ritual sites are all located in the northern half of the country, within the area in which La Tène decorated material occurs most frequently. The fortification of coastal promontories with ramparts placed across narrow necks of land appears to be a new type of site. Called promontory forts, sites such as Drumanagh Fort on the north Dublin coast were certainly in use by the early centuries AD. It is likely that there were many scattered dwellings and family farmsteads throughout the countryside but evidence for them is difficult to detect. A good deal of social organisation appears to have existed as evidenced by the communal efforts invested in the construction of large earthworks and roads. This would include extensive linear earthworks delimiting territorial boundaries and acting as a deterrent against cattle raiding, as well as large enclosures constructed at ritual centres and timber-paved roads to provide access across bogs.

There are a number of different phases to the Iron Age in Ireland, the character of which appears to have been determined to some extent by external happenings. Originating between 350 and 150 BC, the earliest La Tène material found in Ireland has a continental background and direct imports occur. Among the earliest La Tène finds are two gold collars discovered in a bog at Ardnaglug, Co. Roscommon [4:3, 4:4]. The decoration on one collar is comparable with that found on gold ornaments from a grave at Waldalgesheim in the Rhineland, and it is likely that the Ardnaglug collar originated in this general area [4:3]. The second Ardnaglug collar consists of a twisted narrow band of gold with two hollow acorn-shaped terminals and is possibly also an import [4:4].

In the north-east of Ireland a small group of eight decorated sword scabbards has been found that date to the late third century or second century BC. The objects appear to have been produced in a local workshop but their background, and that of a small number of chapes that have also been found, appears to be continental. The scabbards bear engraved designs of the so-called 'Sword Style' that are in the form of stylised plant ornament laid out in a series of S-scroll or lyre shapes. One such plate was found near the River Bann at Toome, Co. Antrim and although it is cruder than other examples it was clearly a much-prized possession [4:5]. A fine example of a cast bronze chape is that from near Roscrea, Co. Tipperary [4:6]. Like the other five known examples it is lozenge-shaped at the end, resembling somewhat a stylised serpent's head, with extensions above the waisted centre. In all, about two dozen Irish Iron Age swords are known. The plate or mount, often decorated, placed at the junction of a sword blade and the haft is known as a quillon. The earliest Irish swords are the closest to continental prototypes, having a characteristic bell-shaped quillon and there is a particularly well-preserved example from Ballinderry, Co. Westmeath.

After around 150 BC, although continental influences continue to be present, material having a British origin becomes increasingly prevalent, perhaps as a result of displacements caused by the invasion of southern England by Gaulish tribes known as the Belgae. More than a dozen related bronze bowls have been found in Ireland that are similar to southern British types and some are actual imports. One such import was found containing a cremation burial within a hill-fort at Fore, Co. Westmeath [4:7]. Originally it had two small bird-headed handles, one of which is now lost. The vessel was made from sheet bronze in two parts, with the joining along the middle decorated with a row of domed studs. The bird-headed form of the handles connects the Fore bowl with another probable import from southern England. This is a handled drinking bowl or cup from Keshcarrigan, Co. Leitrim, that appears to date slightly later than the Fore bowl, perhaps to the early half of the first century AD [4:8]. A cast bronze cup handle was also found at Somerset, Co. Galway, alongside other objects dating to the early centuries AD. Continental Celtic imports of this phase include a south-western French bronze sword hilt recovered from the sea-bed at Ballyshannon

DETAIL OF [4:5]
SWORD SCABBARD PLATE,
NEAR TOOME,
CO. ANTRIM.
Iron Age, second century BC.

DETAIL OF [4:8]
BRONZE BOWL,
KESHCARRIGAN,
CO. LEITRIM.
*Early Iron Age, early first
century AD.*

[4:1]

THREE GLASS RING-BEADS: HAWK HILL, CO. KILDARE; DENHAMSTOWN, CO. MEATH AND CLOUGHWATER, CO. ANTRIM.
Early Iron Age, first century BC.

Bay, Co. Donegal [4:9]. It is cast in the form of a male human figure, perhaps intended to represent a warrior or a god. Other possible imports include large glass ring-beads with whirl or ray designs that are a well-known Late La Tène continental type [4:1].

Imported objects from the Roman world are represented in the most outstanding Irish Iron Age discovery made at the end of the nineteenth century during ploughing at Broighter, Co. Derry [4:10]. This is an unusual group of gold objects which consists of a model boat together with its fittings, a gold bowl with rings for suspension, two chains, two twisted collars and a large decorated collar with buffer terminals.

One of the Broighter gold chains has a single complex strand while the other example has three strands gathered together at the rectangular terminals [4:13]. The chain clasps are of a type which was widespread in the Mediterranean and it is clear that the objects are exotic imports, possibly from Roman Egypt. The two twisted collars [4:14] appear to be of southern English origin and are similar to a pair from an assortment of imported objects found at Newgrange, Co. Meath. The unique gold boat is a model of an ocean-going vessel complete with seats, oars, rowlocks, steering oar and mast [4:11] while the small gold bowl may also be a model, in this case of a cauldron [4:12].

Also found was a large collar with buffer terminals that is of the same general form as one of the Ardnaglug collars, although the ring of the Broighter collar is thicker and decorated sumptuously [4:10]. Apart from its rear moulding the collar is largely complete. The ring is formed from tubular sheets of gold, ornamented with relief decoration on the convex surfaces. The intricate design is of complex symmetry based mainly on the lotus-bud motif but which one authority has proposed, may be a highly stylised representation of a horse. It is truly a masterpiece, from the hand of a master craftsman, and the paucity of other Irish goldwork of the period raises the question as to whether or not it is of Irish manufacture. The fact that all the objects in the Broighter hoard are made from gold which has come from the same source favours an external origin for the collar. This ore source may be located in the eastern Mediterranean in the same general area from where the neck chains were imported, although an origin in the Rhineland is also a possibility. The collar is of a type that originates ultimately on the continent where the mortice and tenon fastening device is also found, although related collars are also found in southern England. However, the decoration on the Broighter collar is Irish and the object can be placed early in the Irish version of the so-called 'boss style' of ornamentation, a style that appears to have its origin in a southern British workshop. A possible but not entirely satisfactory resolution to these apparent contradictions might be found in the proposal that the Broighter collar represents an Irish remodelling of a continental or southern British original. Whatever its origins, the Broighter hoard lay concealed for two millennia near the ancient shore at the entrance to Lough Foyle, Co. Derry. Lough Foyle is associated traditionally with the sea god Manannán Mac Lir and the location of the hoard together with the nature of the objects found — jewellery, model boat and cauldron — strongly argue for it being a votive offering to the ancient Irish deity.

Trumpets made of wood or sheet copper-alloy have been found which may have been used in the context of warfare and ceremony. The form of the instruments is known among the continental Celts and a similar trumpet is represented beside the famous statue of the Dying Gaul, a Roman copy of a bronze casting from Pergamon erected originally around 230 BC. A hoard of four instruments was recovered from a former lake known as Loughnashade, close to the royal site of Emain Macha, Co. Armagh [4:15]. Loughnashade means 'the lake of the treasures', which leads one to conclude that it was a votive site into which offerings to the gods were cast. The surviving trumpet has a finely decorated ring at the flared mouth with repoussé ornament composed of long sinuous tendrils which terminate in spiral bosses in high relief. The tube of the trumpet is in two parts, one of which is clearly a later replacement as it is poorly executed. The quality of the riveting on the other section of tube is of a standard that is only occasionally matched on Iron Age sheet metalwork.

During the middle of the first century BC, Celtic Gaul became incorporated into the Roman Empire and there were two temporary Roman incursions into the south of England. In AD 43 troops of the Emperor Claudius invaded once more and began the process that led to the expansion of the empire as far north as lowland Scotland.

[4:2]

GOLD BAND, PROBABLY
FROM A HEAD-DRESS,
LAMBAY ISLAND,
CO. DUBLIN.

*Early Iron Age, second half of
first century AD.*

The Roman expansion in Britain was contested fiercely and there were numerous revolts and uprisings until the decisive defeat of the north British tribes by Septimus Severus in a series of campaigns from AD 208 to 211.

This period of Roman conquest and consolidation saw British refugees arrive in Ireland, as suggested by finds from a late first-century AD cemetery on Lambay Island, Co. Dublin. There were a number of inhumation burials which contained flexed skeletons, of which at least one was that of a warrior buried along with his sword, shield and unspecified 'ornaments' [4:16]. The typical Irish sword of the early centuries AD is one that has a hilt of organic material with a curved quillon and a short blade, the type probably representing a local development of the La Tène form, although its immediate background appears to lie in Romano-British contexts. The sword from the Lambay burial differed however in that it had a long, heavy, parallel-sided blade which is clearly an import. Three bronze mounts, two with open-work ornament, probably adorned a scabbard of leather or wood.

The ornaments from Lambay included five Roman brooches, two bracelets of jet and bronze, and a worn bronze collar ornamented with hollow bronze beads [4:17]. The collar is of north British type dating to around the middle of the first century AD and it provides an important clue as to the origins of the persons interred on Lambay Island. Between AD 71 and 74 the Brigantes of northern England waged war against the Romans before being heavily defeated, and it is possible that the Lambay burials are those of refugees who fled to Ireland to escape the vengeance of their Roman conquerors. The Roman brooches or fibulae from Lambay are of south-eastern English types, but their possession by wealthy Brigantians poses no difficulty.

The Lambay Island burials were discovered in 1927 during harbour works but there is an earlier find from the island, made some time before the 1860s, when an iron sword and a decorated gold band were discovered. The sword is now lost but the gold band is preserved in the National Museum's collections [4:2]. The decoration of the latter is in low relief consisting of a series of wheel-in-circle motifs within a curvilinear design. It may be a simple headband or decoration from a more complex head-dress. Parallels exist on British decorated bronze strips and the wheel-in-circle motif occurs also on an Irish head-dress known as the 'Petrie Crown' [4:18]. The latter is named after George Petrie, a nineteenth-century antiquarian, in whose collection it was for many years but who left no record of the place and circumstances of its discovery. The components, which were probably sewn to leather or textile, formed part of an elaborate horned head-dress. One cone survives, attached to a dished roundel, and evidence for another can be seen on the back of a second roundel. The designs on the Petrie Crown are based on palmette and lotus-bud motifs consisting of sinuous trumpet forms that terminate in lentoid bosses, as well as spirals that terminate in bird heads. Three different types of bird head are represented and those on the cone are remarkably similar to decoration which occurs on British 'Dragonesque' brooches found mainly in northern Britain. It is to that area, therefore, that one must look to find the immediate source of the designs on the Petrie Crown.

A similar type of head-dress is represented by three bronze horns found in Cork where the River Lee meets the sea, and traces of leather were adhering when the discovery was made. Outside of Ireland closely comparable examples of horned head-dress are unknown, although a Celtic bronze horned helmet is known from the River Thames and representations of Celtic warriors wearing similar helmets are known on the continent, particularly in Roman contexts. The Irish objects suggest a ritual purpose and clues to their possible significance may be gleaned from continental finds, such as a silver cauldron found in a bog at Gundestrup, Denmark, which shows a human figure wearing deer antlers. This is likely to be a representation of the Celtic fertility god Cernunnos. The Petrie Crown and the Cork Horns may have been worn on special ritual occasions where they expressed concepts of fertility and renewal.

A ritual context is likely for a series of decorated Iron Age bone objects discovered in a Neolithic Passage Tomb at Loughcrew, Co. Meath. The most remarkable bone objects discovered were the so-called bone slips, made from animal ribs [4:19]. Close to five thousand fragments were found, of which 138 slips are decorated, and they are generally rectangular in shape with rounded or pointed ends. A date in the first or second centuries AD seems likely. A variety of designs are employed including lotus-like forms, continuous broken-backed scrolls, comma curves, background dotting, concentric overlapping arcs, circles asymmetrically placed within each other and spindly knob-ended triskeles.

It has been proposed that the slips were trial pieces on which metal-smiths worked out designs in advance of applying them to metal objects. However, there is no evidence of metalworking at Loughcrew. Although a portion of a compass was reported to have been found and it appears therefore that the slips may have been decorated on site, the location can hardly be regarded as a workshop. A ritual function is perhaps more likely and the objects may have been used in some activity such as divining or fortune telling. Fourteen pieces of bone combs of a Scottish type were also found in the same tomb, many of which bore incised curvilinear decoration. Further evidence of a Scottish connection is to be seen in an imported bronze armlet of second-century AD date found near Newry, Co. Down [4:20], while coiled snake bracelets found in northern Britain during the early centuries AD may have influenced the design of a coiled armlet from Ballymahon, Co. Meath [4:21].

External artistic comparisons with the Loughcrew bone slips have been drawn with objects found both in northern and south-western Britain. A possible bone gaming piece was found at Loughcrew and similar items from Cush, Co. Limerick and Mentrim Lough, Co. Meath bear decoration similar to that found on the bone slips.

The decoration of the bone slips may also be related to that found on a range of metal objects such as the Broighter Collar, the Petrie Crown and certain tubular bronze spear butts. It is also similar to incised designs that occur on a number of bronze spoon-like objects which likewise may have had a ritual function [4:22]. These spoons appear to occur in pairs, one of each pair having a perforation in the 'bowl' close to the edge. Six examples are known, of which one is likely to be an import from southern Britain, whereas the others are of a form current in Scotland and Ireland around the time that the Loughcrew bone slips were made.

As is the case in Britain and on the continent, stone carvings of Celtic gods have been found in Ireland. Some depict a number of faces of which the finest example is the three-faced head from Corleck, Co. Cavan [4:23]. The faces on the carving are similar but not identical, and each seems to express a different mood. A stone head, said to have been found within an Early Bronze Age stone circle at Beltany, Co. Donegal, appears to wear a collar and this is also likely to be of pagan Celtic origin. The precise cultural affinities of the stone heads is difficult to establish, but both continental Celtic and Romano-British connections have been noted. The continental affinities appear somewhat remote and it is probably within a Romano-British context that the more immediate background to the Irish carvings may be found, probably during the first and second centuries AD.

During these two centuries brooches and coins are the main categories of Roman objects found in Ireland and their presence may also be associated with fleeing Romanised Britons. On the other hand such finds may be connected with Roman commercial activity. Roman copper ingots have been found along the north Dublin coast that point to the probable siting of a major workshop at Drumanagh Fort. This would suggest that, to a certain extent, the production of fine metalwork was connected to trade with Britain. Workshops which may have been few in number turned out a relatively small range of high status ornaments that seem to have catered mainly for the tastes of aristocratic cattle lords on the central plain and the rich lands of Ulster. Although some of the objects are uniquely Irish, the material nevertheless possesses a British background and the direct involvement of British or Romano-British craftsmen in their production, employing imported raw materials such as copper ingots, cannot be discounted.

Small circular bronze boxes [4:24] and mounts were fashioned using a variety of decorative techniques and a circular box found at Somerset, Co. Galway, contained a gold torc. Similar torcs as well as bronze bracelets and amber beads were found in a recent hoard discovered at Dooyork, Co. Mayo [4:25]. A small number of Irish brooches were manufactured to supplement imported ones. However, the commonest and most characteristic Irish Iron Age object was the horse-bit [4:26], normally of cast bronze although a few iron examples are known. They occur in pairs and there exists a basic form consisting of a central figure-of-eight link attached to two flanking links, at the ends of which rings are attached. Some 140 examples are known and they appear to be associated with Y-shaped pieces of which about 100 examples have been found. The Y-shaped pieces may be pendants or leading-pieces or may have performed a practical function in harnessing a pair of ponies to a chariot. Five different types of horse-bits have been proposed although the chronological significance of these is uncertain. As one proceeds through the series the side links become more curved, flatter in cross-section and they project further into the rings. The three types lying earliest in the series are plain, although two bits have settings for red enamel, while another has decoration in the form of owl-like heads that are finished using stippling in a manner comparable with a design that occurs on one of the Loughcrew bone slips. On the final two types, decoration occurs frequently in the form of fine curvilinear lines, cast in relief. Stylised human faces and foliage-based designs are common also. Because of the lack of associated material it is not possible to state when the undecorated horse-bits may have been first used in Ireland. What is clear however is that the decorated bits are associated through their ornament with objects such as the Petrie Crown, Cork Horns and decorated tubular spear butts, and a date in the late first or second centuries AD seems likely.

An unusual enamelled horse-bit was found at Killeevan, Co. Monaghan which may be an import from Britain and with it was found a small repoussé disc which may also be an import of the second century AD [4:27].

A similar date is proposed for large, decorated, copper-alloy discs, of which a number have been found in pairs [4:28]. Each disc has a circular area, placed off-centre, which is defined by a raised ring. The area within may be flat, gently concave or deeply hollowed. On each example, this hollow would form the mouth if the over-all design were seen to represent a stylised human face. The raised curvilinear decoration is made up of *peltae* as well as trumpet-shapes that end in lentoid bosses and, occasionally, bird heads. The background may be stippled or bear series of hammer marks which accentuate the raised decoration. Seven examples are known and their function is uncertain. They may have had a ceremonial or parade function, perhaps suspended from the sides of chariots.

During the Early Iron Age, spears may have been used more commonly than swords, but surviving examples made of iron are not easy to identify unless they are found within a secure archaeological context. However, there is a beautiful example of a cast bronze spearhead from Boho, Co. Fermanagh which can be assigned to the Iron Age on the basis of its decoration [4:29].

The distribution of Iron Age prestige metalwork seems to foreshadow later political realities in Ireland. The areas within which La Tène ornamented material is found are those where the ruling dynasties of Early Medieval Ireland are located at the dawning of the Christian era. The ancient rulers of Connacht, Meath and Leinster were all located on the Central Plain. Meath came to be dominated by a tribal federation known as the Uí Néill who originated in Connacht, while an offshoot moved from Connacht to north-west Ulster where they eclipsed the power of the ancient Ulster kingdom centred on Emain Macha. In the Early Medieval period the High Kingship of Ireland alternated between the two main branches of the Uí Néill, with Tara as their pre-eminent ritual centre. There is a small, but perhaps significant, penetration into north Munster of La Tène metalwork and imported Roman material, such as a first-century AD Roman brooch found at Cashel, Co. Tipperary, a place which later became the royal seat of the Munster kings. North Munster was the heartland of the Eoganacht dynasty who ruled Munster until the end of the first millennium AD and who competed with the Uí Néill for the over-lordship of Ireland.

Generally speaking, Roman imports of third-century date are not present in Ireland, and this may reflect a significant change in the nature of the relationship between Ireland and Roman Britain. A significant factor may have been disruption caused by the well-attested incidence of Irish piracy and raiding on Britain from the third century AD which may have cut off supplies of British raw materials as well as a reflexive trade, possibly in Irish cattle hides and dairy produce. These factors may have been responsible for ending the production of the high-status objects which characterised the late first and second centuries AD. La Tène ornamented material dating from the third to fifth centuries AD is difficult to demonstrate although imported Roman material is present once more during the fourth and fifth centuries at a time when Irish settlement occurs in the north and west of Britain. Overall, the period from the third to the fifth century AD appears to be that during which the Irish assimilated many aspects of provincial Roman technology and culture. Finds such as the hoard of silver ingots and chopped-up fine silver tableware from Balline, Co. Limerick may represent loot from a raid on a Roman province [4:30]. On the other hand, the deposition of Roman artefacts at Newgrange, [4:31, 4:32, 4:33] suggests that the site was used as a shrine in a manner consistent with Romano-British practices, while at Freestone Hill, Co. Kilkenny a shrine has been identified devoted to a cult of healing. The latter is of a type known in Late Roman times from south-western Britain and it contained a range of imported personal ornaments of the fourth or fifth centuries AD. Located within the enclosure of a Later Bronze Age hill-fort, the shrine was focused on a burial cairn of the Early Bronze Age. The adoption of pagan Romano-British practices by the Irish should not be seen as surprising given the adoption in the fifth century of Christianity, the religion that had triumphed finally above all others within the Roman world. Indeed, the adoption of Christianity can be seen as but one further step in the process of the Romanisation of early Irish society, a process that had its roots set firmly in the pagan Iron Age.

ILLUSTRATIONS

[4:1] THREE GLASS RING-BEADS: HAWK HILL, CO. KILDARE; DENHAMSTOWN, CO. MEATH AND CLOUGHWATER, CO. ANTRIM.

Early Iron Age, first century BC.

Two of the beads appear to have been associated with burials. The find circumstances of the Cloughwater bead was not recorded, but it may have been found in or close to the Clough river. They are made either of translucent or dense black glass with yellow inlays that spiral around the rings. Analysis suggests that the Hawk Hill bead may be a native copy of imported continental beads and that the other two are continental imports, possibly by way of southern Britain. 1945:323; 1933:3406; 1907:79. D. 4.1 cm, 3.1 cm and 2.6 cm.

Raftery 1972, 14–18; Raftery 1983, 185–6.

❧

[4:2] GOLD BAND, PROBABLY FROM A HEAD-DRESS, LAMBAY ISLAND, CO. DUBLIN.

Early Iron Age, second half of first century AD.

The gold strip was found with an iron sword on Lambay Island, Co. Dublin in the middle of the nineteenth century. As the strip is broken at each end the decoration is interrupted. The curvilinear relief ornament, which incorporates wheeled cross motifs, shows classical restraint and is not of Irish manufacture, being almost certainly a Brigantian import. W82. L. 23.5 cm.

Wilde 1862, 39; Rynne 1976, 231–2; Raftery 1983, no. 867, 279–80.

❧

[4:3] GOLD COLLAR, ARDNAGLUG, CO. ROSCOMMON.

Early Iron Age, third century BC.

For more than a century, two gold neck ornaments were known as the Clonmacnoise collars before recent research established finally that they were found in a bog at Ardnaglug, Co. Roscommon. The more elaborate of the two is of a type characterised by its 'fused-buffer' terminals, comparable examples of which have been found on the continent. The terminals and flanking cone-shaped mouldings bear repoussé decoration in the form of a continuous series of raised S-shapes and spirals, all of which terminate in round bosses. The background is dotted to accentuate the raised designs. A meandering gold wire frames the edges of a box-like feature at the back of the collar which allowed both halves to pivot, thus enabling the wearer to place it in position. W290. D. 14.7 cm.

Wilde 1862, 47–9; Kelly 1983, no. 26; Raftery 1983, no. 451, 169; Ireland 1992, 123–46.

❧

[4:4] GOLD COLLAR, ARDNAGLUG, CO. ROSCOMMON.

Early Iron Age, third century BC.

The second collar found in Ardnaglug Bog consists of a twisted narrow band of gold with two hollow spherical terminals, perhaps representing acorns. The oak tree had a special significance in Celtic religion and its fruit, the acorn, was an important food source for the wild boar. The terminals may therefore be a reference to the oak tree or to the wild boar, which was a cult animal. The collar may be related thematically to a later (first century BC) stone carving probably representing a god, from Euffigneix, France which shows a male figure wearing a collar with buffer terminals on whose body is carved a large figure of a wild boar. Twisted gold collars are known from La Tène contexts on the continent and both Ardnaglug collars are probably imports. W292. D. 14.2 cm.

Wilde 1862, 47–9; Kelly 1983, no. 27; Raftery 1983, no. 454, 170; Ireland 1992, 123–46.

[4:5] SWORD SCABBARD PLATE, NEAR TOOME, CO. ANTRIM.

Early Iron Age, second century BC.

Found near the River Bann at Toome, Co. Antrim. The plate has a characteristic outline, being bow-shaped at the broad end with a tapering narrow tongue at the other extremity. The decorated surface faced outwards originally but the scabbard plate was reversed later and shortened, perhaps because of damage to the end. Subsequent abrasion by a sword as it was withdrawn and replaced has worn the decorated surface. An engraved, stylised foliage design of which the basic form is a spiral, is repeated along the plate. At the sides of the plate the spirals thicken into wide crescentic areas that are divided longitudinally, decorated with a herring-bone pattern. Hatched lines are used to decorate lentoid areas that terminate the spirals. 1937:3634. L. 44.5 cm.

Kelly 1983, no. 34; Raftery 1983, 267.

[4:6] SCABBARD CHAPE, NEAR ROSCREA, CO. TIPPERARY.

Early Iron Age, second century BC.

This is recorded as having been found near Roscrea, Co. Tipperary in 1880. Originally a chape such as this would have been attached to the end of a scabbard similar to that represented by the Toome scabbard plate. The chape, which may be unfinished, is cast in the form of a serpent's head. Circular settings, representing the serpent's eyes, may have held studs, possibly of red enamel. It is of a continental type, the prototype of which appears to occur in the region of north-east France. 1881:38. L. 10.5 cm.

Raftery 1983, no. 274, 105; Raftery 1984, 87–8.

[4:7] BRONZE BOWL, LACKILL AND MOORETOWN, FORE, CO. WESTMEATH.

Early Iron Age, second century BC.

When found in a burial within an inland promontory fort the bowl contained the cremated remains of an older adult male. The vessel is an import from Britain and compares closely to a bowl found in a burial at Spettisbury Rings, Dorset. To the north and east, the promontory fort overlooks an extensive and important medieval ecclesiastical complex. At a short distance to the south lies Lough Lene where a small wooden boat built in the Mediterranean was recovered and which dated to the same period as the bowl. Important imports such as these suggest that the promontory fort was one of considerable importance during the Iron Age and this may have had a bearing on the subsequent importance of Fore during the medieval period. The vessel has an elegant profile and was made in two parts from sheet bronze, the joining along the middle being decorated with a row of domed studs. 1988:172. Max. D. 29.5; H. 16.1 cm.
Lanting and Brindley 1998, 6.

❧

[4:8] BRONZE BOWL, KESHCARRIGAN, CO. LEITRIM.

Early Iron Age, early first century AD.

Found at Keshcarrigan in the stretch of water between Lough Scur and Lough Marrive, Co. Leitrim. Although slightly later in date, like the Fore bowl the one-handled bowl from Keshcarrigan is likely to be an import from south-west England. It was probably a drinking cup and it has the same profile as the example from Fore, the vessel turning in at the shoulder and having an out-turned rim. The metal from which it was made was first beaten into shape and then finished by the exertion of pressure on the surface while the object was being spun in a wooden mould. The rim is decorated with a zig-zag line in false relief produced by hammering while the cast handle is in the form of a duck-like bird, the eye sockets of which probably held red enamel. W37. Max. D. 15.3 cm; H. 7.2 cm.
Mulvany 1852, lix; Wilde 1861, 534; Kelly 1983, no. 33; Raftery 1983, no. 567, 213–214.

❧

[4:9] SWORD HILT, BALLYSHANNON BAY, CO. DONEGAL.

Early Iron Age, first century BC.

Of direct continental origin, probably in south-western France, the remarkable cast bronze sword hilt was dredged up by a trawler from the sea-bed at Ballyshannon Bay, Co. Donegal, around 1916. When found it was attached to a short iron blade about 37.5 cm in length. The hilt is cast in the form of a male human figure and classical influence is manifest in the style of the modelling of the face, although the hair is depicted with the typically Celtic technique of vertical ridging. The eyes are slanted. A raised triangular panel occurs on the front and the back, below the neck. The grip is ridged by three short, reel-shaped mouldings, the surfaces of which are decorated with short, etched lines such as are known from the handles of bronze flagons found in a Celtic burial at Basse-Yutz, France. SA 1926:47. L. 13.4 cm.
Anon 1925, 137–8; Kelly 1983, no. 29; Raftery 1983, no. 244, 89.

❧

[4:10] HOARD OF GOLD OBJECTS, BROIGHTER, CO. DERRY (*ABOVE*),
GOLD COLLAR, BROIGHTER, CO. DERRY (*BELOW*).

Early Iron Age, first century BC.

Found in a hoard of gold objects deposited close to the ancient shore at the entrance to Lough Foyle, Broighter, Co. Derry. There is an elaborate, raised, curvilinear design on the convex areas of the ring. The area between the raised decoration is filled with concentric arcs of circles incised with a compass in a fashion that serves to emphasise the raised decoration. The ends of the tubes adjoining the terminals each bear a single row of small punched-up pellets and a zone of raised ornament with trumpets, lentoid and circular bosses. The terminals are fitted with a mortice and tenon device which fastened the collar and the T-shaped tenon is surrounded by raised lines resembling a sun-burst. Each of the terminals has a recess on the circular face into which an openwork strip of three rows of conjoined raised bosses has been fitted. The use of rows of pellets to disguise rivet heads is reminiscent of earlier sheet-bronze work while the use of chasing rather than repoussé to fashion the raised decoration on the ring might also be seen as representing continuity of native craft traditions from the Later Bronze Age. On balance, however, the technique of decoration may be due mainly to the technical difficulties involved in producing the object. Moreover, by contrast with the large assemblage of Late Bronze Age goldwork, the Broighter collar stands without any comparable body of Irish Iron Age goldwork. 1903:323. D. 19.4 cm.
Praeger 1942, 29–32; Warner 1982, 29–38; Kelly 1983, no. 30; Raftery 1983, no. 450, 167–8.

❧

[4:11] GOLD MODEL BOAT, BROIGHTER, CO. DERRY.

Early Iron Age, first century BC.

The presence of this unique model boat made of beaten sheet gold provides one of the clearest indications that the Broighter hoard is a votive deposit to the sea-god Manannán Mac Lir. It is probably a model of an ocean-going vessel, of wood rather than hide-covered, complete with seats, oars, rowlocks, steering oar and mast. 1903:323. L. 19.6 cm.
Praeger 1942, 29–32; Warner 1982, 29–38; Raftery 1983, no. 834, 268–70.

❧

[4:12] GOLD MODEL CAULDRON, BROIGHTER, CO. DERRY.

Early Iron Age, first century BC.

Made of beaten sheet gold, the small bowl from the Broighter hoard is almost certainly meant to represent a cauldron. Originally there were suspension rings at the cardinal points on the rim. Bronze cauldrons were plentiful during the Later Bronze Age while cauldrons made of wood, iron and bronze are known from the Early Iron Age. It seems likely that cauldrons were used at meals for social groups larger than a family unit and in contexts that were of a ceremonial and ritual nature. The former ritual significance of cauldrons may underlie the widespread European folk traditions relating to magic cauldrons which are ever bountiful. 1903:323. D. 10.5 cm; H. 5.7 cm.
Praeger 1942, 29–32; Warner 1982, 29–38; Raftery 1983, no. 575, 216–17.

❧

[4:13] TWO GOLD NECK CHAINS, BROIGHTER, CO. DERRY.

Early Iron Age, first century BC.

The necklaces are made from gold wire, the chains being constructed in the loop-in-loop technique, which gives more flexibility than true plait. The triple-strand necklace is of the simplest single-loop chain whereas the single-strand chain is of more complex multi-loop construction. The technique of manufacture of these chains originated in the Middle East from whence it spread to the Mediterranean world. The clasps can be paralleled in Etruscan and Roman contexts. 1903:323. The complex necklace is 39.6 cm in length. The single-strand example is 34.8 cm.

Praeger 1942, 29–32; Warner 1982, 29; Raftery 1983, no. 458–9, 172–3; Raftery 1984, 191.

[4:14] TWO GOLD TWISTED BAR TORCS, BROIGHTER, CO. DERRY.

Early Iron Age, first century BC.

It is in the south east of England that parallels for these twisted bar torcs can be found; however, the terminals of the British torcs are looped rather than the hook-in-loop variety on the Broighter torcs. There is a further difference in that the twisted wire within the torsion grooves of the Broighter torcs is not found on the British torcs. Nevertheless, the nature of the gold used in their production suggests that the Broighter torcs are imports and this is supported by the finding of a similar torc among a hoard of Roman objects at Newgrange, Co. Meath. 1903:323. One of the Broighter torcs is incomplete and the other has a diameter of 18.6 cm.

Praeger 1942, 29–32; Warner 1982, 29; Raftery 1983, 171–2; Raftery 1984, 190.

[4:15] TRUMPET, LOUGHNASHADE, CO. ARMAGH.

Early Iron Age, first century BC.

Found in a former lake, the Loughnashade, Co. Armagh trumpet is the only one to survive of a hoard of four found originally. Classical writers have left accounts of the unnerving effect on Roman armies which the continental Celts achieved by blowing their war trumpets before battle and we can assume a similar martial function for the splendid trumpet from Loughnashade. However, it is likely that the trumpet was also used on ceremonial and ritual occasions. It consists of two curved tubes, the joining of which is concealed by a ridged ring. At the flared mouth there is a decorated ring and its ornament is executed in the repoussé technique, based on the classical lotus-bud motif. The quadrants are mirror images of each other and the design is composed of long, sinuous tendrils which terminate in spiral bosses in high relief. A number of trumpet curves are incorporated into the design. Both tubes are riveted along their length. One tube, which is clearly a later replacement, is poorly executed, while the other is a masterpiece of the riveter's craft, the quality being only matched occasionally on other fine metalwork such as the Petrie Crown and the Cork Horns. W8. L. along convex edge 186.5 cm; D. of mouth 19.3 cm.

Browne 1800, 11–12; Kelly 1983, no. 31; Raftery 1983, no. 781, 239–40; Raftery 1984, 134–43.

[4:16] THREE BRONZE SCABBARD MOUNTS, LAMBAY ISLAND, CO. DUBLIN.

Early Iron Age, second half of first century AD.

The mounts, which were seemingly found in the grave of a warrior on Lambay Island, Co. Dublin, are all from the same scabbard. Two of them have openwork triskele designs and the third is a plain cross-bar type. The openwork mounts were first cast and then tooled and polished, the style of the design being paralleled on a Brigantian type of scabbard found at Morton Hall, Edinburgh. The internal dimensions of the open work mounts indicate that they were fitted to a scabbard with a cross-section of 5.5 cm x 1.25 cm. L1947:198–200.

Macalister 1929, 243; Rynne 1976, 237–8; Raftery 1983, no. 276–8, 105–106.

[4:17] BRONZE COLLAR, LAMBAY ISLAND, CO. DUBLIN.

Early Iron Age, second half of first century AD.

Found with inhumation burials on Lambay Island, Co. Dublin. The collar is constructed in two main parts: there is a C-shaped, cast bronze strip with bead-like terminals into which fits a curved rod mounted with eight bronze beads alternating with seven washer-like discs. There are oblique grooves on the beads and cast terminals. The collar is of a type found in the north of England and lowland Scotland and is a well-known Brigantian type. 1947:195. Int. Dims. 13.9 cm x 12.6 cm.

Macalister 1929, 243; Rynne 1976, 238–9; Raftery 1983, no. 455, 171.

[4:18] BRONZE HEAD-DRESS KNOWN AS THE PETRIE CROWN, UNLOCALISED.

Early Iron Age, second century AD.

The find-place is not recorded. It is a complex object which was assembled expertly using rivets and solder. The components, which were probably sewn to leather or textile, formed part of an elaborate horned head-dress. One cone survives attached to a dished roundel and evidence for another can be seen on the back of a second roundel. The roundels are attached to plates which have openwork voids creating the impression that they are composed of running semi-circles. Cast sinuous trumpet forms terminating in lentoid bosses and spirals ending in bird heads achieved low-relief ornament. The bird heads on the cone and discs of the crown were once filled with red enamel, as were settings in the bosses on the discs, one of which still contains an enamel stud. P869; P870. D. of roundels 5.1 cm.

Stokes 1883, 473–80; Kelly 1983, no. 36; Raftery 1983, no. 821, 260–61.

[4:19] DECORATED BONE SLIPS, LOUGHCREW, CO. MEATH.

Early Iron Age, first century AD.

A group of low hills at Loughcrew, Co. Meath is the location of a Neolithic Passage Tomb cemetery. From the 1860s onwards, sporadic investigations at one of the tombs, Cairn H, has revealed the presence of Iron Age as well as Neolithic material. The site was excavated scientifically in 1943 but the results remain unpublished. The Iron Age finds included beads of glass, bone and amber, bone combs and pins, rings of iron and bronze, as well as the remarkable worked bone plaques or slips, most of which were polished and plain, but of which a large number bore incised decoration. Of the two bone slips illustrated, the perforated example bears a decorative scheme similar in layout to the raised decoration on the Broighter collar, while decoration on the smaller bone slip is closely comparable to carved ornament on a stone from Derrykeighan, Co. Antrim. It has been suggested that the bone plaques may be identified with the metal leaf- or feather-shaped plaques found at Roman shrines and that they represent votive deposits. The discovery of similar leaf-shaped plaques of polished bone from a structure identified as a shrine at Cadbury Congresbury, Somerset, supports this interpretation and it is perhaps significant that south-western England is an area for which external artistic comparisons with the decoration on the slips have been drawn. It seems likely therefore that the Loughcrew Passage Tomb was used during the late first and second centuries AD as a cultic shrine in a manner reflecting Romano-British practice. Neither of the slips illustrated is complete. 1941:1222. L. 13.1 cm. 1941:1223. 11.5 cm.
Ratz et al 1992, 242; Raftery 1993, no. 622–623, 235–238; Raftery 1994, 251–263; Swift 1997, 20.

[4:20] BRONZE MASSIVE ARMLET, NEWRY, CO. DOWN.

Early Iron Age, second century AD.

The large, cast bronze penannular armlet, with circular terminals, found near Newry, Co. Down, is an import from eastern Scotland. The decoration is dominated by a repetitive series of transverse lentoid bosses. 1875:120. Int. Dims. 9.0 cm x 8.2 cm; W. 6.7 cm.
Simpson 1968, 252; Raftery 1983, no. 470, 177; Raftery 1984, 194–6.

[4:21] BRONZE BRACELET, BALLYMAHON, CO. MEATH.

Early Iron Age, second century AD.

Found in drainage work at the junction of the Deel and Boyne rivers at Ballymahon, Co. Meath. The bracelet is formed by bending a Y-shaped strip into circular form, thus giving a pseudo-spiral effect. The bracelet shows north British influences both in its form and decoration. There are bird-like perforated triskeles at the junction of the Y and on one circular terminal similar to those represented on the Lambay Island openwork scabbard mounts. One of the coils was broken off in antiquity and a botched attempt was made to repair it, using rivets. W504. D. 9.9 cm.
Wilde 1861, 570; Rynne 1964, 69–72; Raftery 1983, no. 473, 178–9; Raftery 1984, 196, Youngs (ed.) 1989, no. 27.

[4:22] PAIR OF BRONZE SPOONS, UNLOCALISED.

Early Iron Age, first to second century AD.

Find-place not recorded. Six objects of this type are known from Ireland. One is a British import and the remainder appear to derive from prototypes that occur mainly in the south and west of Britain. At least two British finds and the only known pair from Gaul accompanied burials, and some sort of ritual function is suspected for the Irish examples. A spoon of similar shape, though seemingly of fourth- to fifth-century date, made from jet, was found in a burial monument at Carbury Hill, Co. Kildare, which is the source of the River Boyne. The two spoons illustrated appear to be a pair but they are not exactly similar and differ slightly in size. The handles of both are decorated on the top and bottom surfaces with lightly incised compass-drawn designs including a triskele and the designs are highlighted using fields of stippled dots. One spoon is perforated near the rim at the broadest part of the bowl while the other bowl has centrally placed, inscribed concentric circles at the centre of a simple cross. W6;W7. L. 14.4 cm and 14.3 cm.

Way 1869, 67–8; Raftery 1983, no. 822–3, 262–3; Raftery 1984, 242, 264–7.

[4:23] CARVED STONE HEAD, DRUMEAGUE, CORLECK, CO. CAVAN.

Early Iron Age, first to second century AD.

Known since it came to scientific attention in 1937 as the Corleck Head, this three-faced stone idol was found in the townland of Drumeague, Co. Cavan around the year 1855. It appears that it was one of a number of carvings found, including a bearded bust now known as the Corraghy Head which was later built into a barn in the nearby townland of that name. Thomas Barron, the local historian who brought the three-faced head to the attention of the National Museum, spent a lifetime researching the local traditions concerning the find and he concluded that the figures were associated with a shrine located at Drumeague Hill. Nearby is Corleck Hill, where it appears that between 1832 and 1900 a Passage Tomb surrounded by a stone circle and a circular embankment seventy yards in diameter were dismantled. The site of these monuments was the centre of an important Lughnasa festival that celebrated the harvest, an ancient Celtic tradition which survives into modern times. Other Celtic stone heads have been found in the vicinity such as those from Corravilla and Cavan Town and the find-place of the three-faced idol is only twelve miles from Loughcrew, Co. Meath. A little further north there is another group of Iron Age stone carvings which appear to be centred on the vicinity of Emain Macha, the main political and ritual site of ancient Ulster.

The likelihood is that the Corleck Head was associated with a shrine reflecting Romano-British traditions located close to where the carving was discovered. The three-faced carving is the finest of its type and there is a small hole in the base to help it stand securely, perhaps on a pedestal. One of the faces is heavy browed and all of them have bossed eyes, a broad nose and slit mouth. One of the mouths has a small circular hole at the centre and this feature is also found on two of the Co. Armagh carvings and on another from Woodlands, Co. Donegal. There are several examples of this feature from Yorkshire, the best known occurring on two three-faced idols from Greetland, near Halifax. The feature also occurs on a stone head from Anglesey, Wales. 1998:72. H. 33 cm.

Rynne 1972, 84–5; MacNeill 1962, 26, 172, 426; Barron 1978, 3–16.

[4:24] THREE BRONZE CIRCULAR BOXES, CORNALARAGH, CO. MONAGHAN; NAVAN FORT (EMAIN MACHA) CO. ARMAGH AND SOMERSET, CO. GALWAY.

Early Iron Age, first to second century AD.

The beautifully decorated lid found in a bog at Cornalaragh, Co. Monaghan has a wide, raised, circular area, at the centre of which there is a smaller raised disc bearing an openwork design. A sinuous strap, which narrows at each end, spans the central space and divides the disc symmetrically. Two opposed spiral patterns emerge from the edge at right angles to this. Each curls around and ends in a small knob linked to the rim by a reinforcing bar. The area surrounding the central disc is pierced with a lattice arrangement of lozenges with curved sides. The apertures regularly decrease in size inwards towards the centre. Shirley Collection, no. 33. D. 7.4 cm.

Anon, 1852, 14; Kelly 1983, no. 32, 106; Raftery 1983, no. 813, 255–6; Raftery 1984, 284–7.

A circular lid found near Emain Macha has a reserved triskele in a field of red enamel as the central design. This is surrounded by a series of large and small reserved concentric circles which are also set in a field of red enamel. 1906:129. D. 7.3 cm.

Raftery 1983, no. 805, 253; Raftery 1984, 284–7.

The Somerset, Co. Galway box contained a twisted gold collar and was part of a large hoard. The box lid is decorated with repoussé ornament consisting of a trumpet pattern which coils around a small central boss and terminates in a lentoid boss. Fields of punched dots and incised concentric circles highlight the raised ornament. 1958:156–7. D. 8.1 cm.

Raftery 1960, 1–5; Kelly 1983, no. 28a, 102–103; Raftery 1983, 806, 253–4; Raftery 1984, 284–7.

❧

[4:25] HOARD OF GOLD TORCS, AMBER BEADS AND BRONZE BRACELETS, DOOYORK, CO. MAYO.

Early Iron Age, 300 BC–200 AD.

This hoard was found in 2001 on the beach at Dooyork, Co. Mayo. The hoard contains four gold ribbon torcs (three complete and one fragment) made from narrow bands of gold very tightly and evenly twisted. The terminals were simply made by forming small conical terminals from the ends of the bars. Found at the same place were seven amber beads and three bronze bracelets (two complete and one fragment). The bracelets were made from thin rods of bronze decorated by carefully incising a series of lines across the rod which gives the impression that the rod has been twisted. The amber beads differ slightly in size and shape and may have been part of a necklace of graduated beads. 01E1140:1–14. L. of largest torc 30.46 cm; total wt. of gold 36.0g.

Cahill 2002, 118–21.

❧

[4:26] PAIR OF BRONZE HORSE-BITS, ATTYMON, CO. GALWAY.

Early Iron Age, second century AD.

These horse-bits were found with a pair of Y-shaped pieces in a bog at Attymon, Co. Galway and probably represent a votive deposit. All bear decoration in the form of fine cast lines in relief. The bits show considerable wear and have been repaired. The inner ends of the side links are cast in the form of bird heads. The opposite ends are splayed and bear a palmette design. Stop studs in the side rings formerly held settings, probably of red enamel. 1891:9, 9a. L. 31.8 cm.

Haworth 1971, 38–40; Kelly, 1983, no. 38 a–b; Raftery 1983, no. 102–3, 40–1.

[4:27] DECORATED BRONZE DISC AND ENAMELLED HORSE-BIT,
KILLEEVAN, ANLORE, CO. MONAGHAN.

Early Iron Age, second century AD.

An unusual disc was found in a bog at Killeevan, Anlore, Co. Monaghan along with an elaborately enamelled horse-bit. Each of the side rings of the bit has a reserved design, which differs in each case. A fretwork design occurs on one ring and there is series of S-shapes on the other. The bit is of an unusual type and may represent either an import or an Irish copy of a British type. 1883:385. L. 27.6 cm.

Anon. 1856–7, 422–3; Lloyd-Morgan 1876, 217–22; Raftery 1983, no. 803; Raftery 1984, 42–4.

The disc is thought to be a decorative mount for a horse harness. The decoration is in repoussé. In the central circular area a series of spiral bosses define a four-limbed whirligig. Between the centre and the edge of the disc there is a series of continuous S-scrolls. A similar type of disc was found with other important antiquities on Lambay Island, Co. Dublin and the Killeevan disc has also been compared with discs found in the area of the Lower Rhine and in Britain. 1883: 123. D. 11.6 cm.

Anon. 1856–7, 422–3; Raftery 1983, no. 132, 47–8; Raftery 1984, 42.

[4:28] BRONZE DISC, MONASTEREVIN, CO. KILDARE.

Early Iron Age, second century AD.

One of a pair found at Monasterevin, Co. Kildare. It appears to have been beaten from a cake of bronze and then decorated in the repoussé technique. The design in high relief, which may be a stylised head, incorporates two C-shaped scrolls or *peltae* and a ring within which there is an elliptical aperture. The layout of the design compares closely with that which occurs on the terminals of the Attymon Y-shaped pieces and may also be compared with the design on one of the discs on the Petrie Crown [4:18]. Seven discs of the Monasterevin type are known and they are named after the find-place where the only provenanced examples were found. W3. D. 30.6 cm.

Wilde 1861, 639; Kelly 1983, no. 35; Raftery 1983, no. 786, 244–5; Raftery 1984, 276–9.

[4:29] Decorated bronze spearhead, Boho, Co. Fermanagh.

Early Iron Age, first to second century AD.

This remarkable decorated bronze spearhead found in a bog at Boho, Co. Fermanagh, has a leaf-shaped blade while the socket is octagonal in cross-section. Both faces of the blade are decorated with incised angular and concentric-circle motifs. Four small sub-triangular openings are an integral part of the decorative scheme. Straight-line and concentric-circle motifs also occur on the socket. 1901:45. L. 14.8 cm.

Coffey 1898, 120; Raftery 1983, no. 284, 110; Raftery 1984, 108, 289.

[4:30] Roman silver ingots and cut plate, Balline, Co. Limerick.

Early Iron Age, late fourth century AD.

Found in a gravel pit at Balline, Co. Limerick. There are four cow-hide-shaped silver ingots, of which two are incomplete. Official Roman stamps are present on three of them and these carry the letters EX OFFI ISATIS, EX OFC VILIS and EX O NONT. The second of the three bears the Christian Xhi Rho symbol and the stamp on it is the same as that found on a cow-hide ingot from the Roman fort of Richborough in Kent, England. The plate with the beaded rim and the corner of a rectangular dish are probably Romano-British, while the fragment showing the scene with three horsemen may be of Mediterranean workmanship. The items may have been concealed by a raider returning via the Shannon estuary. 1940:1 a–g. The complete ingots weigh 317 g and 318 g respectively.

Ó Ríordáin 1947, 43–53; Macalister 1949, 354; Bateson 1973, 73–4; Raftery 1994, 215–6.

[4:31] Two silver spiral rings, Newgrange, Co. Meath.

Early Iron Age, second century AD.

The spiral rings are among a large number of pieces of jewellery including gold objects and coins found in the vicinity of three standing stones at the entrance to the Passage Tomb at Newgrange. The coins found range in date from the late first to the end of the fourth century AD and it is clear that during this period Newgrange was an important Iron Age shrine. Both rings have three coils. The central coil of each is decorated, in one case with transverse ribs and on the other with transverse notches on the upper and lower edges. Bronze spiral rings occur in Britain and up to five examples were found in Cairn H, Loughcrew, Co. Meath. E56:947; E56:1712. Internal D. 1.37 cm, 1.6 cm.

Carson and O'Kelly 1977, 51, 53; Raftery 1983, 481–2, 181; Swift 1996, 2–3.

[4:32] OVAL AND CIRCULAR DISC BROOCHES, NEWGRANGE, CO. MEATH.

Early Iron Age, fourth century AD.

Found in the vicinity of three standing stones at the entrance to the Passage Tomb at Newgrange. The brooches are of bronze and their fronts are gilded. The central boss on the oval brooch is of black or very dark glass. The boss is missing from the circular brooch. Around each boss there are two concentric zones filled with minute patterns of running spirals, circles and triangles. The brooches are a common type believed to be of Romano-British manufacture, probably made in the south east of England. E56:976; E56:1711. L. 4.0 cm and 3.3 cm.

Carson and O'Kelly 1977, 52–3; Swift 1996, 2–3.

[4:33] TWO GOLD COIN PENDANTS, NEWGRANGE, CO. MEATH.

Early Iron Age, fourth century AD.

Found in the vicinity of three standing stones at the entrance to the Passage Tomb at Newgrange. Like most of the gold coins from Newgrange the two coin pendants are from the Roman mint at Trier, the main mint for north-west Europe. A simple suspension loop has been attached to the coins. One bears a bust of the Emperor Constantine I while the second is of Constantine II. They were struck between AD 330-7 and AD 320-30 respectively. Given the strong links with Britain indicated by the jewellery from the same site it is probable that this was the immediate source of the pendants and the other gold coins of the period found at Newgrange. E56:657; E56:476. D. 1.77 cm and 2.15 cm.

Carson and O'Kelly 1977, 37–8; Swift 1996, 3.

[4:3]
GOLD COLLAR, ARDNAGLUG, CO. ROSCOMMON.
Early Iron Age, third century BC.

[4.4]
GOLD COLLAR, ARDNAGLUG, CO. ROSCOMMON.
Early Iron Age, third century BC.

[4:5]

SWORD SCABBARD PLATE, NEAR TOOME, CO. ANTRIM.

Early Iron Age, second century BC.

[4:6]

SCABBARD CHAPE, NEAR ROSCREA, CO. TIPPERARY.

Early Iron Age, second century BC.

[4:7]
BRONZE BOWL, LACKILL AND MOORETOWN, FORE, CO. WESTMEATH.
Early Iron Age, second century BC.

[4:8]

BRONZE BOWL, KESHCARRIGAN, CO. LEITRIM.

Early Iron Age, early first century AD.

[4:9]
SWORD HILT, BALLYSHANNON BAY, CO. DONEGAL.
Early Iron Age, first century BC.

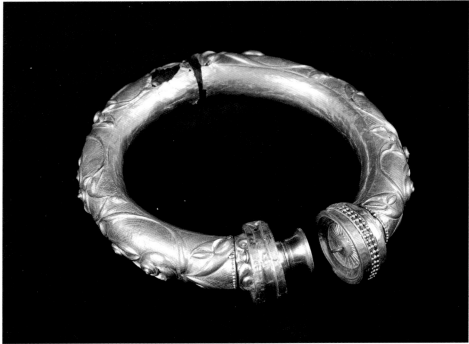

[4:10]
HOARD OF GOLD OBJECTS, BROIGHTER, CO. DERRY (*ABOVE*), GOLD COLLAR, BROIGHTER, CO. DERRY (*BELOW*).
Early Iron Age, first century BC.

[4:11]
GOLD MODEL BOAT, BROIGHTER, CO. DERRY.
Early Iron Age, first century BC.

[4:12]

GOLD MODEL CAULDRON, BROIGHTER, CO. DERRY.

Early Iron Age, first century BC.

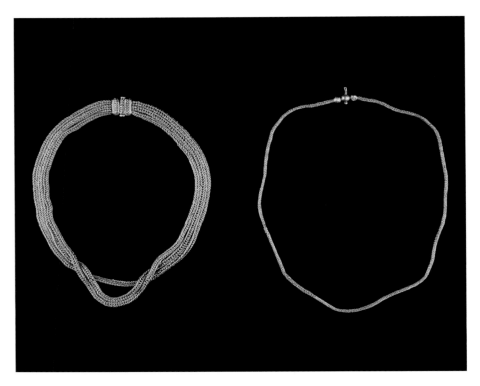

[4:13]

TWO GOLD NECK CHAINS, BROIGHTER, CO. DERRY.

Early Iron Age, first century BC.

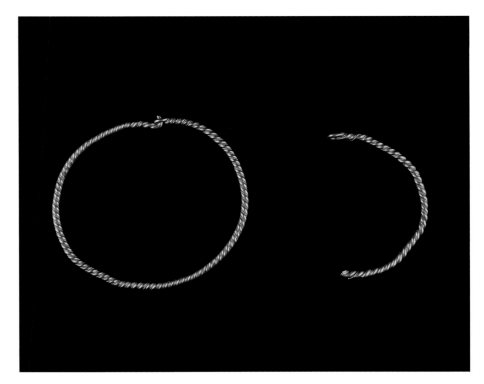

[4:14]

TWO GOLD TWISTED BAR TORCS, BROIGHTER, CO. DERRY.

Early Iron Age, first century BC.

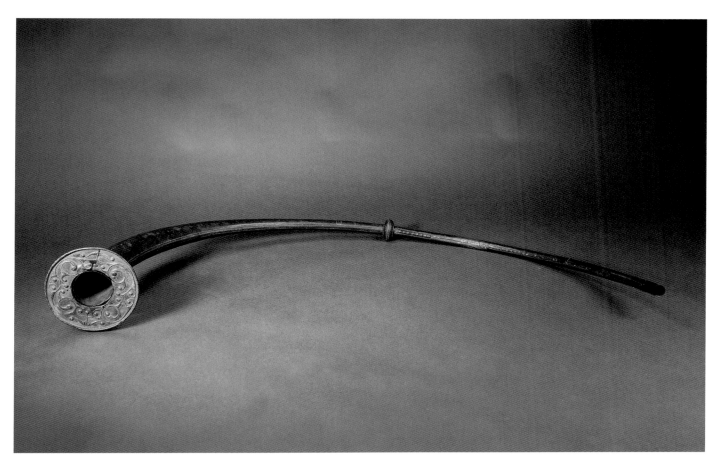

[4:15]
TRUMPET, LOUGHNASHADE, CO. ARMAGH.
Early Iron Age, first century BC.

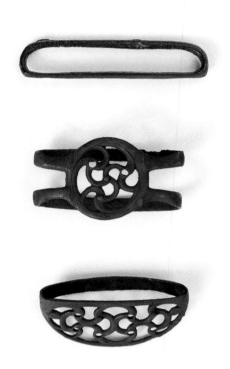

[4:16]

THREE BRONZE SCABBARD MOUNTS, LAMBAY ISLAND, CO. DUBLIN.

Early Iron Age, second half of first century AD.

[4:17]

BRONZE COLLAR, LAMBAY ISLAND, CO. DUBLIN.

Early Iron Age, second half of first century AD.

[4:18]

BRONZE HEAD-DRESS KNOWN AS THE PETRIE CROWN, UNLOCALISED.

Early Iron Age, second century AD.

[4:19]

DECORATED BONE SLIPS, LOUGHCREW, CO. MEATH.

Early Iron Age, first century AD.

[4:20]

BRONZE MASSIVE ARMLET, NEWRY, CO. DOWN.

Early Iron Age, second century AD.

[4:21]

BRONZE BRACELET, BALLYMAHON, CO. MEATH.

Early Iron Age, second century AD.

[4:22]

PAIR OF BRONZE SPOONS, UNLOCALISED.

Early Iron Age, first to second century AD.

[4:24]
THREE BRONZE CIRCULAR BOXES, CORNALARAGH, CO. MONAGHAN;
NAVAN FORT (EMAIN MACHA) CO. ARMAGH AND SOMERSET, CO. GALWAY.
Early Iron Age, first to second century AD.

[4:23] *facing page*
CARVED STONE HEAD, DRUMEAGUE, CORLECK, CO. CAVAN.
Early Iron Age, first to second century AD.

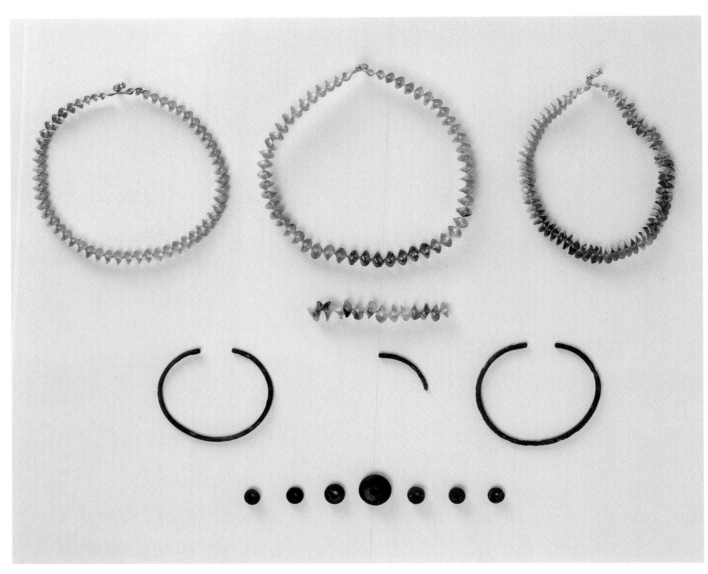

[4:25]

HOARD OF GOLD TORCS, AMBER BEADS AND BRONZE BRACELETS, DOOYORK, CO. MAYO.

Early Iron Age, 300 BC–200 AD.

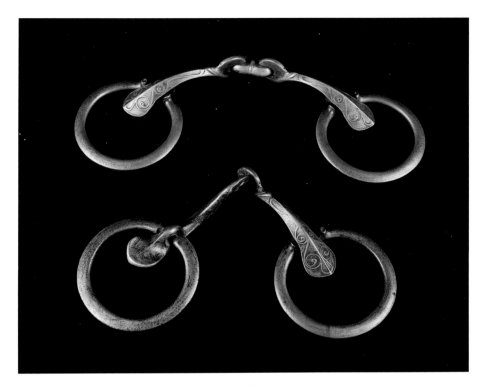

[4:26]

PAIR OF BRONZE HORSE-BITS, ATTYMON, CO. GALWAY.

Early Iron Age, second century AD.

[4:27]

DECORATED BRONZE DISC AND ENAMELLED HORSE-BIT, KILLEEVAN, ANLORE, CO. MONAGHAN.

Early Iron Age, second century AD.

[4:28]
BRONZE DISC, MONASTEREVIN, CO. KILDARE.
Early Iron Age, second century AD.

[4:29]
DECORATED BRONZE SPEARHEAD, BOHO, CO. FERMANAGH.
Early Iron Age, first to second century AD.

[4:30]

ROMAN SILVER INGOTS AND CUT PLATE, BALLINE, CO. LIMERICK.

Early Iron Age, late fourth century AD.

[4:31]
TWO SILVER SPIRAL RINGS, NEWGRANGE, CO. MEATH.
Early Iron Age, second century AD.

[4:32]
OVAL AND CIRCULAR DISC BROOCHES, NEWGRANGE, CO. MEATH.
Early Iron Age, fourth century AD.

[4:33]

TWO GOLD COIN PENDANTS, NEWGRANGE, CO. MEATH.

Early Iron Age, fourth century AD.

5

BEGINNINGS
EARLY MEDIEVAL IRELAND,
AD 500–850

RAGHNALL Ó FLOINN

The Roman conquest of Britain, which began in the first century BC, brought the frontiers of the Empire within view of the Irish coast and, as a result, Classical writers made occasional — if fleeting — reference to the island called *Hibernia* which lay to the west of Britain (Julius Caesar was the first to use the term). The geographer Ptolemy, writing in second-century AD Alexandria, recorded a remarkable list of natural features — rivers, headlands — as well as a number of tribal names and settlements, which provide us with the earliest map of the country. Others wrote of the rich grassland and the cattle which fed on it. These are but straws in the wind and it is not until the advent of Christianity that Ireland emerges into the gaze of history.

Christianity may have come to Ireland from Gaul as early as the late fourth century but it is with the arrival of British missionaries, and of the bishop, Patrick (later to be revered as the national saint), that we have our first written documents [5:2]. Even still, we know little of the process and speed of conversion but it is clear that the missionaries followed lines of communication across the Irish Sea which had existed for centuries. The native peoples of Britain and Ireland shared, to a certain extent, a common language, Celtic, and a common material culture. Trade, settlement and political alliances further strengthened these links. The rich villas and towns of Roman Britain proved irresistible to Irish raiders and pirates, although the amount of Roman loot buried in Ireland in the form of gold and silver is surprisingly small [4:30]. Evidence for Irish settlements in Britain and Scotland exists in the form of origin-legends, place-names and the presence of Ogham stones. We know from later writings that some Irish kings in Patrick's time had British wives. There may also have been treaties concluded between Irish kings and the authorities of late Roman Britain if the Roman historian Ammianus Marcellinus is to be believed when he wrote that the Irish and Picts broke a treaty and threatened the Roman province of Britain in AD 360.

In Ireland, the best evidence for such kinship ties across the Irish Sea is the development of a unique form of writing, principally on stone, known as Ogham [5:3]. This was developed in the south of Ireland in the course of the fourth century. Based on the Latin alphabet, it was clearly designed to imitate late Roman inscribed monumental sculpture. Ogham stones served a variety of functions: memorial stones erected for the dead, ancestral burial markers, boundary indicators or statements of territorial claim. The inscriptions, which preserve the oldest form of the Irish language, usually give the name and descent of the individual commemorated. While it is often claimed that these are Christian monuments, this is far from certain and the earliest may be carved on ancient pillar stones, already revered in the landscape. One carved stone with no Christian symbolism is the decorated pillar stone from Mullamast, Co. Kildare [5:4]. This lies clearly in a direct line of descent from Iron Age carved stelae both in Ireland and elsewhere. Its decoration is multifaceted, partly carved in relief and partly incised, its decorative motifs clearly related to metalwork of the fifth and sixth centuries. The meaning of its curvilinear patterns are now lost to us but its location on the site of a royal stronghold suggests it may have been the focus of outdoor ceremonies.

Irish metalwork in the later Iron Age was characterised by a range of personal ornaments and horse fittings in plain cast bronze with engraved and cast curvilinear decoration, occasionally inlaid with red enamel. Gold was used sparingly and silver seemingly unknown. Through contact with late- and post-Roman Britain in the fourth and fifth centuries, new techniques and forms were introduced. These included a range of new dress ornaments, in particular the penannular brooch — a ring brooch with a gap in the ring to enable a movable pin to be passed through it [5:5]; and the hand-pin, its head resembling the palm of the hand with the fingers bent forward [5:6]. These pins and brooches were developed in the third and fourth centuries by British metalworkers who combined Roman forms with both later Iron Age and Roman motifs and techniques. The use of fine-line enamelling (where the design is reserved against an enamelled background) and ribbed decoration was borrowed from Roman craftsmen while spirals, stylised animal heads and other curvilinear motifs were derived from the repertoire of the late Iron Age metalworker. Archaeological finds indicate that this fusion took place first in south-western Britain and was later introduced to the east of Ireland — the area most prone to external influences and contacts. Their widespread adoption in Ireland suggests that Roman forms of dress were also introduced. We cannot be absolutely certain whether these pins and brooches were worn by men or women or both, but later written texts and images in sculpture and metalwork indicate that brooches were worn singly, by women on the breast and by men on the shoulder. In many early-medieval societies, however, brooches were regarded as part of the dress accessories of women of high status and one possible explanation of their presence in Ireland may be that they were brought by British women of high birth who married into aristocratic Irish families.

It was only in Ireland that the hand-pin and the zoomorphic penannular brooch (so called because of the stylised animal heads at the junction of ring and terminal) found favour, their terminals and pinheads becoming increasingly enlarged fields for ornament. These later brooches added the use of multicoloured inlays of enamel and millefiori glass (decorative glass made from bundles of coloured glass rods fused together) to increasingly more complex curvilinear patterns — a process which led eventually, in the case of brooches, to the baroque extravagance of the 'Tara' and related brooches of the eighth century. In Britain, the penannular brooch appears to have gone out of fashion by the fifth century. However, the same techniques are found on hanging bowls — small, round-bottomed bronze vessels fitted with suspension hooks, some lavishly decorated — which are found mainly in Anglo-Saxon graves of the sixth and seventh centuries. Few have been found in Ireland and the probability is that they are largely products of British Celtic workshops rather than of Irish manufacture as previously thought.

In the first few centuries after the introduction of Christianity overt Christian symbolism is occasionally found on metalwork, but is most evident on stone sculpture and, in particular, on a group of carved pillars from the west and south of the country carved with Maltese crosses or crosses of arcs. The pillar from Aglish, Co. Kerry [5:3] is notable in this respect as the Christian symbolism appears to be secondary: the original Ogham-inscribed monument was inverted and the cross of arcs carved into the thickness of the stone. The pair of swastikas incised below the cross are also Christian symbols and signify the Resurrection. While it has been claimed that the re-use of the Aglish pillar represents a deliberate Christianisation of a pagan memorial slab it may simply be the case of an opportunistic recycling of suitable carving by persons for whom the earlier Ogham script had no meaning.

It is undoubtedly the case that literacy in the form of the written word was introduced to Ireland with Christianity. Latin was the universal language of the Church and its writings opened up a world of learning and literature which was to become one of the hallmarks of Early Medieval Irish culture. Books could only be copied by hand and the inventiveness of Irish scribes is demonstrated by their development of a unique Irish script which survived in altered form into modern times [5:7].

Christian missionaries would have brought with them to Ireland the equipment necessary to carry out their work. This would have included, among other things, vestments, altar furnishings and manuscripts containing the texts of sacred scripture.

Later sources speak of the relics of Peter, Paul and other saints being brought by Palladius, a missionary sent in 431 by Pope Celestine to minister 'to the Irish believing in Christ'. The earliest churches would have been established along diocesan lines as elsewhere in the Christian world, with small territories governed by bishops. By the seventh century, however, a change had occurred in Church administration, which set the Irish Church apart from its neighbours, whereby networks of monasteries linked to a common founder developed in parallel with the episcopal Church. In this system, abbots became the principal administrators of Church affairs while bishops still retained their duties as spiritual advisors and conferring Holy Orders. By the early seventh century one such federation, the Church of Armagh with Patrick as its patron, was using the cult of relics as part of its policy of aggrandisement, dividing and distributing portions of the relics of the early Christian saints and martyrs among its dependant churches.

The earliest pieces of ecclesiastical metalwork are small tomb-shaped reliquaries. They take the form of rectangular boxes with hinged, gabled roofs reflecting the stone sarcophagi of Late Antiquity and are Irish variants of a type of portable shrine found elsewhere in Europe. Comprised of sheets of tinned bronze engraved with late La Tène devices, they are minuscule in size, reflecting the scarcity of such sacred remains from distant places. One such small, undecorated, container was recovered, encased in another, from the bed of Lough Erne, Co. Fermanagh [5:8]. The larger shrine can be dated by reference to its chip-carved ornament to around 800. Both shrines were provided with hinges to enable them to be carried on a chain or strap around the neck. The carrying about of such relics was an important aspect of relic use: they were used to collect dues and were also present to solemnise important political events such as treaties or contracts. Some of these portable Irish tomb-shaped reliquaries have been found on the Continent, either as loot deposited in Viking graves or brought by Irish missionaries to France and Italy. Larger, more massive, fixed reliquaries containing the entire bodies of holy men and women were the focus of veneration in the wealthiest churches. Some were made of the most precious materials such as those of St Brigid and Bishop Conlaed 'adorned with a refined profusion of gold, silver, gems and precious stones' which, according to a seventh-century life of St Brigid, were placed on either side of the main altar of the church at Kildare. All of these larger shrines were plundered over the centuries and only a few fragments survive like the finial from the gable end of a large shrine of an unknown saint [5:9].

Associative relics, consisting of objects believed to be used by or associated with a saint, are far more common than reliquaries which contained the corporeal remains of

DETAIL OF [5:7]
WRITING TABLET;
SPRINGMOUNT BOG,
CO. ANTRIM.
Late sixth/early seventh century AD.

saints. Although known elsewhere in the Christian West, they appear to be a particular feature of the Church in Ireland (and also in Scotland and Wales). The most commonly enshrined objects were those regarded as the saint's insignia of office: staff, hand-bell and book. The practice was sufficiently unusual for it to be mentioned by contemporary writers. The chronicler Gerald of Wales, who came to Ireland in the late twelfth century with the first wave of Anglo-Norman settlers, and himself a churchman of noble birth, describes how 'the people and clergy of Wales and Ireland have a great reverence for bells that can be carried about, and staffs belonging to the saints, and made of gold or silver, or bronze, and curved at their upper ends'. Most of the surviving associative relics and their shrines date from the eleventh century onwards, although a small number from earlier centuries are known. One example is the decorative cresting from a bell shrine which, like the shrine finial mentioned above, may have been found in the ground rather than preserved above ground [5:10]. Dating to the eighth century, it is virtually identical in shape and size to that of the bell shrine known as the *Corp Naomh* ('Holy Body') of some two centuries later [7:33].

The period from the end of the seventh century was one of unparalleled prosperity. During this time control was consolidated among a smaller number of powerful dynasties and patronage of the arts reached new heights. A distinctive Irish art style emerged which was to last, with some variation, into the twelfth century and which to many people represents the archetypal 'Celtic Art' of early medieval Ireland. This combined native curvilinear ornament of the later Iron Age, ribbon interlace which was ultimately of Mediterranean origin (probably introduced through imported manuscripts), and animal ornament and metalworking techniques of Germanic and Anglo-Saxon jewellers. It found its finest expression in manuscripts such as the *Book of Durrow* and the *Book of Kells*, but it is in metalwork that we can chart the changes in the collections of the National Museum of Ireland. These objects are characterised by a brilliant combination of techniques, materials and colours in a unique blend of native and imported methods. The most striking and novel of the techniques borrowed from Germanic jewellery is that of chip-carving as found, for example, on the harness mounts found near Navan, Co. Meath [5:11]. This technique breaks the surface into a series of angled planes which, when gilt, gives added brilliance to the gilt surfaces of these small fittings. The glittering effect was often heightened through the use of inlays of gold filigree, stamped foils, multicoloured studs of glass, enamel and amber. Artists copied other new forms including belt buckles (unknown in Ireland until the seventh century) and fittings for drinking horns, and experimented with new designs: geometric patterns and ribbon and animal interlace in particular. Some of these new forms appear not to have appealed to Irish taste such as the bow brooch from Ardakillen, Co. Roscommon, an experimental piece based on contemporary Continental jewellery [5:1].

[5:1]
BRONZE BROOCH,
ARDAKILLEN,
CO. ROSCOMMON.
Seventh century AD.

The Irish kingdom of Dál Riada in Scotland, and the Columban monastery at Iona in particular, was an important centre in transmitting these new techniques to Ireland. Here, and at Irish foundations in Northumbria (in what is now northern England) were the milieux in which Irish, Pictish, British and Anglo-Saxon taste, style and technique could combine and which produced not only the finest metalwork but also manuscripts such as the *Book of Lindisfarne* and the beginnings of the great series of carved free-standing high crosses, the latter one of the greatest contributions to early medieval European sculpture [5:12].

A good example of the early stages of this development in metalwork is the Moylough belt shrine, made to enclose the remains of a belt or girdle of an unknown saint [5:13]. The belt-buckle was not an Irish dress accessory and the form of the false buckle and buckle plate — rectangular with triangular ends — on the shrine is copied from Anglo-Saxon or Frankish models. Other insular buckles of a similar type are known. The interlocking L- and T-shaped cells of alternating red and yellow enamel interspersed with plates of millefiori glass are combined with Germanic elements such as the stamped silver foils and the circular studs with inset silver grilles. The precise date of the Moylough belt shrine, like most Irish art of the early medieval period, is difficult to establish but it cannot be far removed in date from the great treasures made for secular and church patrons in the eighth century such as the 'Tara' and related brooches and the objects in the Ardagh and Derrynaflan hoards.

We know little of the workshops which produced such fine metalwork. We cannot be sure if objects produced for the service of the church and secular pieces such as the great silver-gilt brooches were produced in separate workshops. Certainly the techniques and motifs are shared by both, indicating that the best were produced in a small number of specialist workshops. The most persuasive evidence for object production comes from excavations of secular sites such as Lagore crannóg, Co. Meath and from ecclesiastical sites such as Nendrum, Co. Down. Excavations in Ireland and Scotland have revealed evidence of fine metalworking in the form of crucibles for melting and pouring metal as well as ingots and ingot-moulds. The complex designs and patterns were often worked out first on pieces of bone and stone and so-called motif-pieces are now, thanks to recent excavations, being recognised at an increasing number of secular and ecclesiastical sites [5:14]. Much early-medieval Irish metalwork was cast, and clay two-piece moulds for the manufacture of inlaid glass studs, brooches and mounts with intricate interlaced patterns have been found. Lumps of enamel, fragments of millefiori glass rods, and pieces of amber for use as inlays have also been uncovered. A particular feature of seventh- and eighth-century

Irish metalwork was the way the craftsman avoided casting a complex object in a single piece. Instead, it was built up from a series of cast, hammered and spun elements and assembled either on a core of wood or metal, with the elements pinned rather than soldered in place. Such a technique is more suited to wood-working and it was from the latter that it was no doubt borrowed. The Ardagh Chalice, for example, is reckoned to be composed of over 350 parts [5:26]. Workshop evidence for the casting of larger objects is lacking but the survival of a number of large, cast, copper-alloy hand-bells indicates that metal founding on a more industrial scale also took place [5:15].

The penannular brooch became the universal dress fastener favoured by the wealthy, but in Ireland changes in fashion and design led to the development of the ring brooch where the terminals were joined by a linking bar or by a solid panel. The resulting brooch thus functioned more as a pin with an enlarged ring which was used as a field for elaborate ornament. A series of over fifty silver and silver gilt brooches of this type survive, as well as a much larger number of humbler bronze brooch pins. The finest of these ring brooches, the so-called 'Tara' brooch, is a virtual compendium of all the techniques known to the jeweller in eighth-century Ireland [5:16–5:17]. Every conceivable surface is covered with ornament, even the inner and outer edges of the ring. As is the case with many other pieces, the spiral and curvilinear ornament are relegated to the back [5:17]. Why this should be so has not yet been fully explained as we do not as yet know what symbolic meaning (if any) the abstract and interlaced animal ornament found on such objects held for their owners [5:18–5:19].

DETAIL OF [5:16]
THE 'TARA' BROOCH
BETTYSTOWN,
CO MEATH.
Early eighth century AD.

We cannot be certain if the great silver brooches of the eighth and ninth centuries were worn exclusively by laypeople or ecclesiastics [5:20–5:24]. In fact, it may be wrong to make such a distinction because in early medieval Ireland, as elsewhere in Europe, the most senior clerics, whether abbots, abbesses or bishops, were often aristocrats in their own right and many were related to the kings and nobles of the locality. These brooches were not merely costly trinkets commissioned by the highest strata of society; they were also statements of power and authority. Although at the highest level these are once-off pieces, many conform to a small number of variants which appear to show distinct regional distributions. Brooches with triangular terminals and interlaced animals as a central motif, such as the 'Tara' brooch and its lesser copies in bronze, are found in the Irish east midlands; while brooches with lozenge patterns on their terminals [5:22] seem to be a south-midland phenomenon. On the other hand, rounded or lobed terminals [5:21, 5:23] are more common in the north-east and in Scotland. In Scotland, the penannular form was never completely abandoned and a distinctive Pictish type can be recognised [5:24]. These variations may therefore represent not so much workshop preference as badges of identity. The sheer weight and bullion value of a brooch such as the 'Tara' brooch goes way beyond what is practically useful and we must begin to regard such pieces as marriage or diplomatic gifts among the élite in early Irish society.

Much of the fine metalwork of the early medieval period was made for the service of the Church. The most important were sacred vessels used for the celebration of the Mass which was at the centre of Christian worship. We are fortunate in that two hoards containing altar vessels have been uncovered. The Ardagh hoard contained, in addition to four silver brooches, two chalices — a plain vessel of bronze and a bigger silver chalice [5:25]. The silver chalice, with its large hemispherical bowl and paired handles is quite unlike other European chalices of the early medieval period and its closest comparisons are, in fact, to be found among Byzantine chalices of the Eastern Church [5:26, 5:27]. The discovery of a chalice of similar form (although somewhat later in date) in a hoard of eucharistic vessels at Derrynaflan, Co. Tipperary, proved that the Ardagh Chalice was not unique [5:28, 5:29]. It was found with a decorated silver paten which, like the two chalices, is best paralleled in Byzantine metalwork [5:30]. This should not, however, be taken as evidence for an eastern influence on the Irish Church but rather indicates a common origin among late-Roman tableware from which vessels used in the Eucharist are derived. It is undoubtedly the case that the Irish craftsmen who produced these vessels copied models similar to those used in the Eastern Church, but it was most likely the rich churches of Rome rather than Constantinople that provided their inspiration.

While the design of these magnificent church treasures came from afar, their decoration and construction was in the native idiom. The hammered and spun silver bowls of the Ardagh and Derrynaflan chalices are in a native tradition of vessel manufacture which goes back to the hanging bowls of the sixth century and later. The Derrynaflan hoard was protected by a plain bronze basin [5:28] which, like the bronze chalice from Ardagh, was made in the same fashion as the more elaborate silver vessels found with them. Likewise, the decorated bronze strainer in the Derrynaflan hoard was designed as a simple ladle, identical in form to a large number of such utilitarian vessels known from both secular and ecclesiastical contexts [5:31].

DETAIL OF [5:29]
THE DERRYNAFLAN
CHALICE, DERRYNAFLAN,
CO. TIPPERARY.
Ninth century AD.

The abstract patterns which characterise early medieval Irish art are often regarded as archaic. It has also been remarked that much of the ecclesiastical metalwork lacks any religious symbolism. The avoidance of naturalistic representations of the human figure in favour of what were perceived as pre-Christian models [5:33, 5:34], the pre-eminence of interlace as a design feature, and the unique form of many object types, have contributed to the notion of a 'Celtic' Church in Ireland, somehow preserving something of the earliest stratum of Christianity overlain with elements of the pagan Celtic past. This is to deny, however, the sheer originality and inventiveness of

DETAIL OF [5:30]
THE DERRYNAFLAN
PATEN, DERRYNAFLAN,
CO. TIPPERARY.
Eighth century AD.

Irish artisans whether in metal, stone, wood or manuscript painting. The brilliant draughtsmanship needed to design, lay out and execute intricate filigree panels on metalwork [5:16, 5:26, 5:29, 5:30] or the complex carpet pages of manuscripts, combined with the sheer variety of technical skills and knowledge of materials are unsurpassed elsewhere in Europe at this time. The naturalistic representations of figured scenes on the high crosses give the lie to the inability of craftsmen to deal with the human figure. Much of this art is found elsewhere in early medieval Europe, as are the technical skills used in its execution. It is clear also that Ireland, far from being a cultural backwater, was very much in touch with developments elsewhere in Europe at this time. Some writers have seen a parallel between the visual ambiguity and intricacy of Irish art of this period and the delight in word play and word patterning found in contemporary prose and verse. There is much to be said for such a viewpoint but our current inability to explain fully the meaning behind early Irish art shows the depth of our ignorance and how little we still understand of the medieval mind.

DETAIL OF [5:30]
THE DERRYNAFLAN PATEN, DERRYNAFLAN, CO. TIPPERARY.
Eighth century AD.

ILLUSTRATIONS

[5:1] BRONZE BROOCH, ARDAKILLEN, CO. ROSCOMMON.

Seventh century AD.

Found in a crannóg at Ardakillen, Co. Roscommon. The brooch is provided with a short pin and catch-plate on the back. The curved bow is fitted with a separately-applied strip decorated with a pattern of ribbon interlace. The ends are likewise made separately and riveted to the backplate. These have raised interlocking C-shaped scrolls. This unique brooch appears to mimic Continental and Anglo-Saxon bow brooches of the sixth and seventh centuries. W476. L. 7.75 cm.

Youngs (ed.) 1989, no. 58.

[5:2] CARVING OF ST PATRICK, FAUGHART GRAVEYARD, CO. LOUTH.

Early sixteenth century AD.

The full-length carving of a bearded ecclesiastic is recessed into the surface of a limestone pillar. He is attired in full episcopal garb including mitre and crook-headed crozier, his right hand raised in blessing. He may be identified as St Patrick from the serpent at his feet. This late medieval carving is one of the earliest representations of the legend which records how the saint banished snakes from Ireland. 1935:167. H. 1.32 m.

Morris 1912.

[5:3] CARVED STONE PILLAR, AGLISH, CO. KERRY.

Fifth or sixth century AD.

From the churchyard at Aglish on the Dingle Peninsula, Co. Kerry. The stone was originally carved with an Ogham inscription, now damaged. The reading is unclear but one possibility is ... MAQI MAQ [I ...] GGODI K[OI] which would translate as 'X [the commemorated person's name] the descendant of ... Got (lies) here'. This formula indicates that this is a memorial to a Christian. It was subsequently inverted and converted into a cross-inscribed pillar. The front face is carved with a Maltese cross set within a circle. Below it is a spear or arrow flanked by swastikas — the latter were ancient symbols of the Resurrection. W1. H. 93.0 cm.

O'Connor 1983, no.42.

[5:4] CARVED STONE PILLAR, MULLAMAST, CO. KILDARE.

Sixth century AD.

Found reused as a lintel in demolishing a castle at the Hill of Mullamast, Co. Kildare. This irregular boulder of limestone is carved with different spiral designs, some incised and some in relief. The designs are close to those found on dress-pins and brooches of the period. The precise meaning of these motifs is unclear, but Mullamast was the centre of the territorial kingdom of the Uí Dúnlainge kings of Leinster and the stone served no doubt as some form of memorial or marker. 1903:254. H. *c.* 1.0 m.

Kelly 1983, no. 37.

[5:5] ZOOMORPHIC PENANNULAR BROOCHES,
TOP: UNLOCALISED; *BOTTOM*: ARTHURSTOWN, CO. KILDARE.
Fifth to sixth century AD.
X1675; 1934:10863. L. of pins, 16.8 cm; 14.2 cm.
Youngs (ed.) 1989, nos. 17, 19.

[5:6] TWO SILVER PINS, CASTLETOWN KILPATRICK, CO. MEATH.
Late fourth/early fifth century AD.
Found in 1848 the larger is known as a hand-pin, its head resembling the palm of the hand with the fingers
bent forward; the larger, with a beaded rim, is an ancestral form. The fine-line spiral patterns on both pinheads, derived from contemporary Celtic metalwork, were originally highlighted with red enamel. This
form of small dress-pin originated in south-western Britain and these ones may represent imports from
late Roman Britain. Silver hand-pins are comparatively rare but examples in bronze with elaborately
decorated heads were made in Ireland into the sixth century. 7W24; P634. L. 8.5 cm and 14.1 cm.
Youngs (ed.) 1989, nos. 2, 3.

[5:7] SET OF WRITING-TABLETS, SPRINGMOUNT BOG, CO. ANTRIM.
Late sixth/early seventh century AD.
The set of six tablets of yew held together by leather straps was found in Springmount Bog, Co. Antrim,
at a depth of four feet. The recesses in the tablets contain wax and texts consisting of parts of the Psalms
are written on them. The Springmount tablets are the earliest examples of Irish handwriting in a script
known as Insular minuscule. The letters were cut into the soft wax with a pointed metal stylus and the
quality of the lettering indicates that it was the work of an experienced scribe. The text shown in the detail
on page 174 is part of Psalm 31. SA 1914:2. L. 21 cm; W. 7.5 cm.
Mullarkey 1991, no. 64.

[5:8]. TWO TOMB-SHAPED SHRINES, LOUGH ERNE, CO. FERMANAGH.
Late eighth or early ninth century AD.
Found by a fisherman in Lough Erne near Tully, Co. Fermanagh, the smaller, plain shrine was found
inside the larger. The form of the shrines is derived from Late Antique sarcophagi and was chosen as a
suitable shape to house the relics of the dead. It is probable that the smaller shrine contained rare
fragments of the remains of Continental saints and was itself enshrined in the larger reliquary. 1901:46a, b.
L. of larger, 16 cm; of smaller 10.6 cm.
Youngs (ed.) 1989, nos. 130a, b.

[5:9] ENAMELLED SHRINE MOUNT, UNLOCALISED.

Eighth century AD.

This cast copper-alloy heart-shaped mount has a broad raised border with geometric cells of alternating red and yellow enamels and panels of blue and white millefiori glass. The scrolled ends enclose studs of blue glass. Its shape can be compared with representations of the gable ends of churches or tombs on stone sculpture and manuscript painting and enables it to be identified as part of the end of the lid of a tomb-shaped shrine. 1906:38. W. 7.2 cm.
Mahr and Raftery 1932–41, 111.

[5:10] CREST OF BELL SHRINE, UNLOCALISED.

Eighth to ninth century AD.

Find-place unknown. The hollow body of the D-shaped composite gilt and tinned copper-alloy casting was designed to accommodate the curved handle of a hand-bell. The scene on the front is truncated and depicts the upper bodies of a human between two animals. Between the figures are disc shapes with amber studs surrounded by interlace. The human is cowled and is shown in a frontal pose with an elaborate garment. He is placed between a pair of long-necked animals viewed in profile whose lower jaws he appears to grasp. This may be a representation of *Daniel in the Lions' Den*. 1920:37a. L. 13.2 cm.
Youngs (ed.) 1989, no. 137a.

[5:11] HARNESS MOUNTS, NAVAN, CO. MEATH.

Eighth century AD.

Found, along with a horse-bit and other objects, as well as human and horse bones, near Navan, Co. Meath. The find is almost certainly that of a pagan Viking horseman. This set of cast and gilt copper-alloy mounts were once attached to leather straps, the cruciform mounts being fitted where two straps met or crossed. The interlace and animal ornament is typical of such fittings which have been found widely throughout Britain and Ireland, as well as in Viking graves in Norway. W558–564. L. of largest plaque, 6.9 cm.
Youngs (ed.) 1989, no. 113.

[5:12] SHAFT OF DECORATED CROSS, BANAGHER, CO. OFFALY.

Late eighth century AD.

The panels on the cross-shaft show (*from top to bottom*), a lion; a horseman carrying a crozier or crook; a stag with its foot caught in a trap and a whirlygig consisting of four interlaced human figures. Wooden traps of the same form have been recovered from Irish bogs. The figures of the lion and stag symbolise Christ, but the identification of the horseman, perhaps a saint, abbot or bishop, is unclear. 1929:1497. H. 1.48 m.
Harbison 1992, no. 20.

[5:13] MOYLOUGH BELT SHRINE, MOYLOUGH, CO. SLIGO.

Eighth century AD.

This reliquary, found in a bog at Moylough, Co. Sligo, takes the form of a set of four hinged metal plates which enclose fragments of a leather belt, no doubt associated with an early Irish saint. Such wonderworking belts or girdles are mentioned in the lives of early Irish saints; they had the power to effect cures or establish truthfulness when placed about the waist. This would account for the extensive wear on this object. The two front plates form a false buckle. The frames of the buckle plates are decorated with bird and animal heads and end in elaborate glass settings. They enclose stamped silver foils with spiral and interlace patterns. 1945:81. W. 45.0 cm.

Youngs (ed.) 1989, no. 47.

[5:14] BONE MOTIF-PIECE, LAGORE, CO. MEATH.

Eighth century AD.

Found in a crannóg at Lagore, Co. Meath. A discarded cattle bone was polished and used to carve a number of panels of animal and ribbon interlace. Some, such as the animal with hatched body gripping its own body, are deeply carved and appear to be finished designs while others are only lightly sketched. Lagore crannóg was the seat of the provincial kingdom of Brega. It was excavated in the 1930s and produced evidence for the production of fine metalworking. W29. L. 22.2 cm.

Youngs (ed.) 1989, no. 153.

[5:15] BRONZE HAND-BELL, CASTLE ISLAND, LOUGH LENE, CO. WESTMEATH.

Early ninth century AD.

Rectangular in section with convex sides and a semi-circular looped handle, this bell weighs around 6.0 kg and is one of the heaviest bronze castings to have survived. The broad faces bear a finely engraved, ringed cross which rises from a band engraved with a geometric fret pattern. 1881:535. H. 33.9 cm.

Ryan 1983, no. 57.

[5:16] THE 'TARA' BROOCH, BETTYSTOWN, CO. MEATH. FRONT.

Early eighth century AD.

Found near the seashore at Bettystown, Co. Meath in 1850. The association with the ancient royal site of Tara was an invention by Waterhouse & Co., a Dublin firm of jewellers, in order to enhance its value. It is made of cast and gilt silver. The front consists of a network of recessed cells filled with panels of gold filigree (some are missing), separated by studs of glass, enamel and amber. The guard-chain of woven silver wires ends in a swivel attachment composed of cast snake and animal heads framing two tiny human heads of cast glass. The detail of the filigree ornament on one of the terminals shown on page 177 above consists of an animal in heraldic pose fitted neatly into a triangular panel, his front paw raised in front of him, his body wound back on itself. The beaded and twisted gold wires and gold granules are soldered to a base of sheet gold. This panel measures only 2 cm end to end.

R4015. L. of pin, 32 cm; D. of ring, 8.7 cm.

Ryan 1989, no. 48.

[5:17] THE 'TARA' BROOCH, BETTYSTOWN, CO. MEATH. BACK.

Early eighth century AD.

The back of the brooch is as ornate as the front. As the back rested against the wearer's clothing, the ornament here is flatter and there are no filigree wires which would catch on the cloth. The hoop and terminals are decorated with designs of scrolls and triple spirals.

❧

[5:18] DECORATED FITTING FOR A HANDLE, DONORE, CO. MEATH.

Early eighth century AD.

Found with other objects in a riverbank near Donore, Co. Meath. This composite fitting consists of a cast copper-alloy animal head grasping a ring in its jaws. This is fitted into a framed disc with finely engraved ornament consisting of an outer band of scrolls and spirals and an inner of interlaced beasts. The workmanship is of the highest quality, on a par with that of the 'Tara' brooch. Although its function is uncertain, it was designed to be fastened to a thick wooden board and it may have been intended as a handle for a church door or an altar fitting. 1985:21b–e. D. of disc, 13.5 cm.

Youngs (ed.) 1989, no. 64.

❧

[5:19] OPENWORK MOUNT, PHOENIX PARK, DUBLIN.

Eighth century AD.

A triangular mount of cast and gilt copper-alloy. The delicacy of the casting and the quality of the ornament of spirals and interlaced animals indicate that this is an exceptional piece, produced in a major workshop. Its shape suggests that it originally functioned as the corner piece of an elaborate object such as a book shrine, book cover or portable altar, although a secular use cannot be ruled out. P782a. L. 8.2 cm.

Youngs (ed.) 1989, no. 145.

❧

[5:20] THE LOUGHAN OR 'DALRIADA' BROOCH, LOUGHAN, CO. DERRY.

Eighth century AD.

Found at an ancient ford on the River Bann at Loughan, Co. Derry. It is unique in being the only brooch made entirely of gold. It is cast and small panels of gold filigree are added to the terminals and pin-head. The terminals are bordered by figures of animals and birds but the finest work is reserved for the shank of the pin. Here, finely engraved pairs of birds, their bodies gracefully intertwined, are highlighted against a finely stippled background. 1878:29. D. of ring, 5.2 cm.

Youngs (ed.) 1989, no. 83.

❧

[5:21] THE CAVAN OR 'QUEEN'S' BROOCH, CAVAN, CO. CAVAN.

Late eighth to early ninth century AD.

Of cast, gilt silver, the matching pin-head and terminal designs consist of circular trays of gold filigree grasped in the jaws of three animal heads. A pair of human heads occupies spaces between the terminals. It was a replica of this brooch, given to Queen Victoria during her visit to the Great Exhibition in Dublin in 1853, which started the fashion for reproduction 'Celtic' jewellery. W43. D. of ring, 11.4 cm.

Youngs (ed.) 1989, no. 73.

❧

[5:22] THE LOUGHMOE OR 'TIPPERARY' BROOCH, LOUGHMOE, CO. TIPPERARY.

Late eighth to early ninth century AD.

Found in 1842, the sparing use of gold on this silver brooch is employed to great effect. The gilt interlace margins of pin-head and terminals shows the technique of chip-carving against the plain silver of the hoop and terminal plates. Gold filigree is confined to discrete, lozenge-shaped recesses and large amber studs add to the overall effect of contrasting colours. 17W42. L. of pin, 24.3 cm.
Youngs (ed.) 1989, no. 78.

[5:23] THE KILMAINHAM BROOCH, KILMAINHAM, CO. DUBLIN.

Late eighth to early ninth century AD.

Found at Kilmainham, Co. Dublin, possibly with a Viking burial. This brooch can be traced back to the late eighteenth century when it was in the possession of Ralph Ouseley, a gentleman-collector living in Co. Sligo. It is of cast silver, with deep cells for panels of gold filigree and glass, although much of the latter is now missing. The lobed terminal form was one which was most favoured by Pictish craftsmen, although this is an Irish piece. W45. D. 9.67 cm.
Youngs (ed.) 1989, no. 74.

[5:24] SILVER PENANNULAR BROOCH, BALLYNAGLOGH, CO. ANTRIM.

Late eighth to early ninth century AD.

Found in a bog at Ballynaglogh, Co. Antrim. The terminals are squared, each with a central amber stud surrounded by four bird heads with long beaks, their eyes set with tiny beads of blue glass. This is the product of a Pictish workshop and was an ancient import into north-east Ireland from Scotland. 1930:495. L. of pin, 13.9 cm.
Youngs (ed.) 1989, no. 85.

[5:25] THE ARDAGH HOARD, REERASTA, CO. LIMERICK.

Eighth and ninth centuries AD.

Found in 1868 hidden under a stone slab in Reerasta Rath, near Ardagh, Co. Limerick, this find may have been placed in the ground for safekeeping. The hoard contained a magnificent silver chalice, a smaller, plain chalice of copper-alloy and four silver brooches. The objects range in date from the mid-eighth century (the silver chalice) to the late ninth. The latest object in the hoard is a silver thistle brooch (*middle right*) and such brooches are also found as scrap in hoards of Viking character. The hoard may therefore have been placed in the ground around the year AD 900. 1874:99–104. H. of silver chalice, 17.8 cm.
Ryan 1983, nos. 51a–f.

[5:26] THE ARDAGH CHALICE, REERASTA, CO. LIMERICK.

Eighth century AD.

The decorative band under the rim appears to be held in place by a series of studs but these are, in fact, purely decorative. This band and the circular medallions on either face may have been inspired by the jewelled metal straps of Byzantine workmanship fitted to Late Antique vessels of glass and semiprecious stone such as those now preserved in the Treasury of St Mark's Cathedral, Venice, brought there from Constantinople during the Crusades. 1874:99. H. 17.8 cm.

[5:27] DETAIL: THE ARDAGH CHALICE, REERASTA, CO. LIMERICK.

Eighth century AD.

Detail of the rim. Above, a panel of gold filigree with a pair of interlocked beasts framed between studs of red enamel and blue glass set in geometric silver grilles. Note, below this, the accomplished geometric letter forms, engraved against a stippled background. The names of the apostles James (IACOBI) and Thaddeus (TATHEVS) can be clearly seen.

[5:28] THE DERRYNAFLAN HOARD, DERRYNAFLAN, CO. TIPPERARY.

Eighth and ninth centuries AD.

This group of altar vessels was found on a church site at Derrynaflan, Co. Tipperary as recently as 1980 by a treasure hunter. It consists of a silver chalice, a silver paten or dish with its stand, a copper-alloy strainer-ladle, all covered by a plain copper-alloy basin. 1980:4–8. D. of basin, 45.0 cm.
Youngs (ed.) 1989, nos. 124–7.

[5:29] THE DERRYNAFLAN CHALICE, DERRYNAFLAN, CO. TIPPERARY.

Ninth century AD.

Its proportions are not as elegant as those of the Ardagh Chalice which it resembles in many respects. Its more muted colours and coarser filigree reflect changes in metalworking practice in the intervening period of some two or three generations. 1980:6. H. 19.2 cm.

[5:30] THE DERRYNAFLAN PATEN, DERRYNAFLAN, CO. TIPPERARY.

Eighth century AD.

In terms of style, technical ability and date this object lies much closer to the Ardagh Chalice [5:26] and may even have been produced in the same workshop, if not under the control of the same master craftsman. The detail of the jewelled rim on page 179 above depicts a pair of kneeling men placed back-to-back. Their beards and hair become entangled in a mesh of interlace. On the side view of the paten on page 179, the foils of thin stamped gold alternate with rectangular studs intricately inlaid with geometric patterns of red and yellow enamel against a blue glass background. These are framed by finely-knitted wires of silver which alternate with copper wires on the upper register. 1980:4. D. 36.8 cm.

[5:31] THE DERRYNAFLAN STRAINER, DERRYNAFLAN, CO. TIPPERARY.

Eighth or ninth century AD.

A decorative rim of pressed silver foils has been added to the bowl. Similar foils along with enamelled studs were added to the strainer-plate. 1980:7. D. of bowl, 11.5 cm.

[5:32] WOODEN BUCKET WITH COPPER-ALLOY MOUNTS, DERREEN, CO. CLARE.

Eighth or ninth century AD.

Found in a bog, this stave-built yew vessel is encircled by three bands of thin bronze and is fitted with a carrying handle. The upper band is engraved with a band of ribbon interlace. It is likely that such vessels were used for both secular and ecclesiastical use. Their small size suggests they were used for serving liquids of value, perhaps wine. 1941:722. H. 16.5 cm.

Raftery 1941; Brady 1989, no. 129.

[5:33] CRUCIFIXION PLAQUE, ST. JOHN'S, RINNAGAN, CO. ROSCOMMON.

Eighth century AD.

Found in a churchyard along with a bronze-coated iron hand-bell. The plaque is made from a thin sheet of copper-alloy hammered into a form, the ornament engraved. The size of the figure of Christ is exaggerated, the cross barely represented. He is flanked below by the sponge- and lance-bearers and above by angels. The most peculiar feature of the composition is the breastplate on the figure of Christ composed of interlocking scrolls and spirals. R554. H. 20.75 cm.

Youngs (ed.) 1989, no. 133.

[5:34] FIGURE OF AN ECCLESIASTIC, AGHABOE, CO. LAOIS.

Eighth century AD.

Found in 1836 in a grave near the ancient churchyard at Aghaboe, Co. Laois. This rectangular plaque of cast and gilt copper-alloy was originally attached to a larger object, perhaps a cross or a reliquary. The standing figure is shown with a tunic which extends below the knees. He holds a short staff or crozier in his right hand while his left displays an object, perhaps a book. The recessed background is decorated with ribbon interlace and spiral ornament. There are patterns of interlace on the sides of the tunic also. The considerable wear on the surface indicates that this object was of some antiquity before it was buried. R2945. H. 12.9 cm.

Ryan 1983, no. 46.

[5:2]

CARVING OF ST PATRICK, FAUGHART GRAVEYARD, CO. LOUTH.

Early sixteenth century AD.

[5:3]
CARVED STONE PILLAR, AGLISH, CO. KERRY.
Fifth or sixth century AD.

[5:4]
CARVED STONE PILLAR, MULLAMAST, CO. KILDARE.
Sixth century AD.

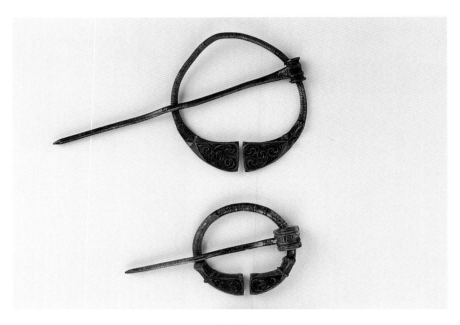

[5:5]
ZOOMORPHIC PENANNULAR BROOCHES,
TOP: UNLOCALISED; *BOTTOM*: ARTHURSTOWN, CO. KILDARE.
Fifth to sixth century AD.

[5:6]
[5:6] TWO SILVER PINS, CASTLETOWN KILPATRICK, CO. MEATH.
Late fourth/early fifth century AD.

[5:7]
SET OF WRITING-TABLETS, SPRINGMOUNT BOG, CO. ANTRIM.
Late sixth/early seventh century AD.

[5:8]
TWO TOMB-SHAPED SHRINES, LOUGH ERNE, CO. FERMANAGH.
Late eighth or early ninth century AD.

[5:9]

ENAMELLED SHRINE MOUNT, UNLOCALISED.

Eighth century AD.

[5:10]

CREST OF BELL SHRINE, UNLOCALISED.

Eighth to ninth century AD.

[5:11]

HARNESS MOUNTS, NAVAN, CO. MEATH.

Eighth century AD.

[5:12]

SHAFT OF DECORATED CROSS, BANAGHER, CO. OFFALY.

Late eighth century AD.

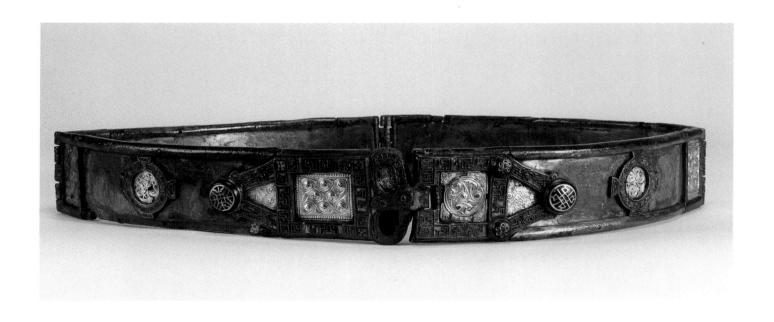

[5:13]

MOYLOUGH BELT SHRINE, MOYLOUGH, CO. SLIGO. COMPLETE BELT (*ABOVE*); DETAIL OF BELT BUCKLE (*BELOW*).

Eighth century AD.

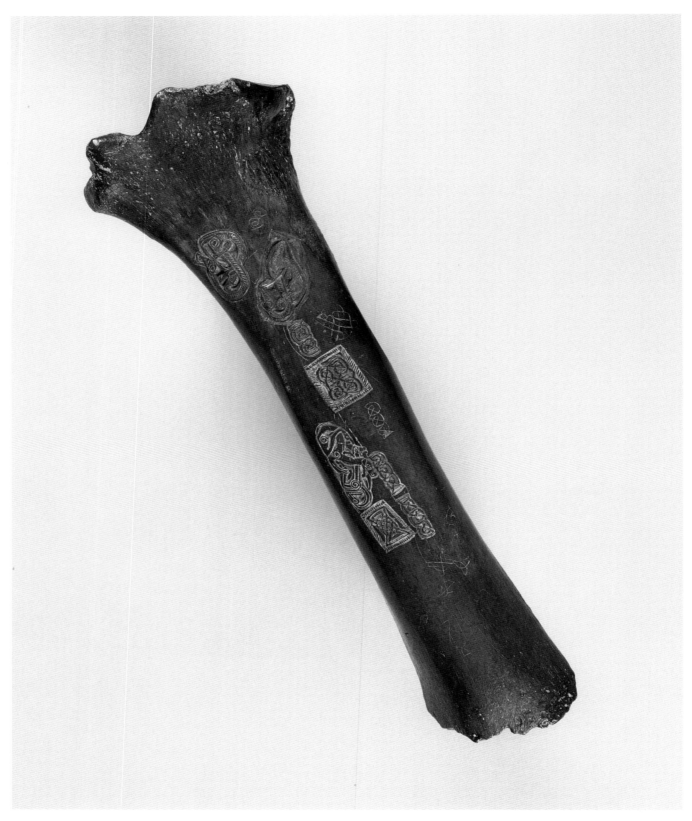

[5:14]
BONE MOTIF-PIECE, LAGORE, CO. MEATH.
Eighth century AD.

[5:15]
BRONZE HAND-BELL, CASTLE ISLAND, LOUGH LENE, CO. WESTMEATH.
Early ninth century AD.

[5:16] *facing page*

THE 'TARA' BROOCH, BETTYSTOWN, CO. MEATH. FRONT.

Early eighth century AD.

[5:17]

THE 'TARA' BROOCH, BETTYSTOWN, CO. MEATH. BACK.

Early eighth century AD.

[5:18]
DECORATED FITTING FOR A HANDLE, DONORE, CO. MEATH.
Early eighth century AD.

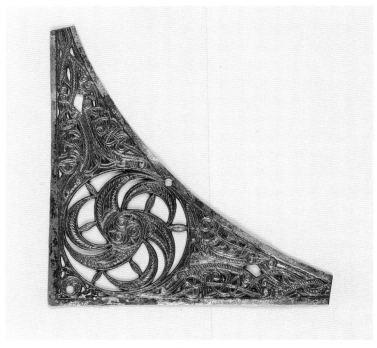

[5:19]
OPENWORK MOUNT, PHOENIX PARK, DUBLIN.
Eighth century AD.

[5:20]

THE LOUGHAN OR 'DALRIADA' BROOCH, LOUGHAN, CO. DERRY.

Eighth century AD.

[5:21]
THE CAVAN OR 'QUEEN'S' BROOCH, CAVAN, CO. CAVAN.
Late eighth to early ninth century AD.

[5:22] *facing page*
THE LOUGHMOE OR 'TIPPERARY' BROOCH, LOUGHMOE, CO. TIPPERARY.
Late eighth to early ninth century AD.

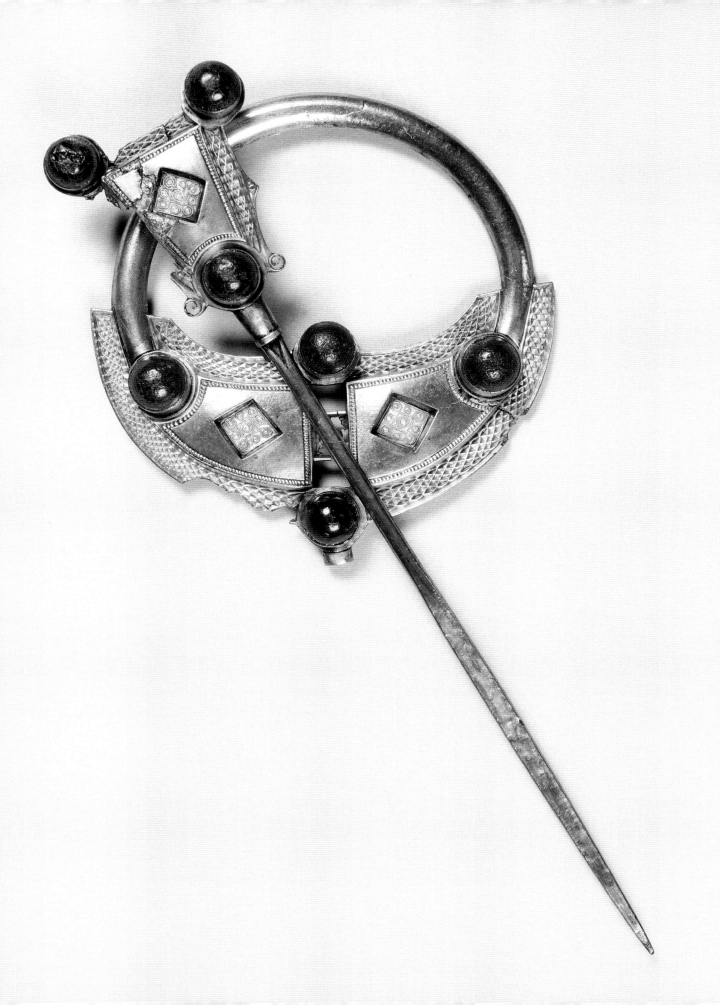

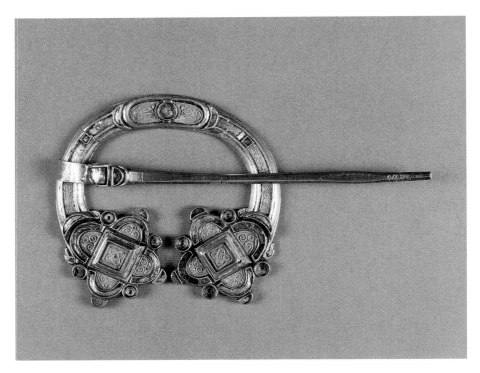

[5:23]
THE KILMAINHAM BROOCH, KILMAINHAM, CO. DUBLIN.
Late eighth to early ninth century AD.

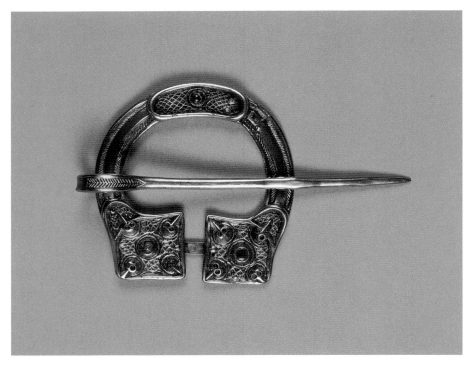

[5:24]
SILVER PENANNULAR BROOCH, BALLYNAGLOGH, CO. ANTRIM.
Late eighth to early ninth century AD.

[5:25]

THE ARDAGH HOARD, REERASTA, CO. LIMERICK.

Eighth and ninth centuries AD.

[5:26] *facing page*

THE ARDAGH CHALICE, REERASTA, CO. LIMERICK.

Eighth century AD.

[5:27] *above*

DETAIL: THE ARDAGH CHALICE, REERASTA, CO. LIMERICK.

Eighth century AD.

[5:28]
THE DERRYNAFLAN HOARD, DERRYNAFLAN, CO. TIPPERARY.
Eighth and ninth centuries AD.

[5:29]

The Derrynaflan Chalice, Derrynaflan, Co. Tipperary.

Ninth century AD.

[5:30]
THE DERRYNAFLAN PATEN, DERRYNAFLAN, CO. TIPPERARY.
Eighth century AD.

[5:31]

THE DERRYNAFLAN STRAINER, DERRYNAFLAN, CO. TIPPERARY.

Eighth or ninth century AD.

[5:32]

WOODEN BUCKET WITH COPPER-ALLOY MOUNTS, DERREEN, CO. CLARE.

Eighth or ninth century AD.

[5:33]
CRUCIFIXION PLAQUE, ST. JOHN'S, RINNAGAN, CO. ROSCOMMON.
Eighth century AD.

[5:34]
FIGURE OF AN ECCLESIASTIC, AGHABOE, CO. LAOIS.
Eighth century AD.

6

VIKING AGE IRELAND

AD 850–1150

PATRICK F. WALLACE

Three main groups of treasures characterise this era, that is, apart from what might be termed the more ordinary artefacts of everyday life recovered from the National Museum's excavations at Wood Quay and other Dublin sites, which may be regarded as treasures of scientific information [6:7, 6:8]. These are the great silver ornaments of the ninth and earlier tenth centuries, the brooches and other ornaments of indigenous type and decoration which continued to be made from the golden age of Irish metalwork described in the previous chapter. They also include the great collection of shrines, croziers and other ecclesiastical treasures which were produced on foot of the Church reform movement of the late eleventh and earlier twelfth centuries and among which the Cross of Cong is the most notable.

Silver is the single most significant surviving phenomenon from the first half of the period under review. It occurs in such volume and is found so frequently that it inspired the art historian Françoise Henry to conclude that for the Vikings the 'cold gleam of silver' was irresistible. Whether in bullion or, as later, in coin, it was the currency of the age, the material in which so many of the ornaments of the period were made. So attractive was it, to both Scandinavian-derived and native-Irish smiths alike, that they produced plain silver ornaments without the decorative applications that had given the jewellery of the preceding age a more coloured and, to a modern eye, a fussier finish. In the new approach it sufficed to add bosses of silver itself or, simply, to stamp, chisel, chase or cast cut-away effects to beautify the silver [6:9, 6:15]. Showing perhaps the degree to which the silver ornaments of Viking Age Ireland were made by native smiths rather than the Vikings in Dublin or the other towns, there is

a marked absence of ornamentation in any of the relevant Scandinavian inspired art styles — *Borre*, *Ringerike* or *Urnes* (the latter two being anyway too late to have featured on the silver which had its floruit before they were developed!). This is in contrast to Dublin, where *Ringerike* became ubiquitous in the earlier eleventh century if the bone motif-pieces and carved wood are anything to go by, and the *Urnes* style which, if we look at the later eleventh- and early twelfth-century metalwork, sculpture and architectural ornament, appears, by then, to have conquered the art of the whole island.

In the ninth and earlier tenth centuries silver flooded into Ireland in such quantities that craftsmen were inspired to produce a range of hitherto unknown ornament forms, such as bossed penannular brooches [6:10, 6:11], thistle brooches [6:11, 6:12], kite-brooches [6:13, 6:14] as well as arm-rings [6:15], neck and finger ornaments and even wire-mesh cones [6:1]. The range of silver ornaments is every bit as evocative of the Viking period as are the great swords, the hilts of which, while lightly ornamented, may, for the most part, have been made abroad [6:16]. The silver jewellery was almost all made in Ireland and, apparently, most of it at non-Scandinavian controlled centres. This pattern was to change later in the Viking Age when, on bone motif-piece and other evidence, craftsmen in Hiberno-Norse Dublin are likely to have manufactured at least a good proportion of the great reliquaries and other ecclesiastical treasures.

Altogether we now have about one-hundred-and-fifty silver hoards which contain combinations of ornaments, hack silver (the small change of the era!), ingots and coins, and in the order of two hundred individual finds of silver objects. While the silver is of varying purity and quality, it is thought that coins from the Islamic world and its trading centres, weighing-scales and weights for use with the silver were the source of its earliest influx into Western Europe, including Ireland, to which it was passed via the Russian rivers and the Baltic to western Scandinavia. Testimony to this Eastern link is provided by Russian 'Permian rings' with their characteristic faceted terminals and also by a female grave from Arklow with its oval brooches linked by a Baltic silver wire chain, and some Kufic (arabic) coins found in Ireland. After about the middle of the tenth century, it is thought silver was being mined in the Hartz Mountain region in Germany, but future spectrographic analysis may indicate that some of the silver originated in the lead-rich ores south of Dublin. Research in the National Museum of Ireland has shown that an ounce unit of 26.6 grams prevailed in tenth- and eleventh-century Dublin [6:17] and this unit is also evident in some of the silver ingots and ornaments found in the Southern Uí Néill strongholds around the midland lakes where they are thought to represent booty, ransom and 'protection money' extracted from Dublin.

[6:1]
SILVER CONES, DUNMORE CAVE, CO. KILKENNY.
Late tenth century AD.

After defeats at Brunanburh (937) and Tara (980) and with the expulsion of Eric Bloodaxe from York (954), Dublin became the main town of the Norse, the capital of the Irish Sea and of the Vikings in the west. It was part of an international trade network as the discoveries of oriental silks, Baltic amber, Arctic walrus, English canal coal/lignite, worsteds and Saxon disc brooches testify. Having started as a ship fortress, a trading base for overwintering, it developed after the mid-ninth century into a slaving emporium and, as recent archaeological evidence shows, by the end of that century, to a town. It is the layout, defences and architectural nature of this settlement which were so graphically unearthed at the Museum's excavations at Fishamble Street, Wood Quay and Christchurch Place.

Having been mediated through the port of Dublin (more than Wexford, Waterford and Limerick — the other Scandinavian urban foundations, in which mints did not develop, in contrast to Dublin which had a mint from about 997), significant amounts of silver found its way to native chieftains whose craftworkers converted it into an exquisite range of ornaments. The silver bossed penannulars, the thistle brooches and most of the kite-brooches are conspicuous for their generous use of plain silver. The thistle type, while inspired from Scandinavia, found very elaborate, though at the same time understated, expression in the hands of Irish silversmiths. Even plaited arm-rings and finger-rings, which were produced in gold and copper-alloy as well as in silver, were for the most part plain; though some of the clenchings were faceted and simply punch-decorated, as in the case of a pair of bracelets from the Dublin excavations [6:8]. Gold was not as scarce as is often thought if we also consider a plaited gold ring from Fishamble Street, Dublin, as well as the several other fragments and strips which indicate the presence of gold working in the Viking town [6:8]. The discovery of a (now lost) five-kilo gold hoard at Hare Island, Co. Westmeath, on the Shannon underlines the relative availability of this precious commodity. The discovery of small copper-alloy, kite-brooches in the Dublin excavations, as well a spectacular specimen from Waterford which has applied gold foil face-masks, underlines the link between the towns and especially their link to Dublin. The hoard, ingot and single finds of silver and gold from the countryside support such a connection, as do the large numbers of lead weights from Dublin [6:15, 6:17, 6:18].

Silver may have poured into Ireland for about a century after the establishment of Dublin in 841, but before that it was less easily obtained. A preference for plain rather than gilded surfaces is evident even before the arrival of the Vikings. This is seen for example in its use on the terminals of the two annular brooches found with the Ardagh Chalice [6:19, top], a trend which continued further with the Killamery brooch where the brooch and pin are of plain silver [6:2]. The glorious brooch from Kilmainham, Dublin [5:23] seems to stand at a cultural crossroads, for whereas its annular form and use of filigree place it in an eighth-century indigenous tradition, its plain silver surface seems to herald a change in taste and, undoubtedly, in availability. The change to the annular form and the use of plain silver rather than gilding in brooch manufacture, finds its best expression in the beautiful brooch from Roscrea which, in true native idiom, still uses gold foil with filigree toppings in the terminals and pinhead as well as large amber studs [6:20]. The silver penannular brooch from Rathlin Island seems to be a curious example of a brooch made in the native idiom by a Scandinavian craftsman [6:21].

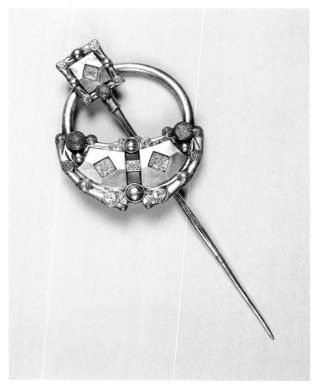

[6:2]
THE KILLAMERY BROOCH,
KILLAMERY,
CO. KILKENNY.
Ninth century AD.

The Scandinavians made hitherto undreamed amounts of silver available to native jewellers who in turn responded by making new brooch types such as bossed penannulars, thistles and kites. These may have been inspired by the taste and technology of the insular Viking world; but native Irish craftsmen, their techniques, tastes and approaches to manufacture, also influenced the Hiberno-Norse workshops, especially in Dublin [6:22]. One has only to consider the dozens of motif-pieces with their mature designs, clay moulds and other techniques associated with non-ferrous metal production, to understand the magnitude of the native influence on Dublin's eleventh-century workshops and to appreciate their debt to the by then centuries-old decorative metalworking traditions of Ireland [6:3, 6:5]. The copper-alloy kite-brooches, which were cast, and the ringed and plain stick pins which were hammer-produced in Dublin in great quantities, also seem to belong with the indigenous tradition, regardless of their forms. The production of a vast range of decorated wood, by contrast, may betray a more Scandinavian influence, as the ubiquitous use of *Ringerike* motifs suggests [6:23]. The comparative absence from native contexts of decorated wooden equivalents of the metalwork objects should not rule out their probable original existence (as a wooden cross boss of native origin from Fishamble Street shows) and possible related native influence on the Dublin carved wood.

With or without the Vikings, the Irish Church could have followed along the lines it had developed since the seventh century. Its established monastic character and missionary endeavour intensified in the ninth and tenth centuries. Ireland's multiplicity of tiny kingdoms continued into this period. Constant warfare with various Viking warrior leaders and, related to this, improvements in warfare, including iron technology, particularly the production of better edges on swords, spearheads and arrowheads, led to the emergence of powerful dynasties who controlled increasingly larger areas of provinces. The Viking Age saw these consolidate into one or two main dynasties in each province before eventually the idea of an overall high kingship became a reality in the reign of Brian Boru. After the Battle of Clontarf in 1014 the main provincial dynasties produced alternating competing kings who ruled with opposition for most of the eleventh century before the concentration of overall power in the lands of Brian's successors, the Uí Bhriain, towards the end of the eleventh century and after them, the O'Connors, the greatest of whom, Turlough, commissioned the most famous treasure of the whole era, the Cross of Cong [6:24].

Made towards the end of the period in question, the Cross of Cong reveals much about that time. It is one of the great treasures of the Museum and, appropriately, occupies a prominent position in a gallery devoted to the art of the late Hiberno-Norse/Romanesque period. It was made, probably in Tuam or Roscommon rather than at Cong, towards the end of the first quarter of the twelfth century, to enshrine a relic of the True Cross that had been acquired in 1122 by Turlough O'Connor, High King of Ireland.

[6:3]
BONE MOTIF-PIECES,
DUBLIN EXCAVATIONS.
*Late eleventh/
early twelfth century* AD.

While in some ways it can be regarded as the last, and one of the finest, artistic achievements of the Early Christian period, the culmination of a tradition of processional crosses that starts with the eighth-century Tully Lough Cross, it also encapsulates several of the strands of influence which comprise the three centuries, 850–1150, particularly the metalwork. Created for devotional display, it preserves the continuity of the earlier metalwork in the choice of a cross type and form that may have been reintroduced as part of the artistic and Church organisational renaissance of the late eleventh and early twelfth centuries. That it was produced under the patronage of one of the great twelfth-century dynasties, the O'Connors, at a time when their greatest son was High King of Ireland evokes the difficult (political and dynastic) background of the previous century and a half, when wars with the Vikings sparked dynastic struggles in various provinces that led to the emergence of a few dominant ruling families.

The Vikings may have been catalysts in the development of a centralised monarchy, thereby, incidentally, making Ireland easier to take later on than when it had dozens of regional kings, but their *artistic* influence is even more tangible. We can see all this in the Cross of Cong. The form of the cross and the religious milieu in which it was produced may have been Irish but the cast openwork plates which cover its surface bear S-shaped, ribbon-like animals intertwined with threadlike snakes which are typical of the Irish version of the international *Urnes* art style named after a Norwegian site in which related designs cover the jambs and lintels of a stave-built church. Like the Scandinavians and much belonging to them, this art style and its predecessors, particularly the *Ringerike* style, was gratefully absorbed by native Irish

[6:4]
SHRINE OF
ST LACHTIN'S ARM,
DONAGHMORE,
CO. CORK.
c. 1120 AD.

craftsmen who made it their own. It can also be seen on the croziers, the Shrine of St. Patrick's Bell, the late high crosses at Kilfenora and Dysert O'Dea, Co. Clare and the sarcophagus at Cormac's Chapel, Cashel, Co. Tipperary.

The Cross of Cong is the artistic and chronological culmination of a series of ecclesiastical metalwork which includes croziers, tomb-shaped shrines and shrines made to encase revered bells, books and other sacred relics. Although shrines were made in Ireland both before and after the three centuries of our concern here, some of the finest examples date from the later eleventh and earlier twelfth centuries. So encrusted are some shrines with the addition of later medieval mounts of semi-precious stones and other adornments, that the viewer often has to look carefully at the sides or for semi-obliterated details on the faces to decipher the sophistication and restraint of the original ornament. Indeed, it is because some of the shrines were redecorated in the conventions of later centuries that they will also find mention in the next chapter. For the Museum visitor, the Shrine of St Patrick's Bell, the Shrine of St Lachtin's Arm, the *Breac Maodhóg* and the Croziers of Clonmacnoise, Co. Offaly and Lismore, Co. Waterford, best preserve the style details and overall integrity of the eleventh and twelfth centuries.

While the cult of relics in Ireland goes back to the introduction of Christianity, the seventh-century Clonmore, Co. Armagh, tomb-shaped shrine probably being the earliest, the more focused devotion of the eleventh and twelfth centuries, probably deriving from the Church reform movement of that time, witnessed an increase in the output of reliquaries. Some of these were made to contain the exhumed bones of Irish saints, as testified by the early twelfth-century arm shrine of St Lachtin from Co. Cork [6:4], with its late Hiberno-Norse *Urnes*-style plates (showing a dense network of interlaced ribbon-like animals separated by a cast copper-alloy openwork band of beasts); and the roughly contemporary Shrine of St. Patrick's Tooth which was later heavily restored. The now much-damaged *Corp Naomh* bell shrine from Co. Westmeath has a cast upper crest featuring tenth-century Hiberno-Norse decoration [7:33].

Two other bell shrines merit special notice: the Shrine of St Senan's Bell, the *Clogán Óir* from Scattery Island, Co. Clare [6:25], and the magnificent Shrine of St Patrick's Bell, Armagh, Co. Armagh [6:26]. The former consists of an eleventh-century copper-alloy core with panels of inlaid silver, typical of the time.

When the popularity of some of the later Scandinavian art styles, particularly the later eleventh- and twelfth-century *Urnes*, is recalled in the context of treasures like the Shrine of St Patrick's Bell and the Cross of Cong, products respectively of Ulster and Connacht ateliers, the question arises of how and in what way some of the earlier expressions of Scandinavian animal interlace found their way on to the *Soiscéal Molaise* [6:27] or on to the sides of the later heavily altered *Cathach* which has cast bronze panels featuring the mid-eleventh century *Ringerike* style [6:28]. Where was the *Cathach* made? Probably at Kells, Co. Meath. We know it was the shrine of the battle standard of the Donegal dynasty of the O'Donnells, who had it made to contain a manuscript thought to have been written by St Columcille himself. The closest parallel to the *Ringerike* panel occurs on a bone motif-piece from the Dublin excavations which has the same hyphenated or deliberately broken motif [6:5]. Carved wood ornaments from Dublin indicate an active school of *Ringerike* ornament that has had to be renamed the 'Dublin style'. These Scandinavian-derived art styles with their English and Irish interpretations flourished in Dublin, through which they must have been first introduced to Ireland. Their appearance on some of the finest metalwork suggests that either the metalwork was made in Dublin — and there is plenty of evidence for sectors of the Hiberno-Norse town being given over to metalworking and woodcarving — or that artists trained in Dublin moved to ateliers in monasteries which operated under the patronage of regional kings.

The Shrine of the Stowe Missal [6:29] actually contained a small manuscript when it was found in the walls of a castle near Lorrha, Co. Tipperary. An extensive inscription calls for prayers for Donnchadh mac Briain, a son of Brian Boru and a claimant for the High Kingship, as well as for its maker, Donnchadh Ua Taccain, and MacCraith Ua Donnchadha, King of Cashel. Again, like the *Cathach* and some of the other book shrines, the early medieval decoration mainly survives on the sides where there are gilt-bronze mounts and bronze open-work plaques covered in silver and backed with sheets of gold foil. A circular medallion features an angel with outstretched wings inset with glass beads containing spirals of silver wire, and beasts with spiralled hip joints grip the heads of the angel. Another side has a bearded figure holding a Viking-type sword flanked by pairs of animals as well as, separately, a bearded, long-haired warrior in short trews. On the opposite side, a plaque shows a pair of ecclesiastics at either side of a seated harp-playing figure. Recalling similar depictions on the roughly contemporary *Soiscéal Molaise* and the slightly later *Breac Maodhóg* from Drumlane, Co. Cavan [6:30], the *Stowe Missal* ecclesiastics are clothed in long tunics and cloaks, one with a handbell and wearing shoes, the other with a crozier being barefoot!

Any notice of our early medieval shrines has to include the house-shaped shrines of the early eleventh century, particularly the *Breac Maodhóg* which is associated with a later medieval leather satchel, and the Shrine of St Manchan which is preserved at Boher Church in Co. Offaly. The latter is the largest surviving reliquary and was transported on poles threaded through rings which still survive near its base. One of

[6:5]
MOTIF PIECE, FROM HIGH STREET, DUBLIN.
Mid eleventh century AD.

its broad faces has a large bossed cross with cast open-work panels of *Urnes* ornament in the bosses and, below the arms of the cross, eleven figures individually nailed to the wooden core. The Museum itself has the related figure of a gilded cast bronze ecclesiastic with holes by which it was, presumably, attached to a similar wooden gable [6:6]; the main difference being the approach to decorating the garments on the Shrine of St Manchan, where the artist's concentration was on the skirt area, in contrast to the Museum figure who seems to be attired in the garments of a clergyman of a more senior rank.

One of the finest examples of Irish representational art on a miniature scale must be the ecclesiastics who appear in an almost carved wood-like effect, so deeply are they

moulded, on copper-alloy plaques applied to the sides and face of the wonderful *Breac Maodhóg* [6:30] which was kept by hereditary keepers, the McGoverns, until the nineteenth century. Recalling the figure on the *Soiscéal Molaise* but invested with a deeper humanity, character and humour, these wool-clad, tuniced and cloaked, bearded and long haired, well-observed figures seem almost to invite the viewer back to the early twelfth century even if the demeanour of some of their number is somewhat remote, pious and haughty!

And, finally, the croziers! Clonmacnoise is the earlier and, in my opinion, the finer of the two highlighted here [6:31]. The hollow crook was cast in one piece and bears on its exposed faces perfect displays of *Ringerike*-style ornament, featuring snake-like animals with ribbon-shaped bodies writhing in figure-of-eight patterns inlaid in strips of silver outlined in niello borders. The animals occur in tightly woven knots, have curled upper jaws and lack the accompaniment of the tendrils which characterise the later *Urnes* style. The crest on top of the crook features a procession of gripping dogs. Others have noted that silver and niello inlays against plain surfaces are characteristic of objects from the south midlands, although the arrangement of animal ornament on the Dublin motif-pieces has to be factored into any search for formative influences, origins and possible places of manufacture.

The contrasting, almost 'baroque', appearance of the Lismore crozier [6:32] is due to the fact that the gold foil decorative panels with their interlaced filigree devices which once clothed the sides of its crook and upper knops no longer survive. Only the domed millefiori glass beads which punctuated these billeted panels remain to indicate the balanced assembly of the original decoration on this object. The crest consists of three open-jawed animals connected in an *Urnes*-style mesh. More complete interpretations of Irish *Urnes* are evident on the bronze plaques of the central knop; this contrasts with the upper knop

[6:6]
FIGURE OF AN
ECCLESIASTIC,
UNLOCALISED.
Twelfth century AD.

which is set with blue and green glass beads inset with geometric millefiori designs in white and red. The use of millefiori glass was a conscious revival of the Irish metalworkers' skill in the later eleventh and twelfth centuries. An inscription on the upper knop of the Lismore crozier tells us that it was made for the Bishop of Lismore (probably about the year 1111 when the Synod of Rathbreasail, Co. Tipperary, confirmed the diocese) by a craftsman called Nechtan. The naming of the craftsmen of so many of these early medieval shrines not only indicates the high regard in which they and their skills were held in Irish society, but must also be one of the earliest instances anywhere of a culture which made such acknowledgment. It was only with the Renaissance that artists in mainland Europe began to sign their work!

In summary, important though the Vikings were in effecting change in different facets of Irish life, politics and culture, their contribution was that of catalyst and influencer rather than of main player. It is true they gave Ireland its first real towns, its earliest mint and money, an expanded commercial network and a coherent pattern of trade contact as well as new weapon types, improved iron technology and methods of horse control with the introduction of spurs and stirrups. The impact of Old Norse on Irish suggests a strong influence on ships and shipbuilding. Their very presence also influenced the organisation of the Church and possibly contributed something to a perceived need for Church reform which was to manifest itself so vigorously and productively in the later eleventh and early twelfth centuries. Independence from the Irish Church of their bishopric in Dublin (their earliest bishops were consecrated at Canterbury), in addition to the mercenary links of their fleet to late Saxon interests and to English politics, was to contribute to the beginning of an enduring English interest in Ireland which was to colour and determine the nature of Irish history almost to the present day. It is for the visitor to the National Museum to judge whether the treasures of the age reflect the cultural and political context of the time in which they were produced and whether, above all, they demonstrate the veracity of the historical and archaeological truth that the Vikings were the catalysts whose impact influenced rather than determined much of what was to follow in Ireland's story.

DETAIL OF [6:31]
CLONMACNOISE CROZIER,
CLONMACNOISE,
CO. OFFALY.
Eleventh century AD.

DETAIL OF [6:26]
SHRINE OF ST PATRICK'S BELL, ARMAGH, CO. ARMAGH.
c. 1100 AD.

Illustrations

[6:1] Silver cones, Dunmore Cave, Co. Kilkenny.
Late tenth century AD.

These conical-shaped objects were made of silver wire and occur in three sizes in a later tenth-century hoard from a cave which has produced other Viking Age material in the past. The hoard also included Anglo-Saxon silver pennies and bracelets, hack silver, bent bars and bronzes, including strap tags of insular origin. The cones probably belonged to a single garment which they were used to fasten and which appears to have been bundled up for subsequent recovery. These only materialised a thousand years later when all traces of the garment, save the silver cones, had vanished. The cones are unusual in the archaeological record although a small woven copper-alloy wire version of one of the smaller sizes was recovered in the Museum's Dublin excavations, suggesting that the cones may have been made in Ireland. The meshed wire pattern in the larger specimen produces a chequered pattern, that on the smallest a quartered effect. The thread for attaching the cones was coated in a very thinly wound silver wire. 1999:274–80. D. of the largest 4.1 cm.
Unpublished.

[6:2] The Killamery Brooch, Killamery, Co. Kilkenny.
Ninth century AD.

Although having some of the characteristics of its ninth-century precursors such as the relative separation of the terminals (here joined by a pair of studs and a small tag with an interlace motif) and the scale, shape and approach to design of the terminals and pin-head, the elongated animals around the edges of the ring and around the square pin-head mark the closeness of the relationship of this partly gilt, silver, annular brooch from Co. Kilkenny to that from Roscrea [6:20]. The fact that the sunken lozenge-shaped panels in the terminals and pin-head feature more accomplished filigree motifs on the backing foil and the comparative absence of amber might suggest this brooch was earlier than Roscrea. The reverse has engraved biting animals at the ends of the ring (like Ballyspellan [6.10]) and the two terminals each have a framed rectangle, within which is a deeply engraved animal motif with a back turned head. R165. L. of pin 31.3 cm.
Ryan 1983, no. 63; Youngs (ed.) 1989, 80.

[6:3] Bone motif-pieces, Dublin excavations.
Late eleventh/early twelfth century AD.

Motif-pieces are usually small, portable, bone or stone pieces which bear carved or raised designs, ranging from the trial runs of apprentices and artists' sketches to the more deeply executed dies and models of metalworkers. This Irish tradition was adopted by the Hiberno-Norse craftworkers of Dublin and other towns. The motif-pieces here are amongst the two hundred or so so far recorded from the excavations. In both cases, a cattle long bone is employed. Apart from the sharp triangular knot, the large squared specimen here (*left*) with the cut ends, features a series of plain interlace panels which recall the ornament arrangement on the Shrine of St Senan's Bell [6:25]. The specimen on the right features a half-finished design in relief on a lightly prepared bone. E71:5706. L. 12.9 cm. E190:148. L. 17.7 cm.
O'Meadhra 1979, 50–51; Graham-Campbell 1980, 136.

[6:4] SHRINE OF ST LACHTIN'S ARM, DONAGHMORE, CO. CORK.

c. 1120 AD.

The shrine is of wood covered with cast and engraved bronze plates in the shape of a forearm. The hand with fingers bent over the palm is cast as a single piece and decorated with an applied silver panel engraved with interlace and plant motifs flanked by panels of gold and gilt wire. Also noteworthy are the cast panels of interlace around the wrist. Most striking are the eight large vertical panels which occur around the forearm. These are held in place by vertical strips and, midway, by a cast, open-work collar featuring beasts threaded with snakes in the Irish *Urnes* style. The densely distributed interlaced pattern of the animals which writhe around the large, vertical, bronze panels also conforms to the style, making this a one-period piece of about 1120 AD. The inscription on the vertical holding strip commemorates Maelsechnaill Ua Cellacháin, King of southern Ireland and Tadg MacCarthaig and his brother Cormac who were Kings of Cashel and Munster. 1884: 690. H. 39.0 cm; D. of base 7.0 cm.
Ó Floinn 1983, no. 80.

[6:5] MOTIF-PIECE FROM HIGH STREET, DUBLIN.

Mid eleventh century AD.

This motif-piece, found at High Street, Dublin has cut ends and is decorated with a number of sunken panels. One of these has a false relief *Ringerike* motif which is similar in its composition to a panel of ornament on the shrine of the *Cathach* [6:28]. The bodies of two interlaced snakes are composed of parallel broad and thin lines arranged in hyphenated loops interwoven with tendrils. E71:708. L. 11.6 cm.
Graham-Campbell 1980, 136; Ó Floinn 1983, no. 74a.

[6:6] FIGURE OF AN ECCLESIASTIC, UNLOCALISED.

Twelfth century AD.

This cast, gilt-bronze figure of a bishop almost certainly comes from the side of a wooden gabled shrine like that of St Manchan from Boher, Co. Offaly, which originally had about fifty such figures nailed to its faces. The figure here is of a bishop with a pointed mitre and wearing a decorated, long-sleeved tunic under a cloak fastened at the breast by a pair of disc brooches. The figure holds a crozier with a spiralled crook with both arms, the ferruled tip resting between his feet which display shoes with central tongues. The relative frequency with which bishops are prominently depicted in bronze and in stone sculpture in the early twelfth century must be connected to a strengthening of the role of the bishop in the Irish Church arising from reforming synods, such as Kells in 1152 which finally set out the dioceses. R 2940. H. 19.0 cm.
Ó Floinn 1983, no. 84.

[6:7] Reconstruction of Dublin.

c. 1000 ad.

Based on the most up-to-date archaeological and topographical evidence available from forty years of excavation, most of which was carried out by and for the Museum, the reconstruction shows the comparative scale of the urban area, its streets, lanes and ports (and the location in them of buildings) and how the whole relates to the waterfront, the tidal confluence of the Liffey and its tributary the Poddle and the hinterland. The location chosen by the Vikings was easily defended especially by a waterborne force that required access to boats to facilitate rapid exit. This drawing, prepared by Simon Dick, is the third to be undertaken by the National Museum to show how Dublin might have looked at this time. *Wallace 1988; Wallace 1992*.

[6:8] Selection of artefacts from the Dublin excavations.

Tenth and eleventh centuries ad.

This selection of artefacts from the Museum's Dublin excavations focuses on the craft, commerce and wealth of the town in the tenth and eleventh centuries. The open-work, wooden finial is carved in the local version of the international Scandinavian-derived *Ringerike* style; the figurine also testifies to the existence of an accomplished wood-carving school in Dublin. The green and red porphyry fragments were brought from Rome as religious souvenirs; amber came from the Baltic to be fashioned locally and the gold ring and bracelet indicate the wealth of the Viking town. E190:792; E172:2081, E172:10120; E40:1671; E172:4309; E122:15790; E71:9008. L. of largest 26.6 cm. *Wallace 1985*.

[6:9] Selection of silver ornaments.

Tenth and eleventh centuries ad.

The Vikings opened up trade routes to the silver- and gold-rich Byzantine and Muslim central- and western-Asian markets. The bullion arising from trade, exchange and plunder was largely in the form of coins which were melted down and often converted into ornaments. This is how Irish native silversmiths procured large quantities of silver which led to the production of bossed penannular and thistle as well as kite-brooches. Both the penannulars and the thistles came from traditional indigenous forms. The penannulars in particular were the local response to hitherto undreamed of amounts of silver, which before the Vikings was of poorer quality and had to be used sparingly. Over one-hundred-and-thirty silver hoards have now been identified in Ireland; these include 54 without coins and 76 with coins. It is not clear for what the Vikings were paying the Irish; apart from ransoms and protection, the possibility of the lucrative slave trade has to be kept in mind. *Graham-Campbell 1976, 51–5; Sheehan 1998*.

[6:10] SILVER BOSSED PENANNULAR BROOCH, BALLYSPELLAN, CO. KILKENNY.

c. 900 AD.

In general, Viking Age silver brooches are heavier and bigger than their predecessors. Made of hammered silver, the flat sunken area of the terminals each has an openwork plate of animal design, separated by grooved bands connecting with four domed bosses. The bosses are highlighted by ribbed wire rings and riveted to the brooch, thereby holding the openwork plates in position. The junction of ring and terminal is marked by a biting animal head incised into the silver. The pin-head is a folded ridged sheet which tucks around the ring. Scratched on the back of the brooch in Ogham characters are four Irish names of people who may once have owned the brooch. It was made about 900 when a very plentiful supply of silver was available to native craftsmen courtesy of trade connections with the Scandinavians in Dublin. R 89. L. of pin 25.2 cm.

Ryan 1983, no. 66; Youngs (ed.) 1989, 89.

❧

[6:11] BOSSED PENANNULAR AND THISTLE BROOCHES.

Late ninth/early tenth century AD.

The two brooches on the right (*top and bottom*) were found in Kildimo, Co. Limerick and Richardstown, Co. Louth respectively, while the find place of the two larger brooches is unknown. Viking Age silver in Ireland was converted into a variety of brooches and arm-rings. The brooches are a development of pre-Viking penannular types and are of two forms: bossed and thistle brooches. W38. L. of pin 25.5 cm. W35. L. of pin 18.2 cm. P742. L. of pin 15.0 cm. 1964.239. L. of pin 16.2 cm.

Armstrong 1915, 297; Bøe 1940, 130; Raftery 1963; Ó Floinn and Cahill 1995, 76–77.

❧

[6:12] THISTLE BROOCH, CELBRIDGE, CO. KILDARE.

Late ninth/early tenth century AD.

Silver-gilt 'thistle' brooch with plain round-sectioned ring terminating in spherical, gilt-brambled knobs. The pin is round with a gilt knob matching those on the terminals and is flattened and widened towards a fluted point. This is a simple version of a widespread and often more elaborately finished type. It is almost certainly of Irish manufacture, made in the late ninth or, probably more likely, the early tenth century when silver was widely mediated through Dublin from the Scandinavians to the hands of native craftsmen. It should be noted that although the pin has a rather widened leaf-shaped aspect and is decorated, this is a relatively plain specimen. W40. L. of pin 25.0 cm.

Armstrong 1920, 297; Bøe 1940, 130.

❧

[6:13] DETAIL OF HEAD: KITE-BROOCH, NEAR LIMERICK.

Early tenth century AD.

In this example of a silver kite-brooch from near Limerick, the second Viking town, the kite-shaped openwork head is attached to the pin by a hinged tag. The head is lozenge-shaped with animal heads at the angles. The heart-shaped opening at the centre recalls contemporary wooden ornaments, such as a harness bow crest. This specimen was found, with another, exceptionally long, oval-headed kite brooch which originally held gold filigree and glass insets in its deep recesses in 1845, during the construction of the Limerick-Tipperary railway line. About half a dozen silver kite-brooches exist. Apart from the large type illustrated here, several copper-alloy brooches of this type have been found in the Dublin excavations. These were made in Dublin, as was a more English inspired, star-shaped, lead-alloy variety for which we also have the stone mould in which it was made. Large kite-brooches were worn on the shoulder with the pin pointing upwards and the ring at the tip securing it to the cloth; the size indicates how plentiful the supply of silver was in earlier tenth-century Ireland. 1874:73. L. of pin-head 7.9 cm. *Ryan 1983, no. 69; Ó Floinn and Cahill 1995; Whitfield 1998.*

[6:14] DETAIL OF HEAD: KITE-BROOCH, UNLOCALISED.

Late ninth/early tenth century AD.

This decorative almond-shaped pendant, which is noteworthy for its inlaid panels of filigree, is a kite-brooch variant less usual than the angular form [6:13]. Both are very large in scale compared to the more usual run and extremely large in contrast to the more commonly found miniature variants in copper-alloy which are found in Dublin from where they are presumed to have been exported. Here, two main panels of a total of five are ranged around a setting for a now missing glass, stone or amber stud. They feature backward looking animals in twisted and beaded gold wire set, as in the other panels, on a gold foil backing and levelled flush with the retaining edges by a paste infill. A lower panel shows an animal head full face, on which there are sockets for now missing studs in the eye and ear positions. Of the two top panels, one is now missing, the other retaining the outline of a filigree inhabitant of which a presumably beaded wire body is mostly missing. All the filigree panels are retained by stitching. The tip of the oval has a cast animal head with a wire ring in its jaws and the central hinged tab which attaches the oval element to the pin features a tiny gold filigree panel. The use of granulated bodies and the filigree animal head in plan, apparently, show similarities with Scandinavian box- and animal-headed brooches. 4W27. L. of pin-head 6.1 cm. *Ryan and Ó Floinn 1983, no 70.*

[6:15] HIBERNO-NORSE SILVER ARM-RINGS, IRELAND.

Late ninth/early tenth century AD.

Over one hundred of these are known from Ireland where they were current during the later ninth and early tenth centuries. Of the various silver ornament types known from Ireland at this time, these most closely correlate to the Dublin weight system which centred around an ounce value of 26.6 grams. They are probably more functional than decorative and were produced in bars which were hammered flat into bands and rings for ease of transport. They were manufactured in Ireland, probably in the Viking settlements, from imported silver coin and other sources of bullion; some have been found in hoards in England, Scotland and Norway.

Graham-Campbell 1976, 51–5; Sheehan 1998.

[6:16] THE BALLINDERRY SWORD, BALLINDERRY, CO. WESTMEATH.

Ninth century AD.

The sword was the principal weapon used by the Vikings, most of the iron blades with their often carborised steel edges probably being imported to Scandinavia where the hilt ornament was generally added. This iron sword from County Westmeath with its silver mounted handle is the finest surviving specimen of a Viking sword from Ireland and one of the most impressive anywhere. It has an elaborate, pattern-welded blade inlaid with the name of the sword-maker VLFBEHRT. Blades inlaid with the name of *Ulfbehrt* were exported from the Rhineland and have been found as far east as Russia. Most swords found in Ireland from this era probably originated in Norway and have been found in graves in the Dublin area (at Islandbridge, College Green, Bride Street and Dollymount) where they appear mainly to have been interred with the extended burials of warriors, although some of the ritually bent examples may have accompanied cremations as they did in Scandinavia. The present specimen is from a crannóg excavated by the Harvard Archaeological Mission to Ireland in 1932, a site interpreted as the homestead of a farmer or local king. SA 1928:382. L. 92.5 cm.

Mahr 1928, 204–52; Walsh 1998.

[6:17] Decorated lead weights, Islandbridge, Dublin.

c. 900 AD.

Balance beams, pairs of pans and weights of Viking age date are known to have been recovered in Dublin in the nineteenth century. The weights and two of the balances came from a gravel pit south-west of Islandbridge in 1866. They are part of an overall assemblage which represents a minimum of four to six male and at least two female graves. They are the only Scandinavian burials in Ireland which produced balance components or weights.

The weights shown here are circular, oblong and semi-circular in shape. The five circular weights include three (D. 1.9 cm; D. 2.2 cm and D. 3.2 cm) topped with gilt-bronze discs (reused from insular ecclesiastical metalwork mounts) and two with enamelled decoration (D. 2.7 cm), one of which has yellow enamel panels alternating with millefiori glass (D. 2.7 cm). The three oblong specimens are topped respectively with two lengths of corded blue glass (L. 2.4 cm), the cut-down bronze mount of an animal head (L. 1.8 cm) and, most impressive of all, a three dimensional, cast gilt-bronze animal head with scrolling on the nostrils and a small triquetra knot on the forehead (L. 3.3 cm). The semi-circular weight is topped with a gilt-bronze mount with alternating copper and silver zig-zags (D. 3.2 cm). The weights were buried around 900. The actual weights seem to have been interfered with somewhat, possibly since discovery, which probably explains why they do not all conform to the Dublin 'ounce' unit of 26.6 grams, which has been worked out from the two hundred or so intact specimens found in the Dublin excavations. R2389, 2399–2401, R2413–7.

Graham-Campbell 1980, 89, no. 308.

[6:18] Gold ornaments: Ardtrea, Co. Tyrone; unlocalised; Rathedan, Co. Carlow; Wicklow, Co. Wicklow and Edenvale Caves, Co. Clare.

Late tenth/early eleventh century AD.

These gold ornaments consist of two finger-rings and three arm-rings. The larger of the finger-rings is from Ardtrea, Co. Tyrone, the other is unlocalised. The arm-rings are from Rathedan, Co. Carlow, Wicklow, Co. Wicklow and Edenvale Caves, Co. Clare, respectively. Gold ornaments are not common as gold was scarce throughout the early medieval world. The massive gold ring (*centre*) from Rathedan, Co. Carlow, which is made of three gold rods, weighs 375 grams and is the largest surviving gold ornament from Ireland. It should also be remembered that the largest gold hoard in the entire Viking world which weighed about 5 kilograms consisted of ten arm-rings and was found in 1802 at Hare Island, Lough Ree. It was melted down soon after discovery. P828. D. 2.2 cm. X4387. D. 2.5 cm. W193. D. 10.0 cm. 1994:23. D. 3.0 cm. 1902:110. D. 6.2 cm.

Armstrong 1920, 94, 95, 98.

[6:19] TWO ANNULAR BROOCHES, ARDAGH HOARD, REERASTA, CO. LIMERICK.

Ninth century AD.

The magnificent Ardagh hoard contained the celebrated silver chalice and a plain bronze chalice, a silver-gilt annular brooch (*bottom*), a pair of later silver-gilt annular brooches (one of which is the subject here) and a thistle brooch with gilt brambled terminals [5:25]. In one brooch (*top*) the ring is of silver and the terminals of ring and pin-head bears sunken diamond-shaped depressions to carry filigree insets. An amber stud survives in the corner of one of the terminals. The filigree panels have not survived. Most impressively, the margins of the terminals feature elongated open-work animals with hip joints highlighted in chiselled spirals. The joints of their counterparts on the tops of the terminals have brambled bosses. The animals on the margins of the terminals here are typical of the time and find many parallels, including those on a small silver brooch from Cahercommaun, Co. Clare. The second brooch (*bottom*) is broadly of Tara type. The ring is completely closed and the terminals are covered in panels of interlace with raised birds. The pinhead's decoration echoes that of the plate and contains an empty triangular and round setting. Only one stud survives on the terminal; it is of silver, hemispherical and has four glass inlays. 1874:102 and 1874:104. L. of pins 26.4 cm and 33.55 cm.

Ryan 1983, 51e and 51c.

[6:20] THE ROSCREA BROOCH, ROSCREA, CO. TIPPERARY.

Ninth century AD.

This annular brooch is of cast silver engraved with stylised animals and embellished with gold filigree panels and amber settings which combine to result in a well-proportioned and attractive brooch in the Irish tradition. The abundant use of plain silver and of amber in place of the more traditional glass or enamel for the settings, and the roughness of the filigree, suggest a date well into the Viking age, probably the later ninth century. The margins of the terminals and the pin-head are engraved with elongated animals, while outside them on the edges are conjoint D-shaped cells, alternatively featuring amber settings and crude gold filigree panels. The terminal and pin-head panels also bear crude filigree which has been seen as copying earlier, more sophisticated work, such as the raising of small bosses on the surface of the backing gold foil, simulating the way granules of gold used to be surrounded by rings of beaded wire.

Presumably, the replacement of glass by amber reflects the relative ease with which amber could be procured from the Baltic by the Vikings. The pin has flanged sides, back and front, and the point has incised chevrons. The elongated animals resemble those on the Killamery brooch [6:2]. P737. L. of pin 18.3 cm.

Ryan 1983, no. 62; Youngs (ed.) 1989, 79.

[6:21] SILVER PENANNULAR BROOCH, RATHLIN ISLAND, CO. ANTRIM.

Ninth century AD.

It has been suggested that this, probably ninth-century, silver brooch from Co. Antrim was made by the Vikings themselves, a possibility strengthened by its coming from a Viking cemetery at Rathlin Island. It is interesting in that, while it is of plain silver and of open-work design and the biting animals on the ring suggest affinities with the Killamery brooch [6:2], the overall approach of restoring the gap between the terminals is a feature of the probably contemporary bossed penannular brooches [6:10] which harks back to a more archaic Irish brooch tradition! The centre of the open-work terminals each has a plate (like that on the pin-head), surrounded by rings of beaded filigree. The open-work areas around these plates feature zoomorphic interlace in which the stippled bodies of the animals are outlined by engraved borders. The pin-head is barrel shaped with a central boss of spiral coils of beaded silver wire surrounded by bands of silver. R87 and IA/L/1963:3. D 12.3 cm.
Cone (ed.) 1977, 179.

❧

[6:22] WOODEN GAMING BOARD, BALLINDERRY, CO. WESTMEATH.

Tenth century AD

A fine example of one of several types of game board from the Viking Age, this one from the same crannóg in Co. Westmeath which produced the decorated sword [6:16] is thought to have been used with the pegged conical-shaped gaming pieces which frequently turn up in the Dublin and other town excavations, and were used in a game known as *hnefatafl*. The boards from the Dublin excavations tend to be more of simple draught-board design with some cancelled squares which were used with the variety of flat-based, domed or discoidal or conical gaming pieces of bone, antler, jet/lignite, stone and wood recovered from the excavations. The Ballinderry board is roughly square, has forty-nine holes, is of yew, and is ornamented with projecting heads as well as with eight panels of interlace and triangular fret ornament on its raised margin. Two panels have plain five-and six-strand interlace and two at opposing corners have ring-chain interlace of so-called Scandinavian *Borre* type. The latter used to be associated mainly with the Isle of Man, from where it was thought the board might have originated, but now, because this also occurs in Irish metalwork and on Dublin motif-pieces, it is thought more likely to have been made in Dublin or Limerick, the second most important Viking town in Ireland, Ballinderry being centred between both towns. 1932:6533. L. 24.9 cm; W. 24.3 cm.
Graham-Campbell 1980, 23.

❧

[6:23] CARVED CROOK (OR FINIAL), FISHAMBLE STREET, DUBLIN.

Early eleventh century AD.

This carved wooden crook was found in a building within a plot on an early eleventh-century level at Fishamble Street, Dublin. Its ornament conforms to what the late James Lang named the 'Dublin school' of the international *Ringerike* style, which was derived from Scandinavia to flourish in Dublin. In Dublin it appears in metalwork, as the trial- or motif-piece evidence indicates, as well as in the output of a remarkable school of wood carving, of which this is the supreme example. In Lang's words 'the Dublin style is primarily foliate, with tendrils, often in groups terminating in a volute. In some cases these tendrils serve as appendages to a head, either animal or human, but are none the less unmistakably vegetal'. He saw insular, including southern English, origins in terms of motif and especially in layout. It is possible that the crook was a whip handle. E172: 5587. L. 17.1 cm.

Wallace 1983, no. 73a; Lang 1988, 63–64.

❧

[6:24] CROSS OF CONG, CO. MAYO.

Early twelfth century AD.

This shrine from Co. Mayo, which was designed for processional use, was made towards the end of the first quarter of the twelfth century, to enshrine a relic of the True Cross that had been acquired in 1122 by Turlough O'Connor, High King of Ireland. In many ways, it may be regarded as both the last and one of the finest artistic efforts of our entire Early Christian period. The large rock crystal on the front, at the junction of the arms and shaft, was intended to protect the fragment of the Cross. It is set in a conical mount surrounded by a flange that is decorated with gold filigree, niello and blue and white glass bosses. The surfaces of the cross, apart from the area around the crystal and its mount, are divided into decorative panels made of cast openwork bronze plates with S-shaped Irish *Urnes* type, ribbon-animals intertwined with thread-like snakes, all fastened to an oak core. R2833. H. 76.5 cm.

Henry 1970, 74; Cone (ed.) 1977, no. 63.

❧

[6:25] SHRINE OF ST SENAN'S BELL, SCATTERY ISLAND, CO. CLARE.

Late eleventh and fourteenth centuries AD.

The bell shrine of St Senan of Scattery Island, Co. Clare, is known as the *Clogán Óir* 'Little Golden Bell'. The original bell is missing, but the two outer casings of the shrine survive, the most spectacular and complete being of the later eleventh century, the other being of the fourteenth century. The shrine was in the hands of descendants of its hereditary keepers until the early twentieth century. The inner bronze shrine was cast in two pieces: a body divided into four panels (of niello-bordered zoomorphic interlace) by a cross with expanded terminals which is outlined with an inlaid silver strip, and a curved top with a crest which was divided into triangles of interlace. The panels on the crest were once covered in gold foil. The shapes of the panels and their knots of snake-like animals have been compared to a trial piece from the Dublin excavations (6:3, left). 1919:1. H. 12.2 cm; W. 6.0 cm.

Ó Floinn 1983, no. 90a–b.

❧

[6:26] SHRINE OF ST PATRICK'S BELL, ARMAGH, CO. ARMAGH.

c. 1100 AD.

The Shrine of St Patrick's Bell was made about 1100 to preserve a much earlier, bronze-coated, iron bell, reputed to have belonged to the saint himself. The shrine was made when Domhnall, one of the Uí Lochlainn dynasty, was High King of Ireland. The openwork panels on the trapezoidal sides feature exquisite examples of *Urnes* ornament with characteristic large beasts interlaced with small ribbon-like snakes. This is covered with a silver-gilt frame which originally held thirty gold filigree panels in position. These panels are ordered in the shape of a ringed cross. Two of the four quarters of the space made by the cross feature distinctive figure-of-eight animals in gold filigree of a most complex type — beaded bronze wire overlaid with plain wire and a layer of beaded gold wire, all set in gold foil sheets bordered by beaded gold wire. The plainer silver backplate features a series of openwork interlocked crosses which reveal a bronze background and an inscription running around the margins. The inscription on the margins of the backplate tells us that it was made by Condulig Ua hInmainen and his sons for Domhnall Ua Lochlainn (King of Ireland, 1094-1121). Domhnall MacAmhalgadha was then bishop of Armagh, and Cathalan Ua Maelchallain was the 'keeper of the bell', a position his family was to retain until the end of the eighteenth century. R4011. H. 26.7 cm, base 15.5 cm.
Ó Floinn 1983, no. 79b.

❧

[6:27] *SOISCÉAL MOLAISE* SHRINE, DEVENISH, CO. FERMANAGH.

Early eleventh century AD.

This box, believed to be the oldest of the eight surviving Irish book shrines, was made to enshrine the gospels of St Molaise of Devenish, Co. Fermanagh. It is now almost all of early eleventh-century construction. The shrine was acquired from the O'Meehans, its hereditary keepers. The front face (shown here) is laid out as a ringed cross with rectangular terminals, with panels of gold filigree and gilt silver framed by the silver grille of the cross device. The figures represented in the panels are symbols of the four Evangelists, whose names appear in Latin on the margins. R4006. H. 14.75 cm; W. 11.70 cm.
Ó Floinn 1983, no. 75.

❧

[6:28] SHRINE OF THE *CATHACH*, SIDE PANEL, KELLS, CO. MEATH.

Late eleventh century AD.

The *Cathach* ('battler') from Co. Meath was the battle standard of the O'Donnells, the manuscript it contained having been thought to have been compiled by St Columcille (the patron and distant kinsman of the family) himself. The shrine was hinged to allow access to the relic and was made between 1072 and 1098 but embellished in the later middle ages. It does have eleventh-century side panels in cast metal which consist of a typical *Ringerike* animal ornament, made by a craftsman with the Scandinavian-derived name of Sitric. While the *Cathach* was almost certainly made at the Columban monastery of Kells, the name of the maker probably betrays his origin and where he learned his trade, which must surely have been Dublin. Conveniently enough, there is a motif-piece from the Dublin excavations [6:5] which appears to be a 'dead ringer' for the panel. R2835. W 25.1 cm.
Mahr and Raftery 1932–41, 155 and pls 113–14; Cone (ed.) 1977, 188.

❧

[6:29] Shrine of the Stowe Missal (detail of side), Lorrha, Co. Tipperary.

Early eleventh century AD.

This shrine once contained an eighth-century Latin mass-book, which was thought to have been compiled at the monastery of Lorrha, Co. Tipperary, near where it was discovered, sealed up in the walls of Lackeen Castle. It is called the Stowe Missal because it was formerly kept at Stowe House, Buckinghamshire, England.

The shrine, which is made of wood and covered with metal plates, is mainly of the mid-eleventh century, but it was severely embellished in the fourteenth century when an entire face was redesigned with the addition of a cross jewelled with rock crystals, glass studs and an ivory bead. Plates of gilt silver show the Crucifixion and other scenes. This side of the shrine shows a bearded figure holding a Viking sword between a pair of animals. 1883:614a. H. 18.7 cm, W. 15.8 cm.

Ó Floinn 1983, no. 76.

[6:30] *Breac Maodhóg* **Shrine (details), Drumlane, Co. Cavan.**

Eleventh/twelfth century AD.

This house-shaped shrine from Drumlane, Co. Cavan, of which the O'Farrellys were the traditional keepers, dates to the eleventh/twelfth century. It is of particular importance due to the applied panels with well-observed, relief figures, as well as details of ecclesiastical and social historical interest. These details from the plaque on the side of the shrine show a series of clerics whose tunics are clearly delineated. A late-medieval leather satchel for this shrine is also on display at the National Museum. P1022. H. 30.5 cm; W. 12.7 cm.

Henry 1970, 117, 119.

[6:31] Clonmacnoise Crozier, Clonmacnoise, Co. Offaly.

Eleventh century AD.

Traditionally associated with the abbots of Clonmacnoise, Co. Offaly, the crozier consists of a crook and two tubular lengths of sheet bronze wrapped around a wooden staff, with three biconical spacer knops. Mainly of the eleventh century, with some fifteenth-century refurbishment, it is especially notable for the wonderfully bold snake-like animals in figure-of-eight arrangements, executed in inlaid silver and outlined with niello decoration on both faces of the bronze crook, and for the animals in the cast open-work ring under the topmost knop. The crook was cast in one piece with an open-work crest comprising a procession of gripping dogs on top. (The figure of a mitred bishop slaying a monster with his crozier is late medieval.)

The animal ornament on the sides of the crook is a version of the mid-eleventh-century international style known as *Ringerike*. The discovery of similar designs among the Dublin motif-pieces suggests that items such as this could have been made in Dublin. R2988. L. 97.1 cm.

Ó Floinn 1983, no. 77.

[6:32] LISMORE CROZIER, LISMORE, CO. WATERFORD.

c. 1100 AD.

This crozier from Co. Waterford which contains a wooden staff, was made about 1100 and was found in 1814 in a blocked-up doorway at Lismore Castle. The name of the smith who made the crozier and the bishop of Lismore who commissioned it are inscribed on a strip under the crook. The crook was cast in one piece and is hollow, except for a small box-shaped reliquary inserted through a side in the drop. Typically, the crozier also has slightly decorated upper and middle knops, as well as a lower knop cast in one piece with the ferrule. The border around the (now missing) front of the drop consists of panels of zoomorphic interlace which were originally covered in gold foil and separated by rectangular panels of blue and white millefiori glass in chequerboard arrangements. Distinctive blue glass beads with red and white millefiori insets are set between the sunken panels at the sides of the crook. The crest consists of three animals linked in open-work *Urnes* style interlace. L1949:1. L.116 cm.

Ó Floinn 1983, no. 81.

[6:7]

RECONSTRUCTION OF DUBLIN.

c. 1000 AD.

[6:8]

SELECTION OF ARTEFACTS FROM THE DUBLIN EXCAVATIONS.

Tenth and eleventh centuries AD.

[6:9] *facing page*

Selection of silver ornaments.

Tenth and eleventh centuries AD.

[6:10]

Silver bossed penannular brooch, Ballyspellan, Co. Kilkenny.

c. 900 AD.

[6:11]

BOSSED PENANNULAR AND THISTLE BROOCHES.

Late ninth/early tenth century AD.

[6:12]

THISTLE BROOCH, CELBRIDGE, CO. KILDARE.

Late ninth/early tenth century AD.

[6:13]

DETAIL OF HEAD: KITE-BROOCH, NEAR LIMERICK.

Early tenth century AD.

[6:14]

DETAIL OF HEAD: KITE-BROOCH, UNLOCALISED.

Late ninth/early tenth century AD.

[6:15]

HIBERNO-NORSE SILVER ARM-RINGS, IRELAND.

Late ninth/early tenth century AD.

[6:16] *facing page*

THE BALLINDERRY SWORD, BALLINDERRY, CO. WESTMEATH.

Ninth century AD.

[6:17]
Decorated lead weights, Islandbridge, Dublin.
c. 900 AD.

[6:18]
Gold ornaments: Ardtrea, Co. Tyrone; unlocalised; Rathedan, Co. Carlow;
Wicklow, Co. Wicklow and Edenvale Caves, Co. Clare.
Late tenth/early eleventh century AD.

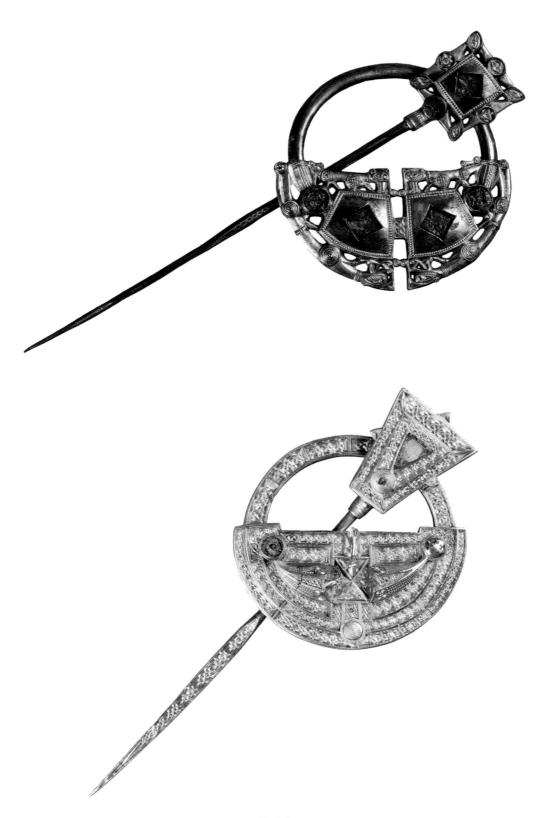

[6:19]
TWO ANNULAR BROOCHES, ARDAGH HOARD, REERASTA, CO. LIMERICK.
Ninth century AD.

[6:20]

THE ROSCREA BROOCH, ROSCREA, CO. TIPPERARY.

Ninth century AD.

[6:21]
SILVER PENANNULAR BROOCH, RATHLIN ISLAND, CO. ANTRIM.
Ninth century AD.

[6:23]

CARVED CROOK (OR FINIAL), FISHAMBLE STREET, DUBLIN.

Early eleventh century AD.

[6:24]

CROSS OF CONG, CO. MAYO.

Early twelfth century AD.

[6:22] *facing page*

WOODEN GAMING BOARD, BALLINDERRY, CO. WESTMEATH.

Tenth century AD.

[6:25]
SHRINE OF ST SENAN'S BELL, SCATTERY ISLAND, CO. CLARE.
Late eleventh and fourteenth centuries AD.

[6:26]
SHRINE OF ST PATRICK'S BELL, ARMAGH, CO. ARMAGH.
c. 1100 AD.

[6:27] *facing page*
SOISCÉAL MOLAISE SHRINE, DEVENISH, CO. FERMANAGH.
Early eleventh century AD.

[6:28]

SHRINE OF THE *CATHACH*, SIDE PANEL, KELLS, CO. MEATH.

Late eleventh century AD.

[6:29] SHRINE OF THE STOWE MISSAL (DETAIL OF SIDE), LORRHA, CO. TIPPERARY.

Early eleventh century AD.

[6:30]

Breac Maodhóg Shrine (details), Drumlane, Co. Cavan.

Eleventh/twelfth century AD.

[6:31]

CLONMACNOISE CROZIER, CLONMACNOISE, CO. OFFALY.

Eleventh century AD.

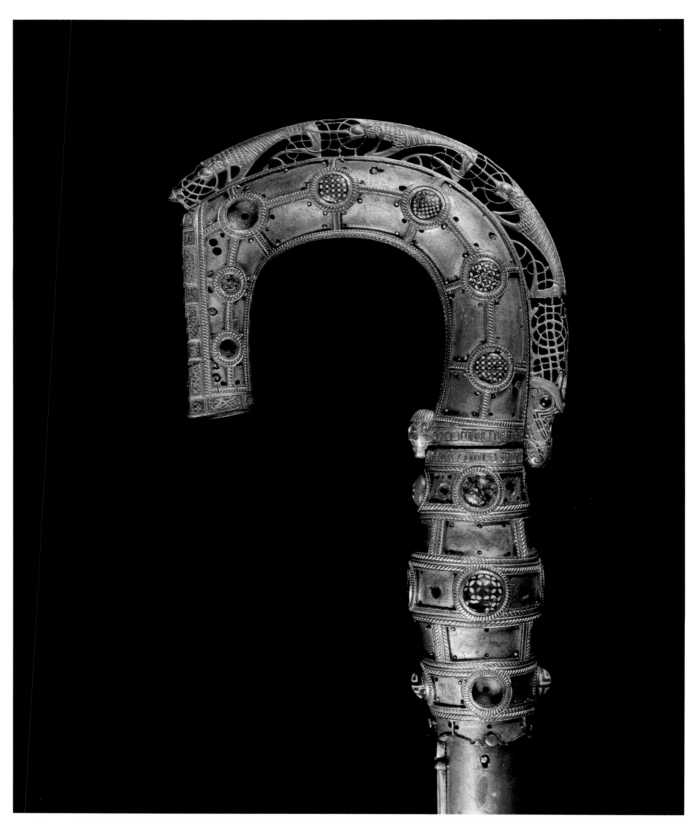

[6:32]
LISMORE CROZIER, LISMORE, CO. WATERFORD.
c. 1100 AD.

7

LATER MEDIEVAL IRELAND

AD 1150–1550

RAGHNALL Ó FLOINN

In the mid-twelfth century, Ireland was to a great extent culturally and ethnically homogenous, with the exception of a small, but economically powerful, Hiberno-Norse population based in and around the main port towns of Dublin, Waterford, Wexford, Limerick and Cork. The archaeological evidence and historical sources suggest that in the course of the eleventh and twelfth centuries these towns engaged in increasing foreign trade, especially with the English ports of Chester and Bristol and further afield with Continental ports such as Rouen. As a result, the importation of English and Continental influences and luxury goods had an increasing effect on Irish craftsmanship and taste.

The Irish Church was also looking outwards. In common with other parts of Europe it was undergoing a process of re-organisation and reform designed to bring it in line with Church practices elsewhere in the Christian West [7:1]. Supporters of the reform movement included most of the prominent kings and dynasts of the day who promoted the new territorially-based diocesan structure for their own political ambitions. These new dioceses required church-building on an unprecedented scale, as did the foreign monastic orders (most notably the Cistercians) which were introduced as part of the same reform process. Outward-looking patrons and churchmen introduced building and sculpture in the Romanesque, and later the Gothic, style to cater for the new liturgical practices required under the reforms. New liturgical texts and novel forms of liturgical vessels and vestments were required and it would appear that most of these were, of necessity, imported [7:6].

[7:1]
SEAL OF THE CATHEDRAL
CHAPTER OF LEIGHLIN,
CO. CARLOW.
Thirteenth century AD.

[7:2]
FORGED SEAL MATRIX OF
HENRY II, IRELAND.
c. AD 1200.

Political instability in Ireland led one provincial Irish king, Diarmait Mac Murchada, the expelled King of Leinster, to recruit knights and adventurers to reclaim his kingdom. The latter, drawn from Anglo-Norman warrior lords in south-western England and south Wales, proved so successful militarily in Ireland that the English King, Henry II, was drawn into Irish affairs in 1171 to curb their growing power [7:2]. Ireland thus came to be ruled by English kings.

This English colonisation accelerated the momentum of change already in progress. It brought in its wake a wave of English and Welsh aristocrats, retainers and churchmen who were responsible for the importation of goods on a scale hitherto unknown and for the introduction of foreign, notably English, craftsmen who catered for the new market. This influence is particularly evident in relation to architecture where the hand of English (specifically West Country) master masons can be detected in many Irish buildings, especially the Gothic cathedrals of the thirteenth century. This is hardly surprising considering that many leading churchmen and patrons in the centuries after the Anglo-Norman incursion were themselves English-born.

The settlement was so successful that by the end of the thirteenth century over two-thirds of the country was in the hands of the English colonists. After 1300, however, the colony was in decline and the succeeding centuries saw a revival of the fortunes of Irish kings and nobles. For the first time in recorded history, a significant minority of the country's population was of non-Irish birth and practised a radically new lifestyle. English lords founded many new towns and manorial villages populated by tenants brought from Britain and beyond. They also established a new agricultural economy and, in a period of economic boom, the thirteenth century saw the Irish landscape transformed on an unprecedented scale with monumental church and castle building and the widespread foundation of towns.

It is now increasingly evident that the concept of two conflicting cultural monoliths — the so-called 'two-nation' theory, whereby late-medieval Ireland is regarded as having been divided culturally between 'Anglo-Irish/English' and '(Gaelic) Irish' — is no longer a valid model. Cultural exchange and indeed fusion did occur and problems of identity existed from the outset. Gerald of Wales, chronicler of the first wave of English colonists put it thus: 'to the English we are Irish and to the Irish we are English'. The history of later medieval Ireland is one of a complex series of interactions and conflicts — military, political and cultural — which did not always run along neat ethnic lines.

This is reflected in the study of the material culture of the period. One of the chief difficulties is to determine what is of local production, what is imported and what made in the country by foreign craftsmen. Initially, much was undoubtedly imported from England or from further afield. The small hoard of silver drinking vessels hidden in the churchyard at Taghmon, Co. Westmeath, may once have graced the table of a wealthy Anglo-Norman household [7:7]. Made in southern England or Germany in the late twelfth century, they are of a type known throughout Western Europe and are testimony to the growth of international trade which blurred stylistic differences between regions and led to an increasing Europeanisation of material goods, especially among the wealthy.

[7:3]
GOLD FINGER RING,
CASTLETOWN MOUNT,
CO. LOUTH.
*Twelfth or thirteenth
centuries AD.*

Throughout history, items of secular and altar plate and jewellery were regarded as an investment which could be cashed in as the need arose. Given the prized nature of the raw materials used, much of it would have been melted down or recycled. Only the smallest pieces of jewellery have survived through casual loss. The quantity of jewellery of the period found in Ireland is modest and few pieces are exceptional, reflecting the fact that later medieval Ireland was not particularly wealthy by comparison with countries such as England or France. The surviving jewellery consists in the main of ring brooches and finger rings [7:3, 7:8]. Made of gold and silver, set with precious or semi-precious stones, many of these can be paralleled in collections across northern Europe, from England to Scandinavia, and are probably the products of goldsmiths' workshops of metropolitan centres such as London and Paris. A particular characteristic of Irish fifteenth-century silverwork is the use of filigree wire in various combinations. This can be seen on a group of silver jewelled pendant crosses and reliquaries which use twisted and beaded silver wires, combined with silver granules and settings of glass or semi-precious stone [7:4, 7:9].

[7:4]
SILVER RELIQUARY, UNLOCALISED.
Fifteenth century AD.

Irish kings and nobles adopted the trappings of courtly power found throughout medieval Europe. Seals designed to authenticate written documents were first used by Irish kings in the mid-twelfth century, employing designs copied from contemporary English seals. Their Latin inscriptions carry the names of their owners while equestrian figures or heraldic beasts were used to emphasise their aristocratic rank [7:10]. Noblemen fought on horseback and the knight or mounted horseman was symbolic of the ideal warrior, although Irish and English styles of warfare differed. The precise function of the sadly mutilated figure of a mounted knight from Knocknaman, Co. Offaly, is unknown, but as it is carved in the round it may have decorated an elaborate free-standing monument [7:11]. The dispersed nature of Irish settlement and the rugged landscape dictated that warfare in medieval Ireland would be conducted in a different fashion to that prevailing elsewhere in Europe. Pitched battles were relatively uncommon while running skirmishes in which speed and mobility were essential were the norm. While the weapons and armour used often appeared old-fashioned to outsiders, they were better adapted to Irish conditions and some are characteristically Irish. The most distinctive of these is a group of swords with open ring pommels [7:5]. Irish lords also made use of mercenaries brought in from western Scotland from the thirteenth century onwards. These 'gallowglass' (foreign soldiers) of mixed Gaelic and Viking descent from western Scotland, were heavily armed footsoldiers, much feared by the English. Their weapons included a form of iron axe derived from late Viking types, some examples of which are inlaid with geometric designs in silver. Similar axeheads are depicted on Scottish West-Highland carvings where they are shown mounted on long shafts [7:12].

The only secular piece of metalwork to have survived the medieval period in Ireland is associated with a great Irish family. This is the Kavanagh 'Charter' Horn, preserved at Borris, Co. Carlow, since late medieval times [7:13]. It was so called because it symbolised the MacMurrough-Kavanagh family's claim to the kingship of Leinster. It consists of a carved elephant-ivory tusk held in a brass stand. These late mounts mask the presence of earlier mountings indicating that it was a valued heirloom. The craftsman Tighearnan O'Lavan who inscribed his name on the rim may well have been belonged to a family of hereditary artisans of the Kavanaghs.

Music and poetry were important aspects of courtly life and both Irish and English lords kept retinues of poets and musicians. Some commissioned the gathering together of poems, historical texts and family genealogies in 'great books' which today are one of our primary sources for medieval literature, especially in Irish [7: 14, 7:15]. The playing of board games was another popular lordly pursuit throughout the Middle Ages, the most common being 'tables' (a form of backgammon) and chess. The game of chess was introduced into Europe in the eleventh century from the Middle East. Early sets copied the shapes of Arab chess-pieces but soon figured

[7:5]
IRON SWORD,
TULLYLOUGH,
CO. LONGFORD.
Sixteenth century AD.

examples, representing European courtly life, like the figure of a queen from Co. Meath, were being made [7:16]. This finds its closest parallels among the ivory chess-pieces from Lewis in Scotland, now regarded as being of Norwegian manufacture. Irish and English nobles also maintained great tables and the provision of food, entertainment and hospitality were important means of binding lords and their vassals. Imported tableware of bronze, silver and glass was used along with humbler vessels of wood [7:7, 7:17, 7:18].

One of the distinguishing features of early medieval Ireland was the relatively high social status accorded to craftsmen. This is reflected in two ways: the many references to the deaths of named craftsmen in the Irish chronicles and the fact that it was not unusual for metalworkers and sculptors to sign their work. In areas under Irish control, there is evidence for continuity into late medieval times in the way craftsmen and artisans practised. Like the poets, historians and lawyers, many belonged to families who specialised in a particular craft.

A change can be detected, however, in the later medieval period in that craftsmen (as with the other professions) no longer appear to be based in monastic workshops but were increasingly based in the towns or, in rural areas, attached to particular secular lords. It would appear that by the thirteenth century at the latest, goldsmiths in Ireland, as elsewhere in Europe, were concentrated in towns. Little can be said of how work was commissioned or whether goldsmiths were settled or itinerant, although it is plausible to compare them with poets, who held land, but who travelled from one lordly court to another.

The Church was the greatest patron of goldsmiths during the Middle Ages: every major church and cathedral would have been richly furnished and would have had its own collection of sacred relics enclosed in lavish shrines of gold, silver and precious stones. As with secular plate, examples of Irish medieval goldsmiths' work destined for the Church are rare. The need to recycle precious metals, along with theft and natural disasters, also contributed to the loss of valuable items. For example, in July 1461, the east window of Christ Church Cathedral, Dublin, was blown in by a storm 'and the falling stones broke many chests containing jewels, relics, ornaments and vestments of the altar'. The effects of the Reformation confiscations were devastating and included the destruction of many works of art as with the public burning in Dublin in 1541 of the Staff of Jesus — a relic of St Patrick which was the most venerated relic in Ireland and a prized possession of Christ Church Cathedral [7:19, 7:20].

An early sixteenth-century inventory of the Treasury in Christ Church Cathedral, Dublin, shows just how much has been lost. The list includes, in addition to the Staff of Jesus, a miracle-working cross known as the 'Speaking Crucifix', a marble altar belonging to St Patrick, as well as relics of other Irish saints, including those of Laurence O'Toole, St Brendan and St Brigid. Non-Irish relics included a portion of the True Cross, the Cross and Chain of St Peter, as well as fragments of the Holy Sepulchre. Parts of sacred vestments were also enshrined including those of St Olaf of Norway and St Herbert of Cologne. Relics of the Anglo-Saxon saints Oswald, Wulfstan and Edward the Confessor were obtained, as were those of St Catherine of Alexandria, a popular saint in medieval Ireland whose cult was promoted by the Anglo-Normans.

Much of the church metalwork which survives comes not from the towns but from smaller churches in areas outside English control. It consists of additions or repairs to earlier reliquaries of Irish saints [7:21–27, 7:33]. These were preserved in the hands of successive generations of hereditary keepers who were often descended from the administrators of church property. Throughout their existence, such objects were continually used to effect cures, witness contracts and be touched by the faithful. Consequently they were subject to considerable wear and needed regular repair. One of the finest is a shrine known as the *Domhnach Airgid* [7:24]. Originally made *c.* AD 800 to contain relics given by St Patrick to Macartan, patron saint of Clones, Co. Monaghan, it was completely remodelled around 1350 for the abbot of Clones, John O Carbry. It is decorated with cast and gilt silver plaques bearing figures of saints and apostles. The relief casting of the *Domhnach Airgid* shrine is unusual — most work on shrines appears to be either engraved or stamped on thin sheets of silver using metal dies. The *Domhnach Airgid* bears the name of the craftsman who made it, John O Bardan, and it was probably made in Drogheda where a goldsmith of the same name is known to have lived.

DETAIL OF [7:24] *DOMHNACH AIRGID* SHRINE, CLONES, CO. MONAGHAN. *c. AD 1350.*

The survival rate of pieces of medieval goldsmiths' work is so low that only occasionally can the hand of the same craftsman be seen on more than one piece. A rare example is visible on panels on the Shrine of St Patrick's Tooth and the Shrine of the Stowe Missal [7:26 (*top left*), 7:27]. Both date to the 1370s and were made for patrons based at Athenry, Co. Galway and Lorrha, Co. Tipperary, respectively, locations which are situated only some 50 km apart. The techniques employed on both are very similar. In particular, both carry panels of parcel-gilt sheet silver engraved with human figures against a rock-traced background, the engraved lines being emphasised by a niello inlay (a black metal paste). One of the principal differences between the two objects is that the inscription on the Athenry reliquary is in Latin while that on the Lorrha shrine is in Irish, probably reflecting the different backgrounds — Anglo-Irish and Irish — of the patrons, respectively Thomas de Bermingham, Lord of Athenry and Philip O'Kennedy, king of Ormond.

Women appear for the first time as patrons of the arts in the late Middle Ages. One of the most celebrated was Margaret O'Carroll, daughter of a provincial Irish king, who was a patroness of poets and who also, according to her death notice of 1451 provided 'books, chalices and all articles useful for the service of the church'. Women's names appear increasingly alongside those of their husbands on metalwork inscriptions. The Shrine of the Stowe Missal was redecorated by Philip O Kennedy, king of Ormond and his wife Áine sometime between 1371 and 1381 [7:27]. Other donations by husbands and wives to their family foundations include a silver-gilt processional cross given by Cornelius O'Conor and Avlina (Eileen), daughter of the Knight of Kerry, to Lislaghtin Franciscan Friary, Co. Kerry, in 1479. When Avlina died in 1526 she was described as 'a good, charitable and humane woman' [7:28].

Many of the liturgical objects required for use in church services were imported. Churches who could not afford to commission their own pieces could procure such objects from workshops set up to cater for the increased demand for church furnishings. Enamel was the only means of applying permanent colour to metal and it was used on copper to produce metal objects of great beauty. The enamel industry of Limoges in south-western France dominated the

DETAIL OF [7:28]
GILT SILVER
PROCESSIONAL CROSS,
BALLYMACASEY,
CO. KERRY.
Dated 1479.

European market in the twelfth and thirteenth centuries, producing a wide range of objects including croziers, altar vessels, book covers and gabled shrines in huge quantities [7:6, 7:29].

Ivory was highly prized for its rarity and its rich colour and because it could be easily carved. Two sources were used: walrus and elephant tusks. Ivory workshops located principally in Paris and the surrounding region produced large quantities of carvings including diptychs (two-leafed devotional images) for export during the thirteenth and fourteenth centuries. The most popular images included scenes from the Infancy and Passion of Christ as well as the Life of the Virgin [7:30, 7:31]. Devotional plaques and altar crosses of cast and gilt bronze or brass decorated with symbols of the Evangelists and elaborate foliate borders were imported from England in the fifteenth century and some were copied by Irish craftsmen [7:32].

Given the origins of most of the Anglo-Norman colonists and their successors, it is natural to look to England when studying the visual arts in later medieval Ireland since it is from there that the strongest impulses came. This has led to direct comparisons being made between the two, which marks Ireland out unfavourably. Such comparisons, however, obscure a number of fundamental differences. The first is one of scale. Ireland never had the resources or population density, apart perhaps for a brief period in the first century or so of the Anglo-Norman colony, to undertake building projects on a large scale. The failure of the English crown to establish control over much of the newly colonised lands meant that royal patronage was almost non-existent and therefore no 'court style' emerged. Dublin, the seat of royal government, never became a metropolis on the scale of London or Paris, capable of developing its own specialist workshops to rival the quality of imported goods or expertise. The second difference is one of culture. Only a very small part of the country within the Anglo-Norman colony could be regarded as reflecting English cultural values and aspirations, and only then for a short period in the thirteenth and early fourteenth century. The adaptation of English fashions to Irish taste, social organisation and patterns of patronage is what made late medieval Irish art and architecture distinctive.

The late Middle Ages was a period characterised by increasing external influences in Ireland. It was the age of cathedrals, monasteries and castles; of the colonisation of Ireland by English settlers; of the foundation of most of our towns and a period during which a multi-cultural and multi-ethnic society emerged. The medieval period in Ireland may be said to have come to an end with the Reformation and with the increasing power of the English monarch in Irish affairs through the establishment of Henry VIII as Lord of Ireland. In this way, the later Middle Ages set the pattern and pace of events for the succeeding 500 years of Irish history.

ILLUSTRATIONS

[7:1] SEAL OF THE CATHEDRAL CHAPTER OF LEIGHLIN, CO. CARLOW.

Thirteenth century AD.

Found in a bog near Clara Castle, Co. Kilkenny. This magnificently-cut seal die in bronze shows two figures standing under round-headed architectural niches. On the left is St John the Baptist clothed in a cloak of camel hair and pointing to the Lamb of God; while on the right is a figure of a bishop clothed in ecclesiastical vestments and with a pointed mitre on his head. He holds a crook-headed crozier of early-medieval Irish type in one hand. He may be St Molaise, the patron saint of the diocese of Leighlin. R3057. D. 5.23 cm.

Armstrong 1913, 70.

[7:2] FORGED SEAL MATRIX OF HENRY II, IRELAND.

c. AD 1200.

This seal matrix formed part of the collection of the antiquarian George Petrie and was said to have been found in Ireland. Made of lead, it shows the king enthroned, holding a sword in one hand and an orb, topped by a bird, in the other. This is almost certainly a contemporary forgery of the king's great seal, used perhaps by an Irish monastic house for sealing false charters. X4632. D. 10.0 cm.

Armstrong 1913, 108–109.

[7:3] GOLD FINGER RING, CASTLETOWN MOUNT, CO. LOUTH.

Twelfth or thirteenth century AD.

This tiered filigreed ring with diamond-shaped bezel belonged to someone of the highest rank. Its sunken cells were originally set with red glass and its value was enhanced by being set with an antique gem of red stone showing a running hare. Castletown Mount was the headquarters of the de Veduns, the pre-eminent Anglo-Norman family of Co. Louth. 1984:153. L. 4.13 cm.

Unpublished.

[7:4] SILVER RELIQUARY, UNLOCALISED.

Fifteenth century AD.

The T-shaped (or tau) form of this cross indicates it was designed to protect the wearer from a disease known as St Anthony's Fire, whose symptoms included a burning sensation. It contains a cavity at the back to hold relics or some herbal compound. '35'. H. 7.1 cm.

Unpublished.

[7:5] IRON SWORD, TULLYLOUGH, CO. LONGFORD.

Sixteenth century AD.

This magnificent sword has a slender parallel-sided blade with an acute point. The cross-guard ends in long fan-shaped terminals and the hilt is topped by an open ring-shaped pommel. Like the majority of medieval swords, the blade is probably an import from a Continental swordsmith's workshop while the handle fitting would have been added in Ireland. The distinctive ring pommel is shown in a number of sixteenth-century illustrations of Irish warriors, including a drawing dated 1521 by the German artist Albrecht Dürer. (A&I) 1905:39. L. 97.9 cm.

Halpin 1986, no. 31.

[7:6] ENAMELLED CROZIER HEAD, CASHEL CATHEDRAL, CO. TIPPERARY.

Mid-thirteenth century AD.

Found in a tomb in Cashel Cathedral, Co. Tipperary. The curved crook takes the form of a coiled serpent, its scaled body indicated in blue enamel. This encloses the figure of the Archangel Michael (his wings are missing) and the Dragon, symbolising the struggle of good against evil. Made in Limoges, France, spiral-headed croziers such as this one came into Ireland in the twelfth century. It was probably buried with one of the thirteenth-century bishops of Cashel. P1020. H. 34.7 cm.

Mahr and Raftery 1932–41, 166 and pl. 100.

[7:7] TWO SILVER BOWLS, TAGHMON, CO. WESTMEATH.

Late twelfth century AD.

These shallow, round-bodied bowls are of hammered and engraved silver. Found together with a third (now in the British Museum), they are drinking vessels imported from southern England or Germany. The larger has a central floral pattern with a fluted body. The inside of its bowl is further decorated with pairs of vine leaves, their stems held together by a link. The smaller has a low foot and is decorated with an engraved pattern of a winged dragon which is partly gilt. The central raised roundel inside the smaller bowl is decorated with a two-legged dragon with outstretched wings and spiral tail which ends in the form of a vine leaf. The use of the vine motif on both vessels suggests they were used for drinking wine. (A&I) 1901:115–116. D. 17.0 cm and 12.7 cm.

Mahr and Raftery 1932–41, 143 and pl. 42.

[7:8] GOLD RING BROOCHES: BALLINREA, CO. CORK (*TOP*),
UNLOCALISED (*CENTRE*) AND MARLBOROUGH ST, DUBLIN (*BOTTOM*).

Thirteenth or fourteenth century AD.

Such brooches were used both by men and women to fasten gowns at the neck. The projecting clasped hands symbolised giving. Gifts of jewellery were popular as tokens of affection. The centre brooch is inscribed in Norman French (the language of medieval courtly love) +PAR+AMVR+FIN+SVI DVNE 'I am a gift of fine love'. 1956:7; W86; 1897:26. L. 2.5 cm; D. 2.66 cm; D. 2.9 cm.

Deevy 1998, nos 121, 86, 110.

[7:9] SILVER CROSS PENDANT, CALLAN, CO. KILKENNY.

c. AD 1500.

Found in an old church near Callan, Co. Kilkenny. Made of silver, gilt, the front is set with blue glass and garnet settings surrounded by filigree wires. The back of the cross is engraved with an image of the Crucifixion surrounded by the symbols of the four Evangelists. It is provided with a loop for a chain and would have been worn around the neck. R1427. L. 7.13 cm.

Unpublished.

❧

[7:10] SILVER SEAL MATRICES OF IRISH KINGS AND NOBLES, UNLOCALISED.

Fourteenth century AD.

Seals of kings and aristocrats show mounted knights while those of minor noblemen carry coats of arms or other heraldic symbols. *Clockwise from top left:* Domhnall MacCarthy, King of Desmond (*c.* 1302-6); Macon MacNamara, Lord of Uí Caissén; Brian O Brien and Maurice O Donnell. P1051; R5048; R5046; P1056. D. 2.46 cm; 3.05 cm; 1.84 cm; 3.15 cm.

Armstrong 1913, 11–12, 22–3.

❧

[7:11] FIGURE OF A HORSEMAN, KNOCKNAMAN HILL, CO. OFFALY.

Thirteenth century AD.

Found in 1844 in an enclosure at Knocknaman Hill near Kinnitty, Co. Offaly. This limestone figure (damaged in a fire in the 1920s) is a rare early example of a piece of freestanding figure sculpture with a secular subject. The rider is clad in a long pleated surcoat belted at the waist. He holds reins in his hands. The sword projecting behind identifies him as a warrior, while the high curved saddle and the presence of stirrups suggests that he is an English knight. 1947: 1054. L. 39.2 cm.

Cooke 1875, 153–4.

❧

[7:12] TWO SILVER-INLAID IRON AXEHEADS, BALLINA, CO. MAYO AND CO. DONEGAL.

Thirteenth century AD.

Axes were used instead of swords by many Irish and 'gallowglass' warriors. These broad-bladed battle-axes were developed from late Viking types. Some have inlaid silver decoration which was another Viking tradition. These highly-decorated examples were probably used as status symbols rather than in combat. 1936:1879; 1937:3633. L. of largest, 17.5 cm.

Mahr 1938.

❧

[7:13] THE KAVANAGH 'CHARTER' HORN, BORRIS, CO. CARLOW.

Twelfth century AD with fifteenth-century AD metal mounts.

Preserved at Borris, Co. Carlow by the Kavanagh family. This ceremonial drinking horn, a symbol of the kingship of Leinster, is the only piece of Irish regalia to have survived the Middle Ages. It is made from elephant ivory, an exotic material in medieval Ireland. The brass mounting, inscribed with the name of its maker, Tigernan O Lavan, ends in clawed bird's feet. 1976:2. H. 42.0 cm.

Ó Floinn 1983, no. 89.

❧

[7:14] COVER OF THE *GREAT BOOK OF LECAN*, CO. SLIGO.

Fifteenth century AD.

The *Great Book of Lecan* is one of the most important medieval Irish manuscripts to have survived. It contains genealogies, saints' lives as well as historical and biblical material. It was compiled by Giolla Íosa Mór Mac Fir Bhisigh, a member of the foremost family of historians in medieval Ireland. The manuscript is preserved in the Library of the Royal Irish Academy. The binding is a rare survival and consists of a decorative stamped leather binding with embossed metal mountings. W138. H. 33.5 cm.
Unpublished.

[7:15] WHALEBONE BOOK COVER, DONABATE, CO. DUBLIN.

Sixteenth century AD.

This is recorded as having been found in the parish of Donabate, near Swords, Co. Dublin. The cover bears the coat of arms of the Fitzgerald Earls of Desmond and is decorated with the figure of a mounted knight as well as a group of men engaged in a sword dance. Records such as these are evidence of the popularity of courtly music and dance. X4588. H. 48.8 cm.
Wilde 1861, 319–21.

[7:16] IVORY CHESS-PIECE, CO. MEATH.

Late twelfth century AD.

Found with several others in a bog in Co. Meath. Ivory from walrus tusks was used as a substitute for elephant ivory in northern Europe during the Romanesque period. The figure is that of a queen, seated on a throne. Her left hand (supported by the right) is raised to her cheek in a gesture of surprise or thoughtfulness. It is closely modelled on chess-pieces from the Isle of Lewis, Scotland, which are regarded as of Norwegian origin. P1041. H. 7.25 cm.
Ó Floinn 1983, no. 91.

[7:17] POTTERY 'KNIGHT' JUG, HIGH STREET, DUBLIN.

Thirteenth century AD.

Found in excavations at High St, Dublin. This elaborate green glazed wine-jug was made in the pottery kilns of Redcliffe, near Bristol, in England. The body is decorated with plant-scrolls and around the rim are figures of armed knights and monkeys. It is provided with three spouts, one of which is in the shape of a mask. Complete vessels such as this are rarely found and this example survived having been thrown into a timber-lined rubbish pit. E71:11401. H. 33.5 cm.
National Museum of Ireland 1973, no. 118.

[7:18] WOODEN METHER, UNLOCALISED.

Fourteenth to sixteenth century AD.

Made of sycamore, this is a form of drinking vessel unique to Ireland known as a mether. Methers can have two or four handles and were designed to be passed around the table. The raised lip at each corner helped prevent spills. Although individual examples are hard to date, a mether with jewelled silver mounts, dated 1493 and made for a Maguire lord of Fermanagh, confirms their medieval date. W68. H. 13.0 cm.
Wilde 1857, 217.

[7:19] WOODEN STATUE OF ST JOHN THE BAPTIST, FETHARD, CO. TIPPERARY.

Late fifteenth century AD.

Part of a group of three wooden statues from Fethard, Co. Tipperary, of which this figure is the earliest. It is carved from a solid piece of oak. This tall, gaunt figure, is identified as John the Baptist; he is naked except for his cloak of camel hair and he carries the Lamb of God. The Lamb refers to the words spoken by the saint when he baptised Christ: 'this is the Lamb of God'. (A & I) L1533:4. H. 1.64 m.
MacLeod 1947, 61 and pl. XVI, 3.

[7:20] EMBROIDERED COPE, WATERFORD CATHEDRAL.

Late fifteenth to early sixteenth century AD.

This elaborate embroidered silk and velvet cope — a vestment worn by priests on ceremonial occasions — is part of a set of medieval vestments preserved in Waterford. Made of Italian silk, the embroidery is Flemish. The embroidered panels illustrate scenes from the Passion. On the left, Christ's Agony in the Garden of Gethsemane; the Arrest of Christ; Christ before Pilate. On the right, the Flagellation; Crowning with Thorns; Christ Carrying the Cross. The detail on page 287 above shows Christ guarded by soldiers, one of whom holds a flaming torch. The scene illustrates the moment when Christ healed Malchus, the priests' servant whose ear had been cut off by St Peter. Peter stands to His right, shown in the act of replacing his sword in its scabbard. Kneeling before Christ is the figure of Malchus and Christ is shown replacing his severed ear. (On loan from the Most Rev. William Lee, Bishop of Waterford and Lismore.) L1506B. H. 1.41 m.
MacLeod 1952, 92–95 and pls XIII–XIV.

[7:21] SHRINE OF THE *CATHACH*, BALLYMAGROARTY, CO. DONEGAL.

Late eleventh century, redecorated in the fourteenth century AD.

In the later Middle Ages this shrine was kept at Ballymagroarty, Co. Donegal. Made to contain a manuscript believed to be written by St Columba himself, the *Cathach* ('battler') was one of the chief treasures of the O'Donnells throughout the Middle Ages. They carried it into battle to bring good luck. Its keepers were the Magroarty family, one of whom was killed when the shrine was captured in battle in 1497. The front is decorated with a seated figure of Christ flanked by a figure of a bishop and a Crucifixion scene. R2835. W. 25.1 cm.
Mahr and Raftery 1932–41, 155 and pls 113–14.

[7:22] SHRINE OF THE *MIOSACH*, CLONMANY, CO. DONEGAL.

Late eleventh century AD, redecorated in 1534.

This book shrine was originally associated with St Cairneach, patron saint of Dulane, Co. Meath but in the later Middle Ages it was absorbed into the cult of St Columba. The Irish inscription on the front states that it was re-covered for Brian O Morrison in 1534. The main face bears a series of repeating stamped silver foil panels showing the Virgin and Child and three saints, perhaps intended to represent the three national saints Patrick, Columba and Brigid. Like the Shrine of the *Cathach*, it was used as a battle-standard during the Middle Ages. 2001:84. W. 25.0 cm.
Mahr and Raftery 1932–41, 164 and pls 128–9.

[7:23] THE *MIAS TIGHEARNÁIN*, ERREW, CO. MAYO.

Eleventh, fourteenth and sixteenth centuries AD.

The reliquary, known as the *Mias Tighearnáin* 'Dish of St Tiernan' was discovered in the late eighteenth century at the ancient monastic site of Errew, Co. Mayo. It takes the form of a shallow dish composed of plates of brass with a silver cross on the front. These plates conceal an earlier metal dish, only visible through x-ray photography which may date as early as the eleventh century. Its precise function is uncertain but its form suggests it may have contained a relic of St John the Baptist, whose head was given to Salomé on a dish. The relic would have been set behind a crystal setting, now lost, placed in the centre of the cross. 1999:1. D. 27.4 cm.

Ó Floinn 1998.

❧

[7:24] *DOMHNACH AIRGID* SHRINE, CLONES, CO. MONAGHAN.

Eighth century AD, remodelled c. AD 1350.

The *Domhnach Airgid*, 'Silver Church', was made to enclose a manuscript said to have been given by St Patrick to St Macartan, founder of a church at Clogher, Co. Tyrone. The older part of the shrine belongs to the eighth century. It was substantially remodelled in the mid-fourteenth century by the abbot of Clones, John O Carbry. The front bears figures of saints arranged in two registers around a central crucifixion. Figured scenes are also found on the sides. The detail on page 262 above shows the figure of St John the Baptist holding a disk on which is shown the Lamb of God, outlined in blue enamel. In front of him stands Salomé, the daughter of King Herod, holding a dish with his severed head. R2834. H. 16.7 cm.

Ó Floinn 1983, no. 85.

❧

[7:25] SHRINE OF ST PATRICK'S TOOTH, ATHENRY, CO. GALWAY: FRONT.

Twelfth century AD, substantially altered in the 1370s.

This is a complex piece made up of portions of different objects. Its purse-shaped form dates to the 1370s when it was covered at the request of Thomas Bermingham, Lord of Athenry (who died in 1376). The shrine was used in the early nineteenth century for curing sick animals. St John, the Virgin Mary and figures of Irish saints flank the figure of Christ on the front. R2836. H. 27.7 cm.

Mahr and Raftery 1932–41, 166 and pls 119–20.

❧

[7:26] SHRINE OF ST PATRICK'S TOOTH, ATHENRY, CO. GALWAY: BACK.

Twelfth century AD, substantially altered in the 1370s.

The central ringed cross is of twelfth-century date. The engraved and raised plates around it belong to the fourteenth century. Note the use of die stamps and the figure of a harper *(below left)*.

❧

[7:27] SHRINE OF THE STOWE MISSAL, LORRHA, CO. TIPPERARY.

Early eleventh century AD, remodelled in the 1370s.

This shrine, made to contain an eighth-century mass-book, was regarded as a relic of St Maelruain, patron saint of Lorrha, Co. Tipperary. It was redecorated in the 1370s at the behest of Philip O Kennedy, King of Ormond, his wife Áine and Giolla Ruadhán Ua Maccáin, head of the Augustinian priory at Lorrha. The central jewelled cross is set with rock crystals, glass, silver beads and enamels. Around it are placed figures of the Crucifixion, the Virgin and Child, a bishop and an unidentified saint.
1883:614a. H. 18.7 cm.
Ó Floinn 1983, no. 76.

[7:28] GILT SILVER PROCESSIONAL CROSS, BALLYMACASEY, CO. KERRY.

Dated 1479.

Discovered in ploughing a field, this cross was found in a number of pieces and these have been reassembled. It shows the figure of Christ surrounded by the symbols of the four Evangelists (the symbol for St Matthew, at the foot of the cross, is missing). The inscription acknowledges the patronage of both Cornelius O Conor, Lord of Kerry and of his wife, Avelina (Eileen) Fitzgerald, daughter of the Knight of Glin. This is the finest processional cross from medieval Ireland. It was probably made as a gift for the nearby Franciscan friary of Lislachtin. Figures of Franciscan monks decorate the base of the cross. The detail on page 263 above shows the winged eagle — symbol of St John the Evangelist — standing on a scroll in a four-lobed niche. 1889:4. H. 67.2 cm.
Ó Floinn 1983, no. 88.

[7:29] ENAMELS.

Twelfth and thirteenth centuries AD.

These enamels were not found in Ireland but fragments of similar enamels from Irish churchyards show that such lavish objects were imported and used. *Above and below right* are two thirteenth-century enamels from Limoges, France. *Below right*, a panel showing a standing saint from the gable-end of a house-shaped shrine. (A&I)1894:881. L. 15.3 cm. *Above*, a plaque from a decorative book cover; it shows the Crucified Christ flanked by the Virgin and St John who stand on low hillocks while a pair of angels appear from clouds above the cross. (A&I) 1904:235. L. 22.0 cm. *Below left*, a twelfth-century plaque, depicting the figure of Christ in Majesty, from a cross or book cover made in the enamel workshops of the Meuse in the Low Countries. (A&I)1901:28. L. 10.8 cm.
Plunkett 1912, 7–8.

[7:30] IVORY PLAQUE, THOMAS ST, DUBLIN.

Fourteenth century AD.

Found in nineteenth-century street excavations at Thomas St, Dublin. The quality of the carving is not as accomplished as that on the other ivories. The Crucifixion scene is placed under an architectural triple-arched canopy in the Gothic style. The fainting Virgin is supported by two female figures while two bearded men with hats stand behind the mourning St John. The plaque may have belonged to the nearby Augustinian abbey of St Thomas the Martyr or perhaps to a wealthy merchant family in the area. R2547. H. 8.2 cm.

Mahr and Raftery 1932–41, 164 and pl. 121, 2.

[7:31] IVORIES.

Fourteenth century AD.

These French ivories of the fourteenth century were bought at auction and are not from Ireland. The pair of hinged plaques above bears, on the left, the Virgin and Child flanked by angels with candles; on the right is the Crucifixion. The latter may be compared with the same scene on the ivory from Thomas St, Dublin. (A&I)1945:5. L. 10.04 cm. *Bottom left*: This plaque shows the Nativity with the ass and ox in the foreground and shepherds behind. (A&I)1899:128. L. 6.47 cm. *Bottom right*: Two scenes from the Life of the Virgin are represented: the Crowning of the Virgin (above) and the Presentation in the Temple (below). (A&I)1888:105. L. 21.0 cm.

Unpublished.

[7:32] PROCESSIONAL CROSS, BELL AND CANDLESTICK, SHEEPHOUSE, CO. MEATH.

c. AD 1500.

Found in a quarry at Sheephouse, Co. Meath, this hoard of altar furnishings was found on lands owned by the nearby Cistercian monastery of Mellifont and may have been hidden there for safekeeping. The three pieces are almost certainly English imports. 1899:53–55. H. of cross, 62.6 cm.

Armstrong 1915, 27–31.

[7:33] BELL SHRINE KNOWN AS THE *CORP NAOMH*, TEMPLECROSS, CO. WESTMEATH.

Tenth and fifteenth centuries AD.

This much-damaged bell shrine was extensively repaired in the late medieval period. The semicircular crest belongs to the tenth century and the late-medieval additions include a crude bronze figure of the crucified Christ, a series of stamped silver plates and a polished rock crystal in a silver setting. The naïve figure of Christ is based on earlier, Romanesque models. 1887:145. H. 23.0 cm.

Mahr and Raftery 1932–41, 157 and pl. 68–70; Cone (ed.) 1977, no. 56.

[7:6]
ENAMELLED CROZIER HEAD, CASHEL CATHEDRAL, CO. TIPPERARY.
Mid-thirteenth century AD.

[7:7]

TWO SILVER BOWLS, TAGHMON, CO. WESTMEATH (*ABOVE*). DETAIL OF SILVER BOWL (*BELOW*).
Late twelfth century AD.

[7:8]
**GOLD RING BROOCHES: BALLINREA, CO. CORK (*TOP*),
UNLOCALISED (*CENTRE*) AND MARLBOROUGH ST, DUBLIN (*BOTTOM*).**
Thirteenth or fourteenth century AD.

[7:9]
SILVER CROSS PENDANT, CALLAN, CO. KILKENNY.
c. AD 1500.

[7:10]
SILVER SEAL MATRICES OF IRISH KINGS AND NOBLES, UNLOCALISED.
Fourteenth century AD.

[7:11]
FIGURE OF A HORSEMAN, KNOCKNAMAN HILL, CO. OFFALY.
Thirteenth century AD.

[7:12]
TWO SILVER-INLAID IRON AXEHEADS, BALLINA, CO. MAYO AND CO. DONEGAL.
Thirteenth century AD.

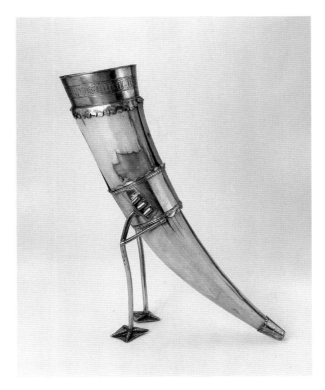

[7:13]
THE KAVANAGH 'CHARTER' HORN, BORRIS, CO. CARLOW.
Twelfth century AD with fifteenth-century AD metal mounts.

[7:14]

COVER OF THE *GREAT BOOK OF LECAN*, CO. SLIGO.

Fifteenth century AD.

[7:15]
WHALEBONE BOOK COVER, DONABATE, CO. DUBLIN.
Sixteenth century AD.

[7:16]
IVORY CHESS-PIECE, CO. MEATH.
Late twelfth century AD.

[7:17]
POTTERY 'KNIGHT' JUG, HIGH STREET, DUBLIN.
Thirteenth century AD.

[7:18]
WOODEN METHER, UNLOCALISED.
Fourteenth to sixteenth century AD.

[7:19]

WOODEN STATUE OF ST JOHN THE BAPTIST, FETHARD, CO. TIPPERARY.

Late fifteenth century AD.

[7:20]

EMBROIDERED COPE, WATERFORD CATHEDRAL, AND (*FACING PAGE*) DETAIL.

Late fifteenth to early sixteenth century AD.

[7:21]
SHRINE OF THE *CATHACH*, BALLYMAGROARTY, CO. DONEGAL.
Late eleventh century, redecorated in the fourteenth century AD.

[7:22]
SHRINE OF THE *MIOSACH*, CLONMANY, CO. DONEGAL.
Late eleventh century AD, redecorated in 1534.

[7:23]
THE *MIAS TIGHEARNÁIN*, ERREW, CO. MAYO.
Eleventh, fourteenth and sixteenth centuries AD.

[7:24]

DOMHNACH AIRGID SHRINE, CLONES, CO. MONAGHAN.

Eighth century AD, *remodelled c.* AD 1350.

[7:25]
SHRINE OF ST PATRICK'S TOOTH, ATHENRY, CO. GALWAY: FRONT.
Twelfth century AD, substantially altered in the 1370s.

[7:26]

SHRINE OF ST PATRICK'S TOOTH, ATHENRY, CO. GALWAY: BACK.

Twelfth century AD, substantially altered in the 1370s.

[7:27]

SHRINE OF THE STOWE MISSAL, LORRHA, CO. TIPPERARY.

Eleventh century AD, remodelled in the 1370s.

[7:28] *facing page*

GILT SILVER PROCESSIONAL CROSS, BALLYMACASEY, CO. KERRY.

Dated 1479.

[7:29]

ENAMELS.

Twelfth and thirteenth centuries AD.

[7:30]
IVORY PLAQUE, THOMAS ST, DUBLIN.
Fourteenth century AD.

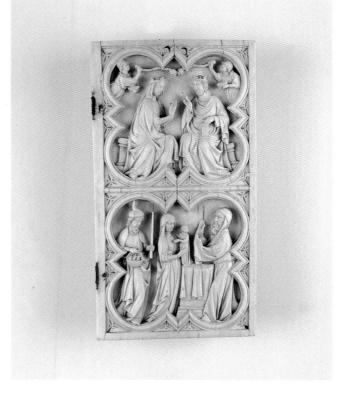

[7:31]

IVORIES.

Fourteenth century AD.

[7:32]
PROCESSIONAL CROSS, BELL AND CANDLESTICK, SHEEPHOUSE, CO. MEATH.
c. AD 1500.

[7:33]
BELL SHRINE KNOWN AS THE *CORP NAOMH*, TEMPLECROSS, CO. WESTMEATH.
Tenth and fifteenth centuries AD.

BIBLIOGRAPHY

Alabaster, E.P. 1910 *National Museum of Science and Art, Dublin. General Guide to the Art Collections. Part XV, Ivories*, Dublin 1910.

Anonymous 1846 'Proceedings of the Central Committee, *The Journal of the British Archaeological Association* 1, (1846), 237–261.

Anonymous 1852 *Descriptive Catalogue of the Antiquities exhibited in the Museum, Belfast*, Belfast 1852.

Anonymous 1856–57 'Proceedings', *Journal of the Royal Society of Antiquaries of Ireland* 1, (1856–57), 422–3.

Anonymous 1925 'La Tène Sword Hilt', *Journal of the Royal Society of Antiquaries of Ireland* 15, (1925), 137–8.

Armstrong, E.C.R. 1913 *Irish Seal Matrices and Seals* Dublin 1913.

Armstrong, E.C.R. 1914–16 Catalogue of the Silver and Ecclesiastical Antiquities in the Collection of the Royal Irish Academy, *Proceedings of the Royal Irish Academy* 32c, (1914-16), 287-312.

Armstrong, E.C.R. 1915 'Processional cross, pricket-candlestick, and bell, found together at Sheephouse, near Oldbridge, Co. Meath', *Journal of the Royal Society of Antiquaries of Ireland* 45, (1915), 27–31.

Armstrong, E.C.R. 1920 *Catalogue of Irish gold ornaments in the collection of the Royal Irish Academy*, Dublin 1920.

Barron, T.J. 1978 'Laragh Parish: I gCeartlár Sliabh na nDee', *I gCeartlár Breifne (The Heart of Breifne)* 1, (1978), 3–16.

Bateson, J.D. 1973 'Roman material in Ireland: A Reconsideration', *Proceedings of the Royal Irish Academy* 73, (1973), 21–97.

Bøe, J. 1940 'Norse Antiquities in Ireland', in Shetelig, H. (ed.), *Viking Antiquities in Great Britain and Ireland, Part III*. Oslo 1940.

Brady, N. 1989 Exhibition entries, in Haus der Bayerischen Geschichte, München (ed.), *Kilian: Mönch aus Irland–aller Franken Patron, 689 –1989*, Würzburg 1989.

Browne, A. 1800 'An Account of some Ancient Trumpets, dug up in a Bog near Armagh', *Transactions of the Royal Irish Academy* 8, (1800), 11–12.

Burgess, C.B. and Gerloff, S. 1981 *The Dirks and Rapiers of Great Britain and Ireland*, Prähistorische Bronzefunde, Abteilung IV, Band 7, München 1981.

Cahill, M. 1983 Catalogue entries, in Ryan, M. (ed.), (1983).

Cahill, M. 1994 'Boxes, beads, bobbins and ... notions', *Archaeology Ireland* 8, (1994), 21–23.

Cahill, M. 1995 'Later Bronze Age goldwork from Ireland – form function and formality', in Waddell J. and Shee Twohig, E. (eds), *Ireland in the Bronze Age*, Dublin 1995, 63–72.

Cahill, M. 1998 'A gold dress-fastener from Cloghernagh, Co. Tipperary and a catalogue of related material', in Ryan M. (ed.), *Irish Antiquities: Essays in Memory of Joseph Raftery*, Dublin 1998, 27–79.

Cahill, M. 2001 'Unspooling the mystery', *Archaeology Ireland* 15, (2001), 8–15.

Cahill, M. 2002 'The Dooyork Hoard', *Irish Arts Review* 19, (2002), 118–121.

Cahill, M. forthcoming 'Roll your own lunula', in Condit, T. and Corlett, C. (eds), *Above and Beyond: Essays in Memory of Leo Swan*.

Cahill, M. and Ó Floinn, R. 1995 'The reprovenancing of two silver kite-brooches probably from Co. Limerick', *North Munster Antiquarian Journal* 36, (1995), 65-82.

Carson, R.A.G. and O'Kelly, C. 1977 'A Catalogue of the Roman Coins from Newgrange, Co. Meath and Notes on the Coins and Related Finds', *Proceedings of the Royal Irish Academy* 77C, (1977), 35–55.

Coffey, G. 1898 'Bronze Age Spearhead found near Boho', *Reliquary and Illustrated Archaeologist* 4, (1898), 120.

Coffey, G. 1906 'Two finds of Late Bronze Age Date', *Proceedings of the Royal Irish Academy* 26C, (1906), 119–24.

Coles, J.M. 1962 'European Bronze Age Shields', *Proceedings of the Prehistoric Society* 28, (1962), 156–90.

Coles, J.M. 1963 'Irish Bronze Age Horns and their relations with Northern Europe', *Proceedings of the Prehistoric Society* 29, (1963), 326–56.

Collins, A.E.P. 1981 'The flint javelin heads of Ireland', in Ó Corráin, D., (ed.), *Irish Antiquity. Essays and Studies presented to Professor M. J. O' Kelly*, Cork 1981, 111–33.

Cone, P. (ed.), 1977 *Treasures of Early Irish Art 1500 BC to 1500 AD*, New York 1977.

Cooke, T.L. 1875 *The Early History of the Town of Birr, or Parsonstown*, Dublin 1875.

Cooney, G. and Mandal, S. 1998 *The stone axe project. Monograph I*, Bray 1998.

Costello, T.B. 1902 'The Lurgan Canoe', *Journal of the Galway Archaeological and Historical Society* 2, (1902), 57-59.

Crooke, E. 2000 *Politics, Archaeology and the Creation of the National Museum of Ireland*, Dublin 2000.

Deevy, M.B. 1998 *Medieval Ring Brooches in Ireland*, Bray 1998.

Dunlevy, M. 2002 *Dublin Barracks, A Brief History of Collins Barracks, Dublin*, Dublin 2002.

Eames, E. and Fanning, T. 1988 *Irish Medieval Tiles*, Dublin 1988.

Eogan, G. 1967 'The associated finds of gold bar torcs', *Journal of the Royal Society of Antiquaries of Ireland* 97, (1967), 129–75.

Eogan, G. 1972 'Sleeve-fasteners of the late Bronze Age', in Lynch, F. and Burgess, C. (eds), *Prehistoric Man in Wales and the West*, Bath 1972, 189–210.

Eogan, G. 1974 'Report on the Excavations of some Passage Graves, Unprotected Inhumation Burials and a settlement site at Knowth, Co. Meath', *Proceedings of the Royal Irish Academy* 76C, (1974), 11–112.

Eogan, G. 1981 'Gold discs of the late Bronze Age', in Ó Corráin D. (ed.), *Irish Antiquity. Essays and Studies presented to Professor M.J. O'Kelly*, Cork 1981, 147–162.

Eogan, G. 1983 *Hoards of the Irish Later Bronze Age*, Dublin 1983.

Eogan, G. 1984 *Excavations at Knowth 1. Smaller passage tombs, Neolithic occupation and Beaker activity*, Dublin 1984.

Eogan, G. 1994 *The Accomplished Art: Gold and gold working in Britain and Ireland during the Bronze Age*, Oxford 1994.

Eogan, G. 1998 'Heart-shaped bullae of the Irish Bronze Age', in Ryan M. (ed.), *Irish Antiquities. Essays in Memory of Joseph Raftery*, Dublin 1998, 17–26.

Eogan, G. 2001 'A Composite Late Bronze Age Chain Object from Roscommon, Ireland', in Metz, W.H., van Beek B.L. and Steegstra, H. (eds), *Patina. Essays presented to Jay Jordan Butler on the Occasion of his 80th Birthday*, Groningen, Amsterdam 2001, 231–40.

Eogan, G. and Richardson, H. 1982 'Two Maceheads from Knowth, Co. Meath', *Journal of the Royal Society of Antiquaries of Ireland* 112, (1982), 123–38.

Gleeson, D.F. 1934 'The discovery of a gold gorget at Burren, Co. Clare', *Journal of the Royal Society of Antiquaries of Ireland* 64, (1934), 138–139.

Gogan, L.S. 1930 'Irish Stone Pendants', *Journal of the Cork Archaeological and Historical Society* 35, (1930), 90–96.

Gogan, L.S. 1932 'A graduated amber necklace, gold-plated rings and other objects from Cnoc na bPoll', *Journal of the Cork Historical and Archaeological Society* 37, (1932), 58–71.

Graham-Campbell, J. 1976 'The Viking Age Silver Hoards of Ireland', in Almqvist, B., Greene, D. (eds), *Proceedings of the Seventh Congress, Dublin, 1973*, Dublin 1976.

Graham-Campbell, J. 1980 *Viking Artefacts: A Select Catalogue*, London 1980.

Griffin, D.and Pegum, C. 2000 *Leinster House 1744-2000: An Architectural History*, Dublin 2000.

Halpin, A. 1986 'Irish medieval swords *c*.1170–1600', *Proceedings of the Royal Irish Academy* 86C, (1986), 183–230.

Harbison, P. 1969 *The Axes of the Early Bronze Age in Ireland*, (Prähistorische Bronzefunde, Abteilung IX, Band 1), Munich 1969.

Harbison, P. 1992 *The High Crosses of Ireland: An Iconographical and Photographic Survey*, 3 vols, Bonn 1992.

Hawkes, C.F.C. and Smyth, M.A. 1957 'On some Buckets and Cauldrons of the Bronze and Early Iron Ages', *The Antiquaries Journal* 37, (1957), 131–199.

Haworth, R. 1971 'The Horse Harness of the Irish Early Iron Age', *Ulster Journal of Archaeology* 34, (1971), 26–49.

Henry, F. 1970 *Irish Art During the Romanesque Period, 1020-1170*, London 1970.

Herity, M. 1974 *Irish Passage Graves. Neolithic Tomb-Builders in Ireland and Britain 2500 BC*, Dublin 1974.

Herity, M. 1982 'Irish Decorated Neolithic Pottery', *Proceedings of the Royal Irish Academy* 82C, (1982), 247–403.

Ireland, A. 1992 'The Finding of the "Clonmacnoise" Torcs', *Proceedings of the Royal Irish Academy* 92C, (1992), 123–46.

Johansen, O.S. 1973 'Bossed Penannular Brooches', *Acta Archaeologica* 44, (1973), 63-124.

Kavanagh, R.M. 1973 'The Encrusted Urn in Ireland', *Proceedings of the Royal Irish Academy* 73C, (1973), 507–617.

Kavanagh, R.M. 1976 'Collared and Cordoned Cinerary Urns in Ireland', *Proceedings of the Royal Irish Academy* 76C, (1976), 293–403.

Kavanagh, R.M. 1977 'Pygmy Cups in Ireland', *Journal of the Royal Society of Antiquaries of Ireland* 107, (1977), 61–95.

Kelly, E.P. 1983 Catalogue entries, in Ryan, M. (ed.), (1983).

Lang, J.T. 1988 *Viking Age Decorated Wood: A study of its Ornament and Style,* (Medieval Dublin Excavations 1962-81. Series B; vol. 1), Dublin 1988

Lanting, J.N. and Brindley, A.L. 1998 'Dating Cremated Bone: the Dawn of a New Era', *The Journal of Irish Archaeology* 9, (1998), 1–8.

Lucas, A.T. 1960 'National Museum of Ireland Archaeological acquisitions in the year 1958', *Journal of the Royal Society of Antiquaries of Ireland* 90, (1960), 1–40.

Lucas, A.T. 1967 'National Museum of Ireland Archaeological acquisitions in the year 1964', *Journal of the Royal Society of Antiquaries of Ireland* 97, (1967), 1–28.

Lucas, A.T. 1968 'National Museum of Ireland Archaeological acquisitions in the year 1965', *Journal of the Royal Society of Antiquaries of Ireland* 98, (1968), 93–159.

Lucas, A.T. 1971 'National Museum of Ireland archaeological acquisitions in the year 1968', *Journal of the Royal Society of Antiquaries of Ireland* 101, (1971), 184–244.

Mac Lochlainn, A., O' Riordan C.E. and Wallace, P.F. 1977 *Science and Art 1877-1977,* Dublin 1977.

Macadam, R. 1860 'Ancient Irish Trumpets', *Ulster Journal of Archaeology* 8, (1860), 99–110.

Macalister, R.A.S. 1949 *The Archaeology of Ireland,* London 1949.

Macalister, R.A.S., Armstrong, E.C.R. and Praeger, R.L. 1912 'Report on the Exploration of Bronze-Age Carns on Carrowkeel Mountain, Co. Sligo', *Proceedings of the Royal Irish Academy* 29C, (1912), 311–347.

Macleod, C. 1947 'Some late medieval wood sculptures in Ireland', *Journal of the Royal Society of Antiquaries of Ireland* 77, (1947), 53–62.

Macleod, C. 1952 'Fifteenth-century vestments in Waterford', *Journal of the Royal Society of Antiquaries of Ireland* 82, (1952), 85–98.

MacNeill, M. 1962 *The Festival of Lughnasa,* 2 vols, Oxford 1962.

Mahr, A. 1928 'Ein Wikingerschwert mit deutschem Namen aus Irland', in *Festgabe für den 70 jährigen Gustav Kossinna von Freunden und Schülern (Mannus,* Ergänzungsband 6, Leipzig, 1928), 204-52.

Mahr, A. 1938 'The Gallóglach Axe', *Journal of the Galway Archaeological and Historical Society* 18, (1938), 66-8.

Mahr, A. and Raftery, J. (eds), 1932–41 *Christian Art in Ancient Ireland,* 2 vols, Dublin 1932–41.

Mc Carthy, P. 2002 'From Torpedo Boat to Temples of Culture, Carlo Cambi's Route to Ireland', *Irish Arts Review,* (2002), 71-79.

McEvansoneya, P. 2000 'A Colourful Spectacle Restored, The State Coach of the Lord Mayor of Dublin', *Irish Arts Review,* (2000), 80-87.

McEvoy, J. 1997 'A Late Bronze Age Collar and Similar Ornament from Ireland', M.A. thesis, National University of Ireland, Dublin 1997.

Mitchell, G.F. and de G. Sieveking, G. 1972 'Flint flake probably of Palaeolithic age, from Mell townland, near Drogheda, Co. Louth, Ireland, *Journal of the Royal Society of Antiquaries of Ireland* 102, (1972), 174–7.

Morris, H. 1912 'A Faughart Monument', *County Louth Archaeological and Historical Journal* 3, (1912), 28–9.

Mullarkey, P. 1991 Catalogue entry, in Webster, L. and Backhouse, J. (eds.), *The Making of England: Anglo-Saxon Art and Culture AD 600–900*, London 1991.

Mulvany, W.T. 1852 'Collection of Antiquities Presented to the Royal Irish Academy by William T. Mulvany, Esq., M.R.I.A., on the Part of the Commissioners of Public Works in Ireland', *Proceedings of the Royal Irish Academy* 5C, (1850–53), xxxi–lxvi.

National Museum Of Ireland 1973 *Viking and Medieval Dublin*, Dublin 1973.

O'Connor, N. 1983 Catalogue entry, in Ryan, M. (ed.), (1983).

O'Dwyer, F., 1987 'The Architecture of the Board of Public Works 1831-1923', in O'Connor, C. and Regan, J., (eds), *Public Works: The Architecture of the Office of Public Works 1831-1987*, Dublin 1987, 23-25

O'Dwyer, F. 1997 *The Architecture of Deane and Woodward*, Dublin, 1997.

Ó Floinn, R. 1983 Catalogue entries, in Ryan, M. (ed.), (1983).

Ó Floinn, R. 1990 'Lisnamulligan Bronze Age cist', in Bennett, I. (ed.), *Excavations 1989: Summary Accounts of Archaeological Excavations in Ireland*, Organisation of Irish Archaeologists, Dublin 1990, 17.

Ó Floinn, R. 1998 'The object known as the "Mias Tighearnáin"', in Ryan M. (ed.), *Irish Antiquity: Essays in memory of Joseph Raftery*, Bray 1998, 151–72.

Ó Floinn, R. 2000 'Freestone Hill, Co. Kilkenny: A Reassessment' in Smyth, A.P. (ed.), *Seanchas: Studies in Early and Medieval Irish Archaeology, History and Literature in Honour of Francis J. Byrne*, Dublin 2000, 12–29.

Ó Raifeartaigh, T. (ed.), 1985 *The Royal Irish Academy, a Bicentennial History 1785-1985*, Dublin 1985.

Ó Ríordáin, B. and Waddell, J. 1993 *The Funerary Bowls and Vases of the Irish Bronze Age*, Galway 1993.

Ó Ríordáin, S.P. 1947 'Roman Material in Ireland', *Proceedings of the Royal Irish Academy* 60C, (1947), 35–82.

O'Riordan, C.E. 1986 *The Natural History Museum, Dublin.* Dublin 1986.

Plunkett, G.T. 1912 *National Museum of Science and Art, Dublin. General Guide to the Art Collections. Part V, Enamels*, Dublin 1912.

Praeger, R.L. 1942 'The Broighter Gold Ornaments', *Journal of the Royal Society of Antiquaries of Ireland* 72, (1942), 29–32.

Raftery, B. 1972 'Some Late La Tène Glass Beads from Ireland', *Journal of the Royal Society of Antiquaries of Ireland* 102, (1972), 14–18.

Raftery, B. 1974 'A Prehistoric Burial Mound at Baunogenasraid, Co. Carlow', *Proceedings of the Royal Irish Academy* 74C, (1974), 277–312.

Raftery, B. 1984 *La Tène in Ireland. Problems of Origin and Chronology*, Marburg 1984.

Raftery, B. 1994 *Pagan Celtic Ireland: The Enigma of the Irish Iron Age*, London 1994.

Raftery, B. 1983 *A Catalogue of Irish Iron Age Antiquities*, 2 vols, Marburg 1983.

Raftery, J. 1940 'Hoard of gold objects from Co. Kerry', *Journal of the Cork Historical and Archaeological Society* 45, (1940), 56–57.

Raftery, J. 1941 'Recent acquisitions from Co. Clare in the National Museum', *North Munster Antiquarian Journal* 2, (1941), 170–71.

Raftery, J. 1960 'A Hoard of the Early Iron Age, Interim Report', *Journal of the Royal Society of Antiquaries of Ireland* 90, (1960), 1–5.

Raftery, J. 1961 'The Derrinboy Hoard, Co. Offaly', *Journal of the Royal Society of Antiquaries of Ireland* 91, (1961), 55–58.

Raftery, J. 1963 'A thistle Brooch from Co. Louth', *Louth Archaeological Society*, 15, (1963), 277-280

Raftery, J. 1967 'The Gorteenreagh Hoard', in Rynne E. (ed.), *North Munster Studies*, Limerick 1967, 61–71.

Raftery, J. 1970 'Prehistoric coiled basketry bags', *Journal of the Royal Society of Antiquaries of Ireland* 100, (1970), 167–8.

Raftery, J. 1970 'Two gold hoards from Co. Tyrone', *Journal of the Royal Society of Antiquaries of Ireland* 100, (1970), 169–174.

Rahtz, P. et al., 1992 *Cadbury Congresbury 1968–73: a late/post-Roman hilltop settlement in Somerset*, (Brit. Arch. Rep. Brit. Ser. 223), Oxford 1992, 242–3.

Ryan, M. (ed.), 1983 *Treasures of Ireland. Irish Art 3000 BC–1500 AD*, Dublin 1983.

Ryan, M. 1983 Catalogue entries, in Ryan, M. (ed.), 1983.

Rynne, E. 1961–3 'Notes on some antiquities found in Co. Kildare', *Journal of the Co. Kildare Archaeological Society* 13, (1961–3), 458–62.

Rynne, E. 1964 'The Coiled Bronze Armlet from Ballymahon, Co. Meath', *Journal of the Royal Society of Antiquaries of Ireland* 94, (1964), 69–72.

Rynne, E. 1972 'Celtic Stone Idols in Ireland', in Thomas, C. (ed.), *The Iron Age in the Irish Sea Province*, (Council for British Archaeology Research Report 9), London 1972, 79–98.

Rynne, E. 1976 'The Late La Tène and Roman Finds from Lambay Island, Co. Dublin: a re-assessment', *Proceedings of the Royal Irish Academy* 76C, (1976), 231–44.

Sheehan, J. 1998 'Early Viking Silver Hoards in Ireland', in Clarke, H.B., Ní Mhaonaigh, M., Ó Floinn, R. (eds), *Ireland and Scandinavia in the Early Viking Age*, Dublin 1998, 166-202.

Shee-Twohig, E. 1981 *The Megalithic Art of Western Europe*, Oxford 1981.

Simpson, D.D.A. 1988 'The Stone Maceheads of Ireland', *Journal of the Royal Society of Antiquaries of Ireland* 118, (1988), 27–52.

Simpson, M. 1968 'Massive armlets in the North British Iron Age', in Coles, J.M. and Simpson, D.D.A. (eds), *Studies in Ancient Europe. Essays presented to Stuart Piggott*, Leicester 1968, 233–54.

Smith, W.C. 1963 'Jade axes from sites in the British Isles', *Proceedings of the Prehistoric Society* 29, (1963), 133–172.

Strickland, W.G. 1921 'The State Coach of the Earl of Clare', *Journal of the Royal Society of Antiquaries of Ireland* 11, (1921), 61-67.

Swift, C. 1996 'Pagan monuments and Christian legal centres in Early Meath', *Ríocht na Midhe, Records of Meath Archaeological and Historical Society* 9, (1996), 1–26.

Swift, C. 1997 *Ogam stones and the earliest Irish Christians*, (Maynooth Monographs: Series Minor II), Maynooth 1997.

Taylor, J.J. 1970 'Lunulae reconsidered', *Proceedings of the Prehistoric Society* 36, (1970), 38–81.

Wallace, P.F. 1983 Catalogue entry, in Ryan, M. (ed.), (1983).

Wallace, P.F. 1985 'The Archaeology of Viking Dublin', in Clarke, H.B., and Simms, A. (eds), *The Comparative History of Urban Origins in non-Roman Europe*, Oxford 1985, 103-45.

Wallace, P.F. 1988 'Archaeology and the emergence of Dublin as the principal town in Ireland', in Bradley, J. (ed.), *Settlement and Society in Medieval Ireland*, Kilkenny 1988, 123-160.

Wallace, P.F. 1992 *The Viking Age Buildings of Dublin*, (Medieval Dublin Excavations 1962-81. Series A; vol. 1), Dublin 1992.

Wallace, P.F. 1992 'The Archaeological identity of the Hiberno-Norse town', *Journal of the Royal Society of Antiquaries of Ireland*, 122, (1992), 35-66.

Walsh, A. 1998 'Viking Age Swords in Ireland', in Clarke, H.B., Ní Mhaonaigh, M., Ó Floinn, R. (eds) *Ireland and Scandinavia in the Early Viking Age*, Dublin 1998, 222-235.

Warner, R. 1982 'The Broighter Hoard: A Reappraisal, and the Iconography of the Collar', in Scott, B.G. (ed.), *Studies on Early Ireland: Essays in Honour of M. V. Duignan*, Belfast 1982, 29–38.

Way, A. 1869 'Notice of certain Relics of a Peculiar Type assigned to the Late Celtic Period', *Archaeological Journal* 26, (1869), 52–96.

Whitfield, N. 1988 'The kite-brooch and its place in Irish metalwork', in Barry, T., Cleary, R.M., Hurley, M.F. (eds), *Late Viking Age and Medieval Waterford, Excavations 1986-92*, Dublin 1998, 490-518.

Wilde, W.R. 1857 *A Descriptive Catalogue of the Antiquities of Stone, Earthen and Vegetable Materials in the Museum of the Royal Irish Academy*, Dublin 1857.

Wilde, W.R. 1861 *A Descriptive Catalogue of the Antiquities of Animal Materials and Bronze in the Museum of the Royal Irish Academy*, Dublin 1861.

Wilde, W.R. 1862 *A Descriptive Catalogue of the Antiquities of Gold in the Museum of the Royal Irish Academy*, Dublin 1862.

Woodman, P.C., Anderson, E. and Finlay, N. 1999 *Excavations at Ferriter's Cove, 1983–95: last foragers, first farmers in the Dingle Peninsula*, Bray 1999.

Youngs, S. (ed.), 1989 *'The Work of Angels': Masterpieces of Celtic Metalwork, 6th–9th centuries AD*, London 1989.

INDEX

Note: Numbers for pages on which illustrations appear are in italics.